A Guide to Sustainable Corporate Responsibility

Caroline D. Ditlev-Simonsen

A Guide to Sustainable Corporate Responsibility

From Theory to Action

palgrave
macmillan

Caroline D. Ditlev-Simonsen
Department of Law and Governance
BI Norwegian Business School
Oslo, Norway

ISBN 978-3-030-88202-0 ISBN 978-3-030-88203-7 (eBook)
https://doi.org/10.1007/978-3-030-88203-7

Cover illustration: Hildegarde
Cover design: eStudioCalamar

This Palgrave Macmillan imprint is published by the registered company Springer Nature Switzerland AG.
The registered company address is: Gewerbestrasse 11, 6330 Cham, Switzerland

Preface

Sustainable Corporate Responsibility is a complex topic involving several fields of knowledge. Good dialogue and constructive feedback from relevant experts, researchers, practitioners, and employees from both small and large companies have been crucial in the process of writing this book. I am very grateful for all their contributions. In addition, I would like to extend special thanks to Emmanuel Chao, Kirsten M Hovi, Kristin A Koppang, Knut Myrum Næss, Atle Andreassen Raa, Nanna Ringstad, Guro Slettemark, Mathilde Emilie Thue, Kristel Tonstad, Elisa Dahl Walderhaug, and Søren Wenstøp. Anna Czerwinska-Andreassen, my research assistant, has been an indispensable help throughout the process of writing this book and has contributed on specific cases. I would also like to thank my employer BI Norwegian Business School, for providing financial support for the book and facilitating its availability via open access; as well as Alec Selwyn, Editor at Palgrave Business and Management and Srishti Gupta, Editorial Assistant, for guiding and managing the formal and practical perspective of the book. Thanks also to the two blind reviewers, who provided invaluable and constructive feedback.

Please note, the contents of this book are all of my own and the aforementioned people and institutions have no responsibility for what is therein written.

My career in the sustainability business started almost 50 years ago, when I as a child collected discarded bottles and returned them for the deposit. This was around the same time that the book *Limits to Growth* was published and about 15 years before *Our Common Future* was published. At the time, my little recycling project was good for my income and good for the environment—which I hope will be the business model for our society going forward as well.

I have watched and participated in the development of sustainability from a time when the majority of people were not aware of or less concerned about environmental degradation, climate change, overconsumption, and so on. I have seen the transition from ignorance to concern, engagement, and willingness to making changes for a more sustainable future. Still, there is so much that has to change to make our future sustainable. There is so much knowledge "out there" and we can make such great steps forward if we manage to combine all. Different fields need to communicate and collaborate—we need bridges between the knowledge silos. Sustainability is complex and requires understanding numerous disciplines. One key scientific contribution of this book might be that it contributes to breaking down the puzzle for a more holistic understanding and facilitates communication.

Writing this book has been a unique experience: lots of struggles, lots of excitement, eye-opening experiences, challenged reflections, extended knowledge, deep frustrations, new inspiration, and much more. Warm thanks to my family who has persevered through this process—and provided great contributions as "non-experts" concerned people and especially our three children, who are the next generation to whom we are leaving the planet.

Oslo, Norway Caroline D. Ditlev-Simonsen

Contents

Acronyms

AA	Arthur Andersen
ACCORD	Accord on Fire and Building Safety in Bangladesh
B2B	Business-to-business
BCSD	Business Council for Sustainable Development
BP	British Petroleum
BRT	Business Roundtable
CARB	California Air Resources Board
CDSB	Climate Disclosure Standard Board
CEO	Chief Executive Officer
CFCs	Chlorofluorocarbons
CFP	Corporate Financial Performance
CO_2	Carbon dioxide
CoP	Communication on Progress
COP	Conference of the Parties
CR	Corporate Responsibility
CSR	Corporate Social Responsibility
CSRD	Corporate Sustainability Reporting Directive
CSV	Creating Shared Value
DJSI	Dow Jones Sustainability Index
DRC	Democratic Republic of the Congo
EMS	Environmental Management System
EPA	Environmental Protection Agency
ESG	Environment, Social, and Governance

ETI	Ethical Trading Initiative
EU	European Union
EV	Electric Vehicle
FCAS	Fragile and Conflict-Affected States
FAO	Food and Agriculture Organization
FSC	Forest Stewardship Council
FT	Financial Times
GDP	Gross Domestic Product
GHG	Greenhouse Gas
GM	General Motors
GMO	Genetically Modified Organisms
GNH	Gross National Happiness
GNI	Gross National Income
GRI	Global Reporting Initiative
IAEA	International Atomic Energy Agency
IAHR	Investor Alliance for Human Rights
ICC	International Chamber of Commerce
ICT	Information and Communications Technology
IEB	International Environment Bureau
IIRC	International Integrated Reporting Council
ILO	International Labor Organization
IMF	International Monetary Fund
IMO	International Maritime Organization
ISO	International Organization for Standardization
kWh	Kilowatt hour
LCA	Life Cycle Analysis
LOHAS	Lifestyles of Health and Sustainability
MDG	Millennium Development Goals
MSC	Marine Stewardship Council
MSCI	Morgen Stanley Capital International
MSF	*Médecins Sans Frontières*
NCP	National Contact Point
NFRD	Non-Financial Reporting Directive
NGOs	Non-governmental Organizations
NOK	Norwegian Krone
NORAD	Norwegian Agency for Development Cooperation
ODA	Official Development Assistance
OECD	Organization for Economic Co-operation and Development

PETA	People for Ethical Treatment of Animals
PETCO	PET Recycling Company
PHL	Post-harvest loss
PMI	Philip Morris International
PRI	Principles for Responsible Investments
PwC	PricewaterhouseCoopers
SAGCOT	Southern Agricultural Growth Corridor of Tanzania
SDGs	UN Sustainable Development Goals
SFAP	Sustainable Finance Action Plan
SME	Small-to-Medium Enterprise
SRI	Socially Responsible Investment
TCFD	Task Force on Climate-Related Financial Disclosures
TISC	Transparency in Supply Chains Act
TNC	Transnational Corporation
UDHR	Universal Declaration of Human Rights
UN	United Nations
UNCAC	UN Convention Against Corruption
UNCED	UN Conference on Environment and Development
UNGC	United Nations Global Compact
UNGP	United Nations Guiding Principles on Business and Human Rights
UNODC	UN Office on Drugs and Crime
USD	United States Dollar
UWV	University West Virginia
VW	Volkswagen
WB	World Bank
WBCSD	World Business Council for Sustainable Development
WCED	World Commission on Environment and Development
WHO	World Health Organization
WICEM	World Industry Conference on Environmental Management
WRI	World Resource Institute
WWF	World Wide Fund for Nature

List of Figures

1

Introduction

Since the Industrial Revolution in late eighteenth century, there have been tremendous increases in both production and population growth. In the 1960s, the society began to consider the relationship between industrial development, environmental degradation, and the costs it imposed on everyone in one way or another. The United Nations (UN) initiated the World Commission on Environment and Development (WCED), later known as the Brundtland Commission, which issued a report in 1987 called Our Common Future. From there, the term "sustainable development" was born. Since then, society has been increasingly concerned with the topic. Yet, global production and consumption continue to grow at an unsustainable rate.

While today around one tenth of the world's population lives in extreme poverty, people in industrialized countries are overconsuming (Si et al., 2020). If everybody in the world enjoyed the same lifestyle as people in the European Union (EU) we would need three planet Earths. Currently, according to the Global Footprint Network, we need an equivalent of 1.7 Earths to provide the resources we use and to absorb our waste. We are living in a world with major economic inequalities, over-pollution and resource depletion. There are currently over 40 million

C. D. Ditlev-Simonsen, *A Guide to Sustainable Corporate Responsibility*,
https://doi.org/10.1007/978-3-030-88203-7_1

people enslaved in the world, greenhouse gas emissions (GHGs) are consistently increasing, and more than 20 percent of the world's animal species are at risk of extinction. Clearly, continuing on this path will ruin our planet, both from a societal and an environmental perspective.

To respond to these global challenges, the UN Sustainable Development Goals (SDGs) were officially adopted in 2015 by 193 UN member states. Efforts to achieve these goals by 2030 are well on their way and the role of business is crucial. Even though environmental and social problems are perceived as challenges, they can also be approached as opportunities. Companies are spending more time, focus, and money on the pursuit of sustainability. Today, 90 percent of CEOs state that sustainability is important to their company's success, 88 percent of business students think social and environmental issues should be a priority, and almost 70 percent want to incorporate environmental issues in their next job (Hoffmann, 2018). Even though corporations are aware of the challenges and opportunities associated with sustainability and want to contribute, many of their efforts are inefficient, leading to time and money wasted.

New business models, sustainable business strategies, system and systemic change, circular economies are all examples of potential solutions, which together with a global change of mindset are necessary to achieve the SDGs. This book sets out to address the role of businesses and their responsibilities for reaching these goals. I have researched these topics associated with sustainability in corporations, organizations, and educational institutions—nationally and internationally—for almost 30 years. I worked for the Business Council for Sustainable Development, which played a key role in engaging the global business community to begin discussing how corporations can contribute and adapt to sustainability, an initiative leading up to the Rio Conference in 1991. Familiar with the realities companies are facing, I share my knowledge on how different corporate approaches to responsibility and sustainability lead to different results. This book builds on business theory and experience to recommend practical steps and strategies for corporations pursuing sustainability in an effective way that is good for business and financially sound. The following section provides a short overview of topics discussed in each chapter of this book.

1.1 A Description of the Content of the Book

This book consists of 12 chapters, which taken together provide guidance on how to move forward and change for a more sustainable future. Each chapter provides a comprehensive overview of different components related to sustainability. A particular challenge in today's society is that so many of these topics have accumulated so much knowledge that research has become too narrow and specialized. Entire books are devoted to only cover small parts of the sustainability concept. This makes dialog between the different areas of expertise quite difficult. People know more and more about less and less, resulting in knowledge-silos. The structure of this book aims to bring cohesion to the body of knowledge in this domain and provide a big picture on the understanding of the topic.

To pursue sustainability, a variety of stakeholders have to be involved and collaborate across the different silos. The SDGs are a key contribution in the field, linking different areas of expertise together. While some criticize the SDGs as being superficial, others argue that the SDGs are the most efficient tool for international cooperation in identifying the key challenges confronting the world and how to approach them together. At any rate, the SDGs are the key references for sustainability worldwide and therefore crucial to refer to.

Along the same line of reasoning, this book puts together key issues and approaches that are relevant for corporations. In order to understand where to go from here and where we are now, we have to understand why we are where we are today. Learning about the past mistakes of other corporates can help others avoid repeating them. But there are also new opportunities which are even more important to focus on and capture.

Chapter 2, "Sustainable Corporate Responsibility", starts by reflecting on the origins and historical context of terms related to sustainability and business, including but not limited to Corporate Social Responsibility (CSR), Corporate Citizenship, and so on. I discuss what they mean, their purpose, and limitations. I explore different, multilateral initiatives and frameworks pertaining to sustainability, in particular ones adopted by UN member states and how these apply to businesses. The role of corporate involvement and contribution, moving from a reactive to proactive sustainability engagement, is addressed. The responsibility of corporations from a philosophical perspective including key ethical schools of thoughts is also addressed.

Chapter 3, "Economic Theories and Sustainable Development", provides a brief introduction of some of the key economic theories and how and to which extent they apply to sustainable development and corporate responsibility. How economics, international trade, organizations, tax, values, banks, governments and so on work today can all be attributed to one or more of the economic theorists introduced in this chapter. Still, these theories were developed at the time when environmental challenges such as climate change and resource depletion were not pressing issues, and therefore not considered. I conclude with an overview of the key economists and philosophers who explicitly consider sustainability and corporate responsibility in their assessment of society and business. This chapter will conclude with discussing new trends and theories capturing the sustainable element of business models.

Chapter 4, "Key Tools for Social and Environmental Performance and the UN Sustainable Development Goals (SDGs)", starts with reflections on the role of corporations in a sustainability setting. Corporate responsibility provides the foundation for sustainable development. It is a complex sphere since there are several confusing initiatives intended to help companies incorporate sustainability. From an international perspective, the UN initiatives have had the most impact. I provide a short introduction to the history of key UN initiatives associated with environmental and social issues and how they relate to business and corporations. As the UN Sustainable Development Goals (SDGs) have a key global framework for sustainable development, they will be discussed in detail with special attention to challenges and practical relevance for corporations. Well known and widely applied initiatives to evaluate corporate performance like Fair Trade Certificate and ISO 14001, Greenhouse and climate reporting initiatives, like the greenhouse gas (GHG) Protocol, CDP, Task Force on Climate-Related Financial Disclosures (TCFD), Sustainable reporting frameworks, like Global Reporting Initiative (GRI) and International Integrated Reporting Council (IIRC), and Supply chain guidance and due diligence like the OECD Guidelines for

Multinational Enterprises, and new laws on transparency, will be presented.

Chapter 5, "The Business Case for Sustainability", discusses how companies address sustainability challenges. First, the chapter begins with examples of different corporate approaches to taking responsibility for sustainability. Second, I explore how companies are viewed from the stakeholder perspective, so how others outside the company view the managers' motivations for engaging in corporate responsibility. Although most companies are still motivated by risk reduction and/or marketing in their sustainability work, this chapter will reframe the motivations into something more positive—a business opportunity. Four cases will be presented, Nike, Arthur Andersen, Volkswagen, and companies involved in the Raana Plaza tragedy, and the companies' approaches relative to the following strategies will be discussed: reacting, defending, accommodating, and finally, a proactive approach in which a business's profitability is anchored in sustainability. This chapter will conclude with reflections on business models for sustainability.

Chapter 6, "Circular Economy: New Business Models", begins with an overview of the key challenges faced by society with a linear economy and proceeds to the concept of circular economy, its potential and associated challenges. Key elements in circular economy will be addressed including issues like "refuse", "reduce", reuse", "refurbish", and "recycle". I provide numerous examples to illustrate the different approaches in practice. The role of different stakeholders in the process of achieving a circular economy is discussed. Lastly, the transition from selling products to providing services is addressed.

In Chap. 7, "Strategy to Approach Sustainability in Companies: A Step by Step Model", I present a strategy for approaching sustainability in a corporation. It emphasizes the importance of anchoring the approach in top management and integrating it throughout the company; getting an overview of the current situation via mapping social and environmental impact, benchmarking relative to the SDGs, and a framework for a materiality assessment. This chapter continues on how to develop a sustainability plan, test among key stakeholders, launching, communicating, and implementing the plan, and finally, reporting on progress. This chapter includes practical advice on progress as well as concrete examples based on experience.

Chapter 8, "Stakeholder Management", addresses the key role of stakeholders in the corporate world, and especially related to sustainability. Even peripheral stakeholders can have great impact on companies. This is an important consideration that companies need to be aware of and consider. In this chapter, I explore the roles of different kinds of stakeholders such as owners, investors, employees, governments, suppliers, customers, NGOs, and the media, and how to communicate and involve these stakeholders in a constructive manner. I address the function of each respective stakeholder as well potential areas for positive collaboration. The power and impact of NGOs on corporations will receive special attention as they often act as representatives for environmental and social interests—and bring such issues to the attention of others. Cases are provided to illustrate the issues presented.

Chapter 9, "Sustainability and Finance: Environmental, Social and Governance (ESG)", addresses the key role and function of finance in the business world. From being included in small and specialized funds, Environment, Social and Governance (ESG), and socially responsible investment (SRI) have become part of the mainstream for investors and analysts. In this chapter, I will address what ESG, SRI, environmental and social risk assessment, and ethical investment are about, as well as different investment strategies taking these into account. Further, dilemmas that arise are introduced such as what is a sustainable sector or product and how this differs based on the values of individuals. The move from addressing sustainability issues as a risk reduction activity to a business opportunity is discussed. Finally, the Norwegian Pension Fund the world's largest sovereign wealth fund, is used as an example to illustrate product-based and conduct-based exclusions in practice.

Chapter 10, "Anti-corruption", is anchored in the challenges associated with sustainability when corruption exists. Representing at least five percent of world GDP, corruption is a great challenge in general, and especially associated with sustainable business, both nationally and internationally. In this chapter, I reflect on how to address corruption and anti-corruption practices. Typical forms of corruption include bribery, facilitation payments, gifts, hospitality and expenses, political contributions, charitable contributions, sponsorships, voluntary community contributions, trading in influence, and conflict of interest and impartiality. Corruption leads to weak institutions and injustice, less respect for rights, denial of basic services. And much of the world's environmental damage and tragedies are associated with corruption. Studies show that almost half of the companies have experienced fraud over the past two years. This chapter addresses the corruption challenges, how they are addressed by corporations and key international laws as well as challenges associated with norms and behaviors. How to detect and avoid corruption receives key attention. As anti-corruption is a huge topic and challenge, yet it is limited space available in the book, the topic is presented from a more general perspective. Even though anti-corruption is often left out when talking about sustainability, it cannot be excluded from a book on sustainability and responsibility.

Chapter 11, "Sustainability in Developing Countries: Case Sub-Saharan Africa", is anchored in Goal #1 of the SDGs: No poverty. In 1995, 10 percent world population lived in extreme poverty. More than one billion, almost 13 percent of the world population, live in Sub-Saharan Africa. This area accounts for two-thirds of global extreme poverty. At the same time, Africa has the fastest growing population with a median age under 20 years, and about 30 percent of the Earth's remaining mineral resources. This dynamic calls for special attention and sustainable development in Sub-Saharan Africa is the focus in this chapter. The chapter begins with an analysis of Africa's current situation in terms of development; it details challenges and opportunities, and through concrete cases and examples summarizes what has worked and what has not worked. Based on this foundation, key issues for a sustainable future in Sub-Sahara Africa is addressed. Examples of businesses built on sustainable resources and business opportunities are also presented.

Chapter 12, "The Way Forward: Is Sustainable Development Realistic?", addresses the future of sustainable development. Given the fact that current consumption in developed countries is unsustainable, and a similar level of consumption in developing countries would be devastating from an environmental perspective, a shift in development is necessary. This chapter touches upon peoples' human needs and discusses to which extent unsustainable consumption is a necessity for a happiness. Alternative approaches to GDP in measuring a country's success, like Gross National Happiness (BNH), and the Happy Planet Index (HPI), are discussed. Shifting focus from increased consumption of natural resources to more attention on development associated with social issues like well-being, health, and happiness will be addressed. This chapter concludes with how sustainable development and happy people is realistic, but it will require a shift associated with revised business models, metrics, and goals.

References

Hoffmann, A. J. (2018). The next phase of business sustainability. *Stanford Social Innovation Review, 16*(2), 34–39. https://ssir.org/articles/entry/the_next_phase_of_business_sustainability

Si, S., Ahlstrom, D., Wei, J., & Cullen, J. (2020). Business, entrepreneurship and innovation toward poverty reduction. *Entrepreneurship & Regional Development, 32*(1/2), 1–20. https://doi.org/10.1080/08985626.2019.1640485. https://search.ebscohost.com/login.aspx?direct=true&db=bth&AN=140851015&site=ehost-live&scope=site

2

Sustainable Corporate Responsibility

In this chapter, I start by reflecting on the origins of terms related to sustainability and what they actually mean. I will explore their historical context and about different, multilateral frameworks pertaining to sustainability, in particular ones adopted by UN member states. The responsibility of corporations from a philosophical perspective including key ethical schools of thoughts will also be addressed.

2.1 The Corporation

To incorporate is to combine into one "body". It has to do with entities, like individuals, joining forces for a common business goal. It is easier to realize a goal together than alone. Corporations have been established for hundreds of years. However, it is only during the last decades that we have seen a substantial growth in their number and size. This is a direct consequence of industrialization, moving from an agricultural society to an economy dominated by mechanized production and services. This transition has also led to the need for laws to regulate corporations.

C. D. Ditlev-Simonsen, *A Guide to Sustainable Corporate Responsibility*,
https://doi.org/10.1007/978-3-030-88203-7_2

In today's society, large corporations play a major role. Measured in revenues, five of the world's largest economies are corporations: Walmart, State Grid, Sinopec Group, China National Petroleum, and Royal Dutch Shell. Their revenues exceed that of Mexico, Sweden, Russia, and Belgium together (Global Justice Now, 2018). This power in the world economy also carries great responsibility.

Corporations have many of the same rights and requirements as individuals. They own assets, pay taxes, take loans, and generate profits and losses. However, there is one major difference between corporations and individuals; the fact that corporations have limited liability. Whereas individuals are personally responsible for actions they take, those who invest in a company are only liable for the amount they invested. When the capital is gone, so are their responsibilities. Companies cannot pay for any damages done in the past, when the company is bankrupt or ceases to exist.

Corporations are usually established by individuals, who as shareholders pursue business endeavors that they themselves could not have started alone. For corporations in general, the goal is to engage in activities that are beneficial for its investors in order to generate profit. Sustainability is not necessarily aligned with this goal. This is where regulations enter into the picture. Governments regulate corporations to ensure that profit is generated without inflicting excessive damage to our society and planet. Corporations have a responsibility to abide by laws and regulations. Still, most regulatory regimes do not provide a framework resulting in sustainable development and many of the goals and targets for improved performance are not implemented.

2.2 Limits to Growth: From an Environmental Perspective

Prior to the Industrial Revolution, there was only about one million people on the planet and most of them were farmers. On a planet with a small population with low consumption and hardly any waste, "sustainable development" was a non-issue. In the 1970s, the global population nearly tripled and for people in the industrialized world, consumption had increased tremendously—mainly based on products manufactured by corporations. This resulted in substantial environmental damage as well as many societal challenges. In this context, realizing the limits of our planet, the relevance and focus on sustainable development merged.

Discussions about the degree of our planet's limitations have been ongoing for several centuries, but mainly from the consideration of scarcity. Already in the 1800s, Thomas R. Malthus claimed that there would be ceaseless resource and food shortages. His argument was that as soon as food production increased, the population would grow and the food surplus would be consumed, eventually leading to famine. This had also been the fact for much of history.

However, the Industrial Revolution was taking place in the same period and the move to factory production changed this situation for at least in the short run. People living in the part of the world engaged in the industrialization process became rich, while those in the non-industrialized part of the world also experienced changes, but mostly the negative consequences.

Books like *Silent Spring* by Rachel Carson, published in 1962, also drew attention to the negative impact of industrialization and its damaging effects on the planet. She was especially concerned about products attempting to control nature, for example, pesticides like DDT, which had long-term ecological impacts. She argued that such insidious products would lead to the extinction of key "actors" within the natural biological cycle, ultimately ruining the basis for our society, resulting in a silent spring. Initially neither corporations nor regulators were aware of these potential long-term negative effects. Not understanding the full scope of the negative environmental impact of products made assessing business risk and regulating them especially challenging. Beginning in the 1970s, the focus on environmental concerns substantially increased.

It was in 1970 that the ecological footprint exceeded the Earth's carrying capacity. In Fig. 2.1, the solid line illustrates the Earth's capacity, whereas the dotted line illustrates the growth in consumption and the collective footprint of the global population.

An Ecological Footprint is a "measure of how much area of biologically productive land and water an individual, population, or activity requires

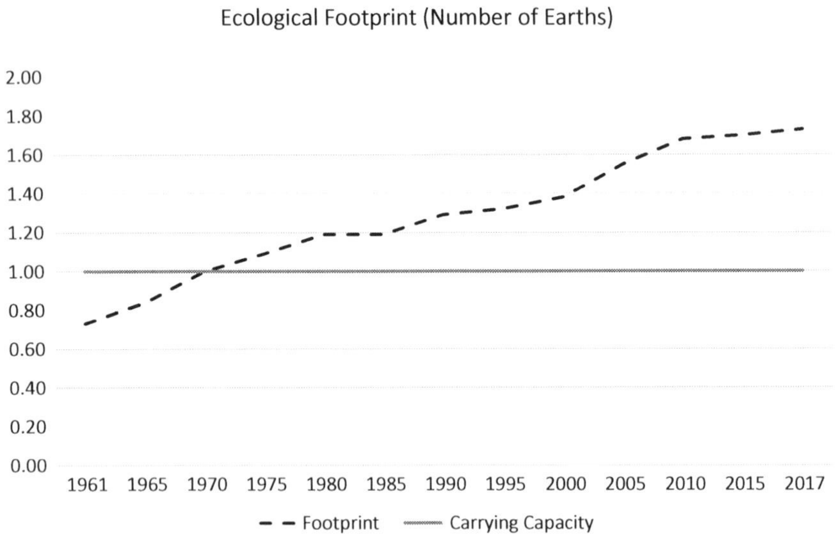

Fig. 2.1 The growth in consumption relative to the planet capacity—Ecological Footprint

to produce all the resources it consumes and to absorb the waste it generates, using prevailing technology and resource management practices. The Ecological Footprint is usually measured in global hectares. Because trade is global, an individual or country's Footprint includes land or sea from all over the world. Without further specification, Ecological Footprint generally refers to the Ecological Footprint of consumption. Ecological Footprint is often referred to in short form as Footprint."[1]

The book *Limit to Growth* published in 1972 is largely considered as the beginning of a new era with regards to awareness and focus on environmental challenges. Thereafter governments and eventually corporations became concerned and consequently many initiatives were launched to confront its associated challenges.

Environmental challenges moving from local pollution to global challenges called for an international approach. The United Nations (UN) is one of the few international organizations, which eventually took on a leading role in addressing global environmental challenges. Still, the UN

[1] https://data.footprintnetwork.org/.

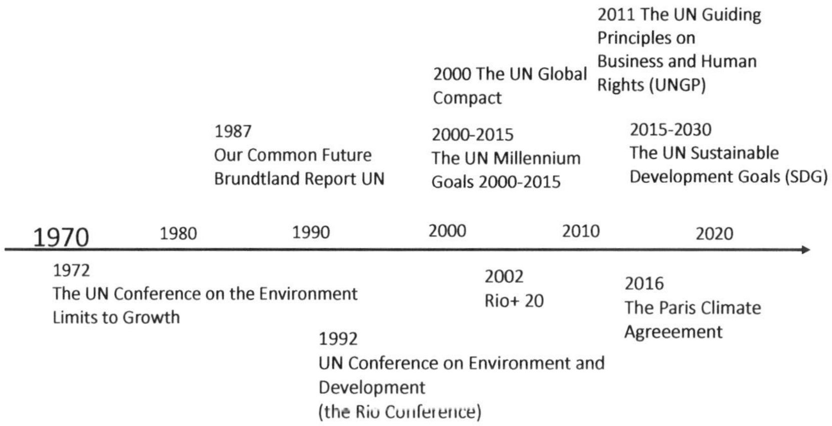

Fig. 2.2 Timeline for key sustainability related events since 1970

was established many years prior for different reasons. The following section provides an introduction to the UN and how it became a key actor in the pursuit of sustainable development.

Figure 2.2 provides a timeline for the key events since the launch of *Limits to Growth.*

2.3 The United Nations

The United Nations was established in 1945 after World War II initially as a forum to maintain peace and for resolving conflicts between countries. The global war was devastating in its aftermath. It incurred significant losses of life, estimated at more than 70 million people and major destruction of industrial production and public infrastructure resulting in negative economic consequences.

Recognizing that many social challenges are global, the United Nations was crucial to identify, collaborate, and develop solutions. In response to the challenges facing humanity, the United Nations (UN) Charter was signed in June 1945. Key elements in Article 1, the purpose of the UN, were in summary to maintain international peace and security, to develop friendly relations among nations, to achieve international cooperations, and to be a center for harmonizing these actions (United Nations, 1945). At the California Conference in 1945, the UN, an "international organization designed to end war and promote peace, justice and better living for all mankind" became a reality. The Universal Declaration of Human Rights (UDHR) was launched in 1948.

UN engagement has changed over time. Focus on issues such as ensuring human rights and avoiding of war, including the Cold War, nuclear weapons, de-colonialization, and so on, which have all received the most attention. From addressing these issues, the gravity shifted and other stakeholders, like non-governmental organizations (NGOs) became involved. Amnesty International was for example established in 1961 and Human Rights Watch was established in 1978. These NGOs drew attention to how nations violated the UDHR and these allegations were later followed up by the UN.

From the 1970s, the UN became increasingly focused on world culture and environmental issues. It expanded its operations and today, the UN is a "family of organizations". The International Monetary Fund (IMF), the World Bank (WB), Food and Agriculture Organization (FOA), International Atomic Energy Agency (IAEA), International Maritime Organization (IMO), International Labor Organization (ILO), World Health Organization (WHO) are some of the 15 independent organizations linked to the UN through cooperative agreements. Today, the UN is the world's largest intergovernmental organization with 193 member nations.

In an international setting, agreements between countries through the UN are important measurements. However, many of these initiatives are not legally binding. Countries can sign up to UN principles, but cannot be fined if the principles are not fulfilled. Still, UN principles often form a basis for national laws in countries and many of these laws affect corporations. From the standpoint of sustainable development, the UN Sustainable Development Goals (SDGs) launched in 2015 is the key contribution, which will be later addressed in Chap. 3. Next, important UN initiatives concerning social and environmental issues are introduced.

2.4 The Universal Declaration of Human Rights (UDHR) 1948

The Universal Declaration of Human Rights (UDHR) is not legally binding but establishes a set of norms for how countries shall operate. It is noteworthy that freedom of speech, religion, and civil rights were great challenges at the time the UDHR was proclaimed. These issues still are today, but, through the UDHR, at least countries have agreed upon a universal goal with regards to rights related to issues as race, color, sex, and so on. The key principle is stated in Article 1. "All humans being are born free and equal in dignity and rights" (United Nations, 1948).

So, why is the Human Rights declaration relevant for corporations? Several of the articles within the declaration are related to work and the rights of employees—even though the term "corporation" or "business" is not included in the declaration. For example, Article 23. "1. Everyone has the right to work, to free choice of employment, to just and favorable conditions of work and to protection against unemployment" and 2. "Everyone, without any discrimination, has the right to equal pay for equal work." Article 24 states that "Everyone has the right to rest and leisure, including reasonable limitation of working hours and periodic holidays with pay." All these clauses concern corporations.

The working conditions in the sweatshop industry are not acceptable with regard to the UDHR. Today, for example, the garments industry represents 80 percent of Bangladesh's total export earnings, and it is still quite typical for employees to work 80 hours per week (Menke, 2017). Sustainability challenges in the supply chain will be addressed in greater detail in Chap. 8.

Today many of the UDHR principles are not met. There are still more than 40 million people trapped in modern-day slavery, most working in corporations, or even more common, providing products and services to corporations. Slaves are at the bottom of the supply chain. This implies that everyone today might wear clothes or carry goods such as cellphones that have been manufactured using slave labor. In that sense, human rights issues are very relevant when it comes to a company's operations and responsibility.

The UN, as an international organization supported by 193 nations, is the most important source of common goals for sustainable development, particularly with regard to human rights and the environment. Chapter 4 will focus on UN initiatives and agreements that pertain to corporations, such as the UN Global Compact (2000), the UN Millennium Goals (2000), and the UN Sustainable Development Goals (2015). These initiatives were all developed in cooperation with corporations. So, they provide a basis for agreements not only between nations, but also between corporations and governments.

2.5 United Nations and Sustainable Development: Our Common Future (1987)

Many of the environmental challenges the world is facing today are international in nature. CO_2 emissions in Europe and North America impact Africa and Asia by contributing for example to extreme weather cycles. Effects are felt whether or not a country is responsible for the emissions. This was a key driver for the first world conference on environmental challenges held in 1972, the UN Conference on the Human Environment—Stockholm Conference.

It was a turning point in the development of international environmental issues and politics. Problems associated with worldwide pollution of air, water, and oceans were acknowledged along with the need to address them at an international level.

A follow-up of this conference was the book *Our Common Future*, commonly referred to as the "Brundtland Report", published in 1987 by the UN. The report was a result of the Brundtland Commission's mandate by the UN General Assembly in 1983:

- "to propose long-term environmental strategies for achieving sustainable development by the year 2000 and beyond;
- to recommend ways concern for the environment may be translated into greater cooperation among developing countries and between

countries at different stages of economic and social development and lead to the achievement of common and mutually supportive objectives that take account of the interrelationships between people, resources, environment, and development;
- to consider ways and means by which the international community can deal more effectively with environment concerns;
- to help define shared perceptions of long-term environmental issues and the appropriate efforts needed to deal successfully with the problems of protecting and enhancing the environment, a long-term agenda for action during the coming decades, and aspirational goals for the world community." (World Commission on Environment and Development, 1987)

The concept of "Sustainable Development" was launched after the publication of this book, which gave it a concrete definition which everybody could relate to and apply. Even though the term is rather broad, it provides an inclusive indication, which eases the dialogue between different stakeholders.

> *Sustainable development is development that meets the needs of the present without compromising the ability of future generations to meet their own needs.* (World Commission on Environment and Development, 1987, p. 41)

Figure 2.3 illustrates the growth in "Sustainable Development" attention in media.

The Brundtland Commission consisted of representatives from 21 nations from both developed and developing countries, politicians, civil servants, and environmental experts. It took about 900 days to write the report. Although corporations were not included in the commission, they were invited to contribute along with other stakeholders.

The role of transnational corporations (TNCs) and their responsibilities were repeatedly addressed in the report. This is an example of such a statement, "Transnational corporations have a special responsibility to smooth the path of industrialization in the nations in which they operate". To illustrate their importance, the report pinpoints three to six of the largest translational corporations and control over 80 percent of trade

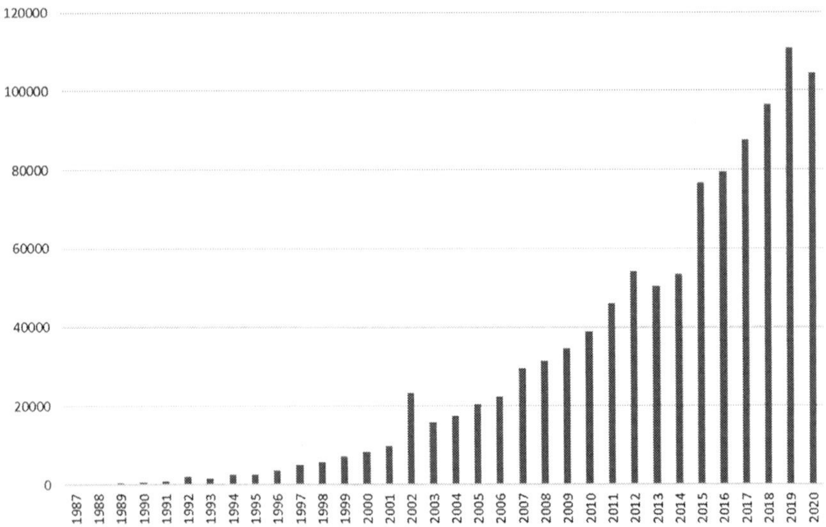

Fig. 2.3 Search on "sustainable development". Factiva database

in key agricultural and metals commodities such as tea, coffee, cocoa, cotton, forest products, copper, iron ore, bauxite, and so on.

However, this focus on transnational corporations in an environmental and social context was not completely new. Whereas the focus was previously on how to regulate them, it shifted toward *cooperating* together in solving challenges. Issues pertaining to pesticides and accident prevention in the chemical industry had already been addressed in the 1970s and the 1980s.

The report picks up and credits constructive initiatives led by corporates to tackle environmental challenges. The 1984 World Industry Conference on Environmental Management (WICEM) is explicitly mentioned. The follow-up of this conference, the International Environment Bureau (IEB), a group of corporations from a number of developed countries committed to assist developing countries with their development needs, is also mentioned. "Such initiatives are promising and should be encouraged" (page 271).

It is disappointing that the challenges the Brundtland report put forward in 1992 are the same challenges we are facing today. The main difference is that the problems associated with these challenges are even more extensive and advanced today than they were 30 years ago. The role of the international economy, population and human resources, food security, endangered species and ecosystems, energy (nuclear energy, wood fuels, renewable energy, and energy efficiency) are all put forward as areas that need action. Fossil fuels are identified as a continuing dilemma, nuclear energy as an unsolved problem, wood fuels as vanishing resources and renewable energy as a source of untapped potential.

Industry is urged to produce more with less. Efforts are needed to manage the commons: oceans, space and the polar regions, peacekeeping, and proposals for regulatory change. Already then, the challenge of CO_2 emissions and global warming were being discussed. The only difference between now and then is that whereas annual CO_2 emission in 1986 was 20 billion tons, in 2019, a little more than 30 years later, the CO_2 emissions have almost doubled to 36 billion tons (Ritchie & Roser, n.d.). Still, alternative and more sustainable energy sources have emerged at a continuous lower price. Solar power cost has, for example, fallen by more than 85 percent in the last decade and is now able to generate electricity at a lower price than the world's cheapest new coal plants (Ambrose, 2021).

Relatively however, there are disturbingly few areas in the world which have improved with regards to the total global footprint since the Brundtland report was released. Still, there are exceptions, and one example is the emissions of gases that contribute to the depletion of the ozone layer. Through a UN agreement, these emissions have almost been entirely phased out. This is an example illustrating how collaboration between companies across borders can have a major positive impact—even, and maybe due to, less interference from nations. This successful case deserves further attention and will be described in greater detail later in the chapter.

2.6 UN and Sustainable Development (UNCED): The Rio Conference 1992

In June 1992, 178 nations, more than 100 heads of states, and over 2000 representatives from non-state actors such as businesses and NGOs, joined together at the UN Conference on Environment and Development (UNCED), also referred to as Earth Summit, in Rio de Janeiro. Prior to the meeting, countries had been working on drafting treaties aimed at preserving biodiversity and the climate to protect the planet. These two issues were perceived as the most challenging from an environmental standpoint. The result of the Rio Conference was, among others, the Framework Convention on Climate Change and Convention on Biological Diversity.

In addition, Agenda 21 was launched, a comprehensive report on actions needed worldwide to attain sustainable development. Reducing unsustainable consumption in rich countries was a key message. Global, national, and local actors were part of this plan. The main focus however was on government actions and there was less focus on role of corporations. In this 351-page report, the term "corporation" was only mentioned 39 times and "business" 69 times. One can argue that to solve the challenges raised, actions involving companies would be crucial—yet their role in developing Agenda 21 was minor.

The Agenda 21 never became an important tool or initiative in the pursuit of sustainable development. In that respect, the UN SDGs, which to a large extent were written with the same purpose as Agenda 21, have become much more prominent and applied. Maybe one of the reasons for this is that corporations were more involved in the process. The fact that the 17 SDG goals are also organized in a simple and colorful way, not in a lengthy report, might also explain the attention they have received.

The 1993 Convention on Biological Diversity and 1996 Convention to Combat Desertification have both had limited effects and are largely considered failures. The absence of good data, funding, and a dedicated body to oversee implementation are typical explanations for the lack of results.

The Framework Convention on Climate Change did not have any specific targets. However, this framework created the basis for the Kyoto Protocol in 1997, which entered into force in 2005. In this protocol, industrialized countries committed to reducing their emissions of all greenhouse gases by about five percent from 1990 to 2012. Few, if any, countries actually reached this goal. As with most conventions, there were no penalties associated with not meeting the set targets.

The fact that the negative effect of rising CO_2 emissions are clearly visible today with sea water levels rising, changing temperatures and bouts of extreme weather, all serve as reminders of its impact on climate change. These clear signals have generated more interest among nations to follow up and take measures to attenuate the situation. At the same time, it can be argued that adapting to the global warming challenges locally by for example changing building codes or constructing further away from the coastline have received more attention and funding than reducing the international global problem of climate change.

Following up the Climate Convention of 1992, and later the Kyoto Protocol, the Paris Agreement was launched in 2015. This was the first legally binding international treaty on climate change. The goal is to limit global warming at least below two degrees Celsius compared to pre-industrial levels. Almost all countries in the world have endorsed the agreement which includes provisions for implementing climate actions. Still, only certain provisions carry legal force and signatories can decide whether or not to fulfil their pledge or withdraw entirely from the agreement as the United States suddenly did in 2019.[2] Luckily, the United States decided to reenter a year later after a change in political leadership.

Annually, there is an international climate meeting called the Conference of the Parties (COP), where there are discussions on implementing the climate convention. The main challenge, however, is to make countries actually follow up on their pledge and commit financial support to developing countries. By 2020, the goal was to raise $100 billion USD annually. By 2017, developed countries had only managed to raise slightly more than $70 billion USD to help developing countries

[2] An agreement among almost 200 nations on how to reduce greenhouse gas emissions, including concrete goals, and finance for poorer nations.

mitigate and adapt to the negative effects of climate change (Laramée de Tannenberg, 2019). Most recently, there is a dramatic need to financial assist developing countries in their efforts to counter COVID-19, which is competing in priority.

2.7 Corporate Engagement on Responsibility: From Reactive to Proactive

For a long time, corporations were responding negatively to environmental and social criticism. Gradually this dynamic changed or at least from an official corporate public relations standpoint. A good example on this process of change is the Montreal Protocol. In the 1970s, it was discovered that fluorocarbons (CFCs, HCFCs, and HFCs), used in for example refrigerators, freezers, and air conditioners, were depleting the ozone layer, resulting in an increase in solar radiation and global warming. Still, major producers of CFCs such as DuPont and Honeywell consistently argued that their products did not cause the hole in the ozone layer. However, after a long process, CFC producers participated in drafting the Montreal Protocol, a plan to phase out ozone depleting substances, which entered into force in 1989. After 25 years, almost 98 percent of these substances had been phased out, and new and less damaging products had been developed to replace them. In retrospect, the agreement could be deemed quite successful and serve as a good example for other international environmental agreements. If the Montreal protocol had not been successfully implemented, it would have added an extra 2.5°C to current global warming projections by the end of the century.

It is suggested that the first time transnational corporations were officially invited to the UN was when the International Chamber of Commerce (ICC), the largest and most representative business organization in the world, gave a 15-minute presentation at the Stockholm conference in 1972 (Gleckman, 1995). The first World Industry Conference on Environmental Management (WICEM I), referred to in the Brundtland report, took place in 1984. The second WICEM conference took place in Rotterdam in 1991. After WICEM II the book, *From Ideas to Action* (Willums, 1992), was published.[3] From lobbying against environmental regulations, large corporations had shifted their strategies to participating in shaping international environmental regulations to be more effective and operational. Corporate involvement in sustainable development also serves to avoid draconian regulations by politicians with no business experience nor competence in the field.

Still, there were actors from outside the business sphere, who were skeptical of the ICC, claiming that the motives behind these corporate initiatives were to avoid controlling regulations which would be good for the environment but bad for business. Corporations on the other hand claimed that the UN was unfitted to develop regulations, which would efficiently lead to a more sustainable world—and companies. The ICC was also struggling with long-time frames in their decision-making processes due to its many members and democratic organization.

To be able to come up with a significant and coherent contribution to the Rio Conference in 1991, a more agile organization was needed. To respond to this challenge, a group of transnational corporations, many of the world's largest corporations at the time, joined forces through the Business Council for Sustainable Development (BCSD), later adding World to the title (WBCSD) in 1991 (Gleckman, 1995). Stephan Schmidheiny, a wealthy business entrepreneur, was appointed as chief adviser for business and industry by the UN Secretary General in association with the Rio Conference. WBCSD was a CEO led organization with initially CEOs from 48 international companies, for example, ENI Italy, Volkswagen Germany, 3M USA, Nippon Japan, ABB Sweden, TATA India, Shell Group UK, Rio Brazil, and Norsk Hydro Norway. The members were carefully selected and joined by invitation only. The fact that the member CEOs spoke in their personal capacities, rather than on behalf of their respective enterprises, made the organization efficient. The BCSD represented a constructive group of leaders, who were keen to work on sustainable development across sectors and borders.

Schmidheiny together with the BCSD CEO members published the book *Changing Course, A Global Business Perspective on Development and the Environment*, in May 1992, in time for the Rio Conference in June

[3] I prepared "most of the background analysis for the first two sections."

the same year. Different companies worked together to provide solutions to key challenges from a business perspective. This was perhaps the starting point for a unified global corporate collaboration for sustainable development and it also coined the concept of eco-efficiency. In the book, each chapter was written by different groups of transnational companies on how to address sustainability challenges. Having worked as the coordinator, administrating the 25 member companies of the Energy Working Group, which formed the basis of the Chap. 3 "Energy and the Marketplace", I witnessed and recognized the true environmental concern and constructive attitude among the all CEOs involved.

However, the main contribution of the book and the WBCSD was perhaps the establishment of a forum for companies pursuing sustainable development, contributing approaches and solutions that would be realistic for the business community. Since 1992 the WBCSD continues to grow, now boasting almost 200 "forward-thinking global companies committed to advance the sustainability agenda", working actively on projects and plans across the world.

It is important to keep in mind that corporations sometimes have the capacity to implement changes more quickly and efficiently than governments, where decisions have to undergo an extensive political process. The top management and the board of directors can make decisions, say to become carbon neutral within 10 years, in just one day, whereas politicians can talk about this for years without committing to an agenda.

The importance of the role of corporations can be illustrated by their sheer size. For example, Walmart is the world's largest company with respect to employees. The company has about 2.2 million employees, which is more than the total populations of Slovenia (2.1 million people), Cyprus (1.2 million people), and Luxembourg (0.6 million people) (Worldometers.info). This underlines the importance of involving and regulating corporations in order to make strides in sustainable development.

Although corporations are the main emitters of substances such as CO_2 and waste, relative to production, it is fair to acknowledge that companies have also made improvements in time. Moving from producing big gas guzzlers to small electric cars is one example. Developing LED light bulbs to replace incandescent light bulbs is another example of sustainable innovation. However, as the global population increases, consumption follows step and the total amounts of emissions and waste have increased as well. Still, the emissions and pollution per product to a large extent have been reduced.

Typical of environmental issues is that there is a lag before we become aware of its negative effects. There are many examples of products that exhibit such characteristics. Asbestos, a mineral exhibiting insulation and fire-resistant properties is one such example. After years of using asbestos in the construction industry, asbestos was many years later found to cause cancer and other illnesses. Now, it is banned in over 60 countries.

2.8 UN Conference on Sustainable Development, Rio+20, 2012

In 2012, another UN conference on sustainable development was arranged, again in Brazil, often referred to as Rio+20. This time, Agenda 21 was followed up and a new document, "The Future We Want", was introduced. This document focuses on the most critical global challenges facing society including poverty eradication; food security and sustainable agriculture; energy; sustainable transport; sustainable cities; health and population; promoting full and productive employment.

The Rio+20 conference did not attract as many heads of states as the Rio conference in 1992 and no legally binding agreements were adopted. Still, a common agreement for a global framework was structured and a call was made for drafting a set of sustainable development goals. This conference in effect was the key driver for the development of the SDGs, which will be further discussed in Chap. 4.

2.9 Responsibility: From an Ethical Point of View

Companies and their employees continuously face situations associated with sustainability where there is no absolute "right" or "wrong" decisions. Such situations can be linked to temptation, crises, and paradoxes. Many of these situations pose ethical challenges. The question often arises; to whom is the company responsible and how far does that responsibility reach?

In such situations, it can be useful to reflect on alternative decisions from a more classical ethical point of view. In this chapter, I will discuss different corporate dilemmas from the point of view of key ethical perspectives: virtue ethics, duty ethics, and utilitarianism. Even though the philosophers with these perspectives lived several centuries ago, from the point of view of decision-making, it is still equally relevant even though the setting has changed.

To illustrate an ethical dilemma, I will use the timeless and well-known Trolley problem. Philippa Foot, a moral philosopher, put forward this dilemma over 50 years ago, and since it has been extended and discussed so much that it has opened a whole field, sometimes referred to as trolleyology. The dilemma is what a bystander can and should do when an out of control trolley is heading toward five people on railroad tracks. The bystander can take an active role, pull a lever which will divert the trolley to an alternative track and lead to only one death. Or, by doing nothing, the bystander will witness the trolley collide into the five people on the tracks, which will result in five deaths. The bystander's dilemma is essentially a question of whether or not to be passive or active, interfered as the events unfold, and to which extent we should act on personal values to change situations. This case can initially seem rather farfetched with regards to corporations; however, today companies are continuously facing similar challenges. They are confronted with situations that have no rules or regulations to guide their decisions. A contemporary example is participating in the nascent self-driving car industry.

Ethical considerations for self-driving cars are becoming increasingly relevant today as the technology advances. On the one hand, such cars can actually reduce accidents and contribute to less traffic problems. However, they also include ethical challenges. If a self-driving car faces an unavoidable accident, who should be saved if the alternatives are either the car owner (the passenger) or a pedestrian, perhaps a child or elderly person. Alternatively, if the child or the elderly person is walking across the road on a crosswalk, should the car automatically go off-road and injure or kill the passenger or hit the pedestrian to protect the car owner? Mercedes-Benz received lot of criticism when they stated that their self-driven cars would be programmed to prioritize saving the life of the car owner (Morris, 2016).

The above example illustrates how ethical dilemmas can be timeless. Based on that, I will discuss three different ethical approaches and link them to more contemporary situations which are relevant in a sustainability setting. This can be useful in clarifying and evaluating different options facing corporations.

Virtue Ethics

Virtue ethics are often associated with Aristotle, who lived in Greece over 2400 years ago.

According to Aristotle, happiness (eudaimonia) is the ultimate goal. However, he argued that indulging in pleasure does not lead to happiness. Happiness is associated with the character of the decision maker. A person, or as we shall see, corporations, with the right character will make the right decision. The right character is developed through experience and is a balance between different virtues. This is often referred to as a "golden mean", not too much or too little of different characters.

The four cardinal virtues are prudence, temperance, courage, and justice. These virtues are regarded as the basis for living a good and righteous life and relevant to managers and leaders as well. Behaving with prudence includes not making hasty decisions. Temperance is for example about not giving up when the company is struggling. Courage is about not always doing what is most convenient and comfortable and an example of justice is treating employees equally, irrelevant of race or gender. Finding the right balance makes us capable to make the right decision in different situations and gives a level of achievement and contentment, thus happiness.

A simplified example of virtuous behavior related to sustainability is what a manager of a company in the fossil fuel sector, like BP, Shell, and Equinor, faces. Given that CO_2 emissions from the industry contribute to global warming, there are many different approaches a manager could take to make the company sustainable. Deciding to dissolve the company could be considered extreme, yet some environmentalists advocate it. Alternatively, the manager could take a more balanced approach. The company could gradually decarbonize its operations, improve its energy efficiency and shift the core business to renewable energies.

Aristotle's perception of the pursuit of happiness reflects the values of the time and place of his life. More than 2000 years later, and with knowledge associated with many different cultures, what is the "right" decision is even more complex than that during Aristotle's time. For individuals today, the understanding of what right behavior entails is often closely associated with belief systems. Different religions can vary greatly in their interpretation of what is right and wrong in the same situation. Sometimes extreme interpretations of religious text for relatively minor offences elsewhere could result in the death penalty. For some suicide, terrorism can be perceived as virtuous martyrdom. This illustrates how the understanding of virtues differs across the world. Variation between what is right and wrong also exists among leaders and in company cultures. All these different interpretations and contexts reinforce the need for and importance of the UN SDGs, adopted, supported, and commonly agreed upon by the majority of world's nations.

Corporations can also be perceived as individuals with rights and responsibilities. To develop its own character, their "virtue", most large companies today have developed mission or vision statements, and a set of accompanying core values conveying what exactly they are pursuing along the lines of sustainability. Patagonia's purpose is to be "in Business To Save Our Home Planet" and IKEA's vision is "to create a better everyday life for the many people—for customers, but also for our co-workers and the people who work at our suppliers." These are examples in which companies acknowledge their virtuous responsibility for a sustainable future. More examples on corporate vision and mission statements are presented in Chaps. 5 and 7.

Key virtuous words in corporate purpose and mission statements are examples of the relevance of Aristotle today. Examples of such key values are typically "honest", "trustworthy", "innovative", "loyal", "reliable", "responsible", "collaborative", "ambitious", "sustainable", and so on. A study analyzing how sustainability in the S&P 500 is reflected in corporate strategic documents found that "generating the profit" appeared in 69 percent of companies surveyed, "caring for the people" appeared in 34 percent and "safeguarding the planet" in 14 percent of the respective companies. Further, 12 percent of the companies included references to the triple bottom line in their strategic documents (Baral et al., 2016).

Duty Ethics Deontological Ethics

Deontological or duty based ethics is associated with several philosophers but in particular, Immanuel Kant, who lived more than two centuries ago. He argued that actions should be judged as "right" or "wrong" in and of themselves, not as the consequences of those actions. What is right or wrong is anchored in supposed universal moral principles of rules, such as it is wrong to steal, kill, and lie. Corporates should abide and make decisions based on local and national laws, even if the results do not lead to an outcome that is best for everyone.

From a deontological perspective, in which stealing is wrong, Robin Hood, taking from the rich and giving to the poor, would be unacceptable. For CEOs today, a deontological dilemma is whether or not their duty is to put shareholders first—or other stakeholders—or society as a whole. Is it acceptable to continue emitting CO_2 as long as it is legal, or does the company has a duty to reduce its CO_2 emissions even if it is not required?

In a corporate setting, companies are expected to follow the law. Breaking the law is rarely perceived as acceptable and based on a deontological approach, abiding by the laws and regulations is sufficient. However, during the last decades, as the level of responsible behavior among corporations has received more attention, the market and customers often expect companies to go beyond what is legally required.

In developing countries, regulations associated with social and environmental issues, such as working conditions and emissions can be less strict or lack systems to enforce compliance. Corporations, especially operating internationally, can be criticized by NGOs and media, even if they were following local laws. In response, several companies have set stricter self-imposed frameworks for operation that go beyond local or even international laws.

A key concept of the deontological ethics is that the laws should be universal. The challenge is that this is not the case. Working to write laws that are fair and just for all is important from a deontological perspective. The UN Human Rights principles are an example of a framework for universal societal laws, anchored in Kant's view. This applies to the UN

Global Compact for corporations and the UN SDGs for society in general. In this setting, the value of duty ethics becomes more evident, even though the concept might seem wrong, when applied to for instance the Robin Hood example.

Utilitarianism and Consequentialism

Utilitarianism and consequentialism are terms often used interchangeably. Both focus on the outcome of a decision, not the decision itself as such. David Hume, Jeremy Bentham, and John Stuart Mill, who lived several centuries ago, are often associated with the concept of decision-making based on bringing about the greatest amount of good or happiness for the greatest number of people.

According to utilitarianism, the result of the action is what matters—or the goal justifies the means. The optimal decision is what amounts to the most happiness for the most people. According to utilitarianism, Robin Hood stealing from the rich and giving to the poor would be ethically right. Helping a terminal ill person, who want to die would be acceptable from a consequentialist perspective. If corporation employs children in developing countries is acceptable when the alternative is begging or prostitution or not enough food to the family. From the consequentialist perspective, the goal justifies the means. While many people believe that child labor is wrong in any form, there are others who think it might be acceptable if the alternatives are even worse.

Still, a problematic area with the utilitarian approach is that it is not explicit whether the goals considered are in the short-term or long-term time horizon. What is best for the most in the short-term perspective might not be the best for the same people in the long term.

Virtue ethics, duty ethics, and consequentialism and utilitarianism are different approaches to the framework for deciding to whom and how the corporation is responsible. At first glance, these approaches to decision-making can seem quite farfetched. However, evaluating alternatives from the different ethical perspectives can prove to be a valuable tool in a tough decision-making process. Corporations might confront a dilemma in deciding to whom they have responsibility. Is it to the shareholders, the employees, or the customers? There is a thin line in determining which philosophy to apply in a constantly changing business environment. Particular to a sustainability setting, the uncertainty of what is right and wrong and to what extent a corporation is responsible is associated with dilemmas and challenges.

2.10 From Environmental Concern to Corporate (Social) Responsibility (C(S)R) and Sustainability: A History

Throughout recent history, there have been a multitude of terms, which have been applied to corporate engagement with environmental and societal challenges such as corporate citizenship, corporate responsibility (CR), corporate social responsibility (CSR), business ethics, Environment Social and Governance (ESG), sustainability, and even philanthropy. These concepts come from different traditions, yet they are often used interchangeably. What is common is that the concepts address the societal responsibility of corporations—with a special focus on environmental and social issues. Much of the discussion associated with these concepts regards how far this responsibility stretches, how it relates to business, and how to measure performance.

Until 2000, little attention was paid to CSR and it was hardly addressed by corporations or mentioned in the media. Figure 2.4 shows how the term gained the attention of the media over time since 1987.

The growth in media coverage of corporate social responsibility does not necessarily indicate an improvement in corporate behavior, specifically responsible companies, but rather the attention was paid to *irresponsible* companies. From the onset, companies' engagement and reporting on responsibility and corporate responsibility was predominately driven by criticism, especially from non governmental organizations (NGOs) such as the World Wide Fund for Nature (WWF), Amnesty International, Green Peace, and so on. It is also seemingly a paradox that the companies which reported the most on environment and social issues were also those

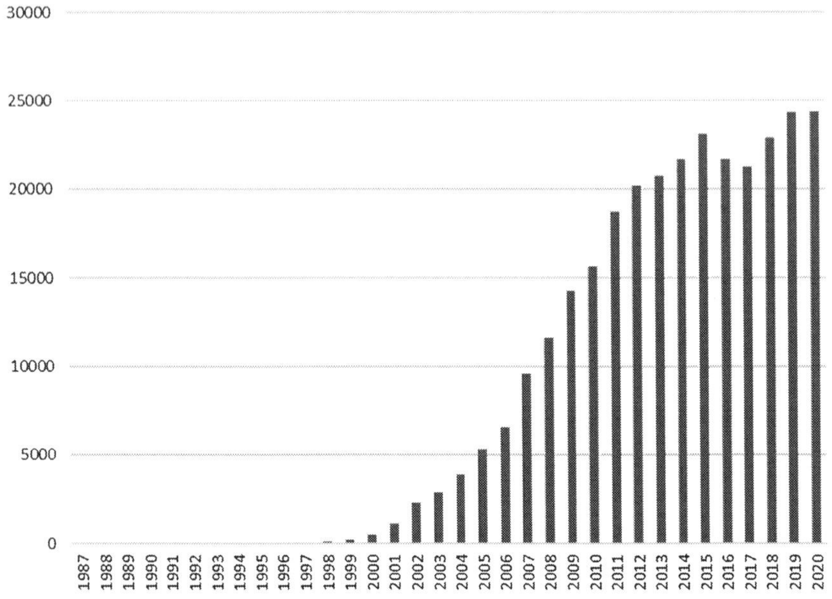

Fig. 2.4 Factiva database search on "corporate social responsibility"

which were most scrutinized. In short, criticism was the driver for non-financial reporting (Ditlev-Simonsen, 2014).

Corporate reporting was probably initially based on pressure to show interest beyond making a profit. The fact that competitors started reporting was also likely a motivating factor. Figure 2.5 provides an overview of the development in "non-financial" reporting for the Financial Times (FT) 500 Top Global Companies. The graph illustrates the growth in such reports between 1989 and 2012. These non-financial reports carried different names which have changed over time. In the beginning, almost all extra-financial reporting was issued as an "Environmental Report". Then around 1998, companies started naming these reports with terms associated with "sustainab-" or "responsib-". After 2000, the term "environment" in the report title declined and was replaced with "sustainability" and "responsibility". This does not imply that companies no longer reported on environmental issues, rather that they began reporting on

Fig. 2.5 Title (and focus) in extra-financial reporting—Financial Times (FT) 500

social issues as well. These new reports included environmental and social issues. It is also evident that "sustainability" became more popular than "responsibility".

By year 2005, around four out of five of these companies issued extra-financial reports, and the growth in reporting flattened out. This does not imply that the companies have levelled out, rather that companies started to include reporting about the environment, sustainability, and responsibility as part of their annual report. This merging of the annual report and sustainability report generally indicates that sustainability is integrated into the core business and operations, rather than a separate nice thing to do.

In the beginning, many companies outsourced their non-financial reporting to external consultants. For several public relations companies, production of non-financial reports became a new field of business. There were ways to detect whether companies were outsourcing their sustainability report. If the report had a different look and layout from the financial report or one was on recycled paper and the other was not, the report production was likely to have been outsourced. If the annual report did not refer to environmental and social issues, then the non-financial report was likely to have been outsourced. The format of the extra-financial reports was also an indicator. If the majority of the content was nice pictures and nice stories, it is more likely the report writing had been outsourced. Concrete goals conveyed with figures and key performance indicators (KPIs) generally suggests that the company takes sustainability seriously. However, the best way to ensure whether sustainability issues are integrated into a company's operations is to check if environmental and social issues are mentioned in the annual report—not only in a separate report.

References

Ambrose, J. (2021, June 23). Most new wind and solar projects will be cheaper than, coal reports finds. *The Guardian*.

Baral, N., & Pokharel, M. P. (2016). How Sustainability Is Reflected in the S&P 500 Companies' Strategic Documents. *Organization & Environment, 30*(2), 122–141.

Ditlev-Simonsen, C. D. (2014). Are non-financial (CSR) reports trustworthy? A study of the extent to which non-financial reports reflect the media' perception of the company's behaviour. *Issues in Social and Environmental Accounting, 8*(2), 116–133. https://doi.org/10.22164/isea.v8i2.85

Gleckman, H. (1995). Transnational corporations' strategic responses to "sustainable development". In H. O. A. Bergesen (Ed.), *Green Global yearbook of international co-operation on environment and development 1995* (pp. 93–106). Oxford University Press.

Global Justice Now. (2018, October 17). 69 of the richest 100 entities on the planet are corporations, not governments, figures show. https://www.globaljustice.org.uk/news/69-richest-100-entities-planet-are-corporations-not-governments-figures-show/

Laramée de Tannenberg, V. (2019). Wealthy countries still failing on $100 billion climate finance pledge. *Le Journal de l'environnement*. https://www.euractiv.com/section/climate-environment/news/wealthy-countries-still-failing-on-100-billion-climate-finance-pledge/

Menke, A. (2017, October 19). Working conditions in the textile industry. *globalEDGE*. https://globaledge.msu.edu/blog/post/54484/working-conditions-in-the-textile-indust

Morris, D. Z. (2016, October 15). Mercedes-Benz's self-driving cars would choose passenger lives over bystanders. *Fortune*. https://fortune.com/2016/10/15/mercedes-self-driving-car-ethics/

Ritchie, H., & Roser, M. (n.d.). CO2 emissions. *Our World in Data*. https://ourworldindata.org/co2-emissions

United Nations. (1945). Chapter I: Purposes and principles. *United Nations Charter*. https://www.un.org/en/about-us/un-charter/chapter-1

United Nations. (1948). *Universal declaration of human rights*. https://www.un.org/en/about-us/universal-declaration-of-human-rights

Willums, J.-O. a. (1992). *From ideas to action—Business and sustainable development*. adNotam Gyldendal.

World Commission on Environment and Development. (1987). *Our common future*. https://sustainabledevelopment.un.org/content/documents/5987our-common-future.pdf

3

Economic Theories and Sustainable Development

Theories have been applied to understand and forecast economic development. Some leading economists and theorists have set the frameworks for the way we run business today—models that in many ways fail as our society are not sustainable in the long run.

In this chapter, I will provide a brief reflection on some of the key economic theories, its "founders", and how this related to a corporate responsibility for sustainable development. How economics, international trade, organizations, tax, values, banks, governments, and so on work today can all be associated with one or more of the famous economic theorists introduced in this chapter. There were also other schools of thoughts which contributed theories that were skeptical to a free market economy and its focus on economic growth, rather more concerned about other limited resources, overconsumption, and the negative consequences of economic growth. The latter theories have, to a lesser degree, been adopted maybe because they were not as "comfortable" allowing less of an increase in growth and consumption.

I will start with introducing the key economists that hold more of a skeptical view, continue on with a brief but more thorough overview of the theories of two of the most "applied" views on the framework of

C. D. Ditlev-Simonsen, *A Guide to Sustainable Corporate Responsibility*,
https://doi.org/10.1007/978-3-030-88203-7_3

economic development. In the second part of the chapter, I will introduce economists, who reflected on the societal responsibility of individuals in a business setting, especially leaders. The third part of this chapter will discuss key economists and philosophers who explicitly take into account sustainability and corporate responsibility in their assessment of society and business. The mounting evidence of environmental and social challenges prompted the incorporation of these issues by economists during their time—along the same time of the publication of the Brundtland Report and the launch of the "sustainable development" concept.

In this chapter, I have selected examples of approaches to economic development and corporate responsibilities. It is necessary to be aware of the history and foundation of economic development in our society (where we come from) to understand how to move on in a more sustainable direction (where we want to go). Still, given limited space, as well as the purpose of the book, this chapter only provides a brief overview and many well-known economists are left out.

3.1 Economists Skeptical to the Societal Pursuit of Economic Growth

Thomas Malthus, a British economist born in 1766, is well-known for his book *An Essay on the Principle of Population*. His view, the Malthusian Law, is that population growth is exponential and will always go beyond what is sustainable for the population. Therefore, there will always be people who are hungry and poor. As soon as food becomes available, birthrates increase and consumption grows beyond what is considered to be enough to feed all. Malthus' thoughts are in line with the English economist W. Stanley Jevons born in 1835, who suggested that the more we get, the more we use. The Jevons Paradox claims that increases in resources availability generate increases in resource consumption. For example, an increase in access to energy, similarly with an increase in energy efficiency, will not lead to surplus energy, rather the extra energy available will be immediately demanded and consumed. Both these theories posit that humans naturally push the limits whenever it comes to consumption, something we definitely see is happening today. Jevons also suggested the concept of marginal utility of consumption which will be addressed in the final chapter "On ways forward".

Thorstein Veblen, an American economist born in 1857, also observed what we are witnessing in today's society—"conspicuous consumption". He pinpointed that the leisure class (rich people who are not working) were overconsuming—something which is even more challenging today with a rapidly growing middle class and an unsustainable way of living.

Arthur C. Pigou was an English economist born in 1877 engaged in welfare economics. In his book *The Economies of Welfare*, he introduced the concept of externalities and that such costs should be corrected by imposing a tax, the Pigovian tax. There are some products today that partly account for external costs via a tax, such as a CO_2 fee—but, based on the unsustainable volume of CO_2 emissions today, the tax is definitely not high enough.

Common for the above economists is that they warned about several of the problems we are facing today: unsustainable population growth, unsustainable consumption, and that there are external costs associated with using natural resources. However, their views have only to a small degree been taken into account in the economic and social development in the centuries to follow. Why is that so? One hypothesis could be that their suggestions were not "comfortable". Reducing consumption and increasing taxes were equally unpopular at that time as it is today.

3.2 Examples of Key Economists Anchored in Economic Growth

Adam Smith, John M. Keynes, and Milton Friedman are three economists whose views are perceived by many over time as laying the foundation of today's society.

Common for the individuals formulating theories and solutions for world development is that they lived in different times. This is especially relevant when it comes to sustainability issues and the current situation. As discussed in Chap. 2, it was not until 1987 that a global agreement emerged that we are facing an unsustainable future, especially with regard to environmental challenges and resource depletion. When the first economic theorists lived, resource depletion was not a real issue. Many people were poor and did not have access to land, however, on a broader scale, the land and resources were there. It was only that individuals did not have access to them. If forests were cut down for heating, people could move to a new forest and cut that down. Two hundred years ago, the world population was just over one billion and CO_2 emissions were not an issue.

The Industrial Revolution took place at the turn of the eighteenth century. Its defining impact on the economy is associated with the move from handmade production to mass production of goods in factories. The invention of steam engines and access to less expensive iron production technologies, only served to speed up the industrialization process. Rural to urban migration to work in factories combined with the growth of international trade formed the basis for the non-sustainable society that we have today.

Describing these three economist views, I will start by reviewing the theories based in their time of departure, and secondly, I will discuss how this relates to corporate responsibility and sustainable development today.

Adam Smith (1723–1790), The Father of Economic Theory

Adam Smith was a Scottish philosopher and moralist born in 1723. He lived parallel to other renowned philosophers such as David Hume, who was actually a good friend to Smith. In his book *The Theory of Moral Sentiments* published in 1759/1976, his focus was based on moral and social behavior of individuals. He recognizes that self-interest forms the basis of human nature and people's behavior. At the same time, he argues that people are not only egoistic, but also care about others. This prudence and justice for people for a societal care is partly based on what is good in a longer term perspective. Smith also claims that we as humans are endowed with natural sympathy toward others. If we see someone in pain, we experience empathy and want to help. Doing so also renders good feelings. In that sense, morality is part of human nature. Smith's views of morals and the good way of living have parallels to Aristotle's views.

Today, Smith is more known as an economist. The fact that Smith's views on economics are anchored in a more philosophical line of thought is often ignored. However, his views on human nature are relevant for his thoughts on people in a business setting. At his time, economics was not a field of research, and, as one of the first thinkers focusing on economics, Smith is later known as the "father of economic theory". His book *An Inquiry into the Nature and Causes of the Wealth of Nations* (The Wealth of Nations) was published in 1776/2008. His concept of economics as articulated in his book almost 300 years ago still prevails today.

Maybe the fact that Smith lived in the early stages of industrialization impacted the relevance and interest in human behavior and morals associated with economics and business. Given that prior to the age of industrialization, most people were farmers or manufacturing simple products mostly by hand, there was an implicit potential for a better life through access to products if production became more efficient. He thus argued for the advantages of "mass production". Even though this would lead to some people, the owners of the capital, getting rich, he also argued that the increase of products would increase the living standards of the majority of the population, the poor people. Suddenly everyone could afford not only one shirt but two.

In his opinion, the government should not intervene with taxes and laws to retain money for the rich. The rich owners of the capital would have empathy with the workers and people in general and share their wealth out of good morals, not because they would have to. Social recognition and respect would be their motivation and gain for such an approach. That the market will correct itself, without intervention of governments, is known by the metaphor "The Invisible Hand". His view was that this type of market liberalism, an unregulated market with unlimited growth, would lead individual interests to fulfil a common goal.

It can be perceived as Smith's view on the morality of individuals was based on a sense by fairness, social concern and care as expressed in Chapter II of his 1759 book *The Theory of Moral Sentiments*: "He is certainly not a good citizen who does not wish to promote, by every means in his power, the welfare of the whole society of his fellow-citizens". Here he claims that the societal responsibility should be anchored in individuals and not in governmental actions. However, relative to the fact that today, for example, the richest one percent of Americans own 40 percent of the country's value, very few act on their societal responsibility along the lines of, for example, Bill Gates (Ingraham, 2017). It might seem like Smith did not expect people to be as greedy as they/we actually are.

Adam Smith and Sustainable Development

During Smith's time, there were no resource limitations, no international mass production and the population was only a fraction of what it is today. Global warming and threats to biodiversity were both non-issues. Today, people still discuss whether the concept of an "Invisible Hand" actually works, but most of us will agree that the premises of Smith's theory, the opportunity of unlimited growth along the same lines as today, is definitely not the case.

His belief that the rich will eventually think beyond their own self-interest and share and do good with their money has to some extent been supported. However, even though Rockefeller, Alfred Nobel, and Bill Gates give back to the poor and support collective goods, these examples are more exceptions than an overall trend (Hodak, 2007).

It is evident that Smith's model, at least the way it is interpreted, misses important elements and facts of our times. Today's unsustainable situation is a proof that the "Invisible Hand" has not guided our development in the direction of sustainability. Smith's model needs to be revisited and extended to be applied to the pursuit of sustainability.

John M Keynes (1883–1946), Macroeconomics

John M Keynes was British and born in 1883. He is known as the founder of macroeconomics through his book *General Theory of Employment, Interest and Money*, published in 1936/2018. The situation society was facing at that time was poverty, unemployment, and depression after the First World War. His argument was that the government had to step in to get society "up and going". With poverty, people did not have money to purchase, and when there were no customers and demand, there was no point in production. According to his theory, the government should go in and create demand with focus on common goods, like construction, roads, rails, and provide loans with low interest. That would generate jobs and eventually demand for other more consumer-oriented goods.

In Keynes' view, the government had a central role to manage and balance the economic development and "steer" with regulations and taxes—that is, seemingly opposite Adam Smith.

Keynes theory was later applied in the Bretton Woods agreement in 1944 at the end of the Second World War. He played a central role in these negotiations for international finance collaboration. His view on regulations nation wise extended to a global level. International interventions and regulations would in his view form a basis for a development that was good for all. Keynes had a key role in the establishment of both the World Bank and the International Monetary Fund in line with his belief in the importance of global collaboration. Neoclassical synthesis combines Keynesian- and neoclassical theories. The economy must be founded on fiscal and monetary policies, but in the long term humans' main focus is on maximizing marginal utility, that is, want the most for the least.

John M Keynes and Sustainable Development

Today the level of government regulations are much more encompassing than when Keynes lived, that is, more in line with Keynes views. At the same time, we also see that with the non-sustainable development we have experienced in the last few decades, government interventions, at least how these have been conducted so far, have not been successful. His argument for international collaboration and steering is however more important than ever. Whereas Keynes argued for global collaboration on a monetary level, additional collaboration on environmental and social issues are crucial to solve global challenges. Furthermore, the neoclassical economic concept, arguing that humans primarily seek to maximize economic utility, is challenged. Today, the social and environmental challenges are very visible. For those who have their primary survival needs met, social and environmental issues are becoming increasingly more important. It could therefore be argued that these variables also should be included in the neoclassical model. Or, alternatively, that the neoclassical model, which overlooks or undervalues ecological concern and value, should be rejected as an obstacle to achieve sustainable development.

Still, his vision, presented in the chapter "Economic Possibilities for Our Grandchildren" in the book *Essays in Persuasion* in 1930 (Keynes, 1930/2010), predicted that a hundred years onward, the standard of living would be at a level where nobody needed to worry about work or making money (Kolbert, 2014). Assuming "no important wars and no important increase in population, the economic problem may be solved". Now, 90 years later, we can confirm that this vision is not fulfilled. Keynes was however right on his prediction of several issues, even though he underestimated the greed of humans. Just as with Adam Smith's, important variables related to environmental challenges and negative consequences of industry are missing in Keynes model. Also, both thought that at a certain level of consumption, when the needs are met, people would be content, help others, and not pursue greed and continuous growth in irresponsible consumption. Unfortunately, people are not as virtuous as they expected us to be.

Milton Friedman (1912–2006), Social Responsibility of Business Is to Increase Its Profits

Milton Friedman is a well-known American economist and a great supporter of the market economy. In that sense, his view is more in line with Adam Smith's belief. In 1976, he received the Nobel Prize in Economics for various contributions to economic analysis. Sustainability and corporate responsibility were not explicitly part of this field of research. However, based on his views on the purpose of corporations and their goals and responsibilities, he has become a cornerstone for corporate responsibility claims.

Friedman's opinion, expressed in a famous and extensively referenced article in the New York Times in 1970, "The Social Responsibility of Business is to Increase its Profits" (Friedman, 1970), is claimed to be out of date and also wrong. This statement is primarily used to support arguments against corporate social responsibility and that business has a responsibility beyond making money. However, I would argue that selective arguments are taken out of context and actually, the article argues that corporations have a social responsibility.

Milton Friedman and Sustainable Development

Like many of the well-known economic theorists, their name often functions as a cue for economic school of thoughts. When referring to Adam Smith, people think of the free market and when mentioning John M Keynes, people think about the need for government regulations. When mentioning Friedman in the context of corporate responsibility and sustainability, people might think his contributions to economics are against such responsibilities. Holding this opinion, it would suggest the person never read the full article in the New York Times that they are referring to.

The article, with the provocative title "The Social Responsibility of Business Is to Increase its Profits", actually, in my view, supports the argument that companies have a social responsibility—as long as it is associated with profit. The following are two excerpts from the article that I think support the argument of a responsible company. However, the key is not just to think philanthropy when profits are available, but rather make responsibility part of the core business. How to do this in practice will be addressed later in the book.

The corporate executive should act as an agent for the company, not a principal, and not spend "the money of his employers or the time or energy he has contracted to devote to their purposes." There is a culture in several countries, and especially in the United States, where philanthropy is common. Many companies donate up to several percentage of its net profit to good causes. By donating to causes that involve, for example, employees' engagement can lead to improvements in employees' corporate affection and commitment. This again can contribute to better work performance and profit. However, if the donations are associated with the CEO's personal interest, which often is the case, this is not an action responsibility that is good for the company in general and its profit.

The corporate executive should "make as much money as possible while conforming to the basic rules of the society, both those embodied in law and those embodied in ethical custom." Most people agree that corporations should follow existing laws and regulations—even though this is not always the case. Friedman made the point that this is a contribution, as following laws is more important than philanthropy. In this quote, Friedman also mentions "ethical custom".

Today, pursuing sustainability is actually becoming an "ethical custom". Later in the book, there are examples of many companies, which go beyond what they are legally required to do—because it is good business. For example, companies are focusing on energy efficiency and reduction of CO_2 emissions. There are limited regulations demanding companies to become more energy efficient. However, investing in more efficient heating technology might be good business as well as good for the environment, thus reducing CO_2 emissions. This is what I would call a "responsible business" and it is in line with Friedman's claim to make profit as well.

3.3 More Views on the Theories of the Responsibility of Individuals and Business Leaders

Prior to Milton Friedman, there were other economists who had reflected on the responsibility of the businessmen. Maurice Clark and Howard Bowen are two such examples. The latter based his explicit reflection of the responsibility of the leaders of corporations that goes beyond generating profit.

J. Maurice Clark (1884–1963), From Individualism to Social Mindedness

John Maurice Clark was a leading American economist. His focus was on institutional economics and responsibilities of different stakeholders, such as individuals and corporations. His reflections on corporate responsibilities are especially relevant with regards to sustainable development. In 1916, he wrote the article "Changing Basis of Economic Responsibility" which addresses the responsibilities of companies and men. At that time, more than 100 years ago, narrow individualism was the standard, and Clark argued for the necessity of moving toward a sense of "solidarity and social-mindedness". This also implied a more encompassing responsibility for doing business: "We have inherited an economics of irresponsibility. We are in an economy of control with which our intellectual inheritance fits but awkwardly. To make control really tolerable we need something more; something which is still in its infancy. We need an economics of responsibility, developed and embodied in our working business ethics" (Clark, 1916, p. 210).

J. Maurice Clark and Sustainable Development

Clark's article on the responsible businessman was one of the first to explicitly address that businessmen have a social responsibility beyond just making money. At that time, the key stakeholder was employees, and, again, the environmental degradation and its international consequences were not issues. His argument that employees should not be treated like "industrial machines", using "charity" to repair the damage originated in poor working conditions. Whereas rights and recognitions are established in the developed world, working conditions in developing countries are in many cases in line with what Clark described. Today, what Clark suggested in 1916 with regards to social responsibility is widely expected of corporations, even though the responsibility is not always fulfilled.

Howard Bowen (1908–1989), Social Responsibilities of the Businessman

Howard Bowen was an American economist. From a sustainability and corporate responsibility point of view his book *Social Responsibilities of the Businessman* published in 1953 was an important contribution to awareness and focus on corporate responsibility (Bowen, 1953). Bowen's understanding of the social responsibility of businessmen was "the obligation of businessmen to pursue those policies, to make those decisions, or to follow those lines of action that are desirable in terms of the objectives and the values of our society". He argued, somewhat in line with Adam Smith, that companies should take responsibility, and not depend upon governmental regulations (which was more in line with Keynes). He argued for establishing a code of practice for corporations to avoid exploiting stakeholders, including customers and labor.

Howard Bowen and Sustainable Development

Bowen's main contribution was at an early stage to put forward and remind about the concept of "responsible businessmen" explicitly as a title of a book. That increased awareness and discussion. It can be argued to which extent his vision was achievable. Is it actually realistic that companies' voluntary would follow a code to reduce competitive struggle and become "well mannered" and let go of business without going out of business? If so, that would be more in line with Aristotle's concept of virtue. Social responsibility today is maybe more based on duty ethics, it is something that is expected and or utilitarianism, that behaving responsible can lead to better profit.

3.4 Economic Growth, Gross Domestic Product (GDP), and Sustainable Development

Economic growth is the increase in the production of goods and service over a specific period. For a country, this is usually measured as Gross Domestic Product (GDP). The pursuit of GDP growth as a "success indicator" might be a challenge with regard to sustainability. GDP was "invented" by Simon Kuznets, associate director of the Bureau of Planning and Statistics at the War Production Board and Nobel Prize laureate, in the 1930s as a means to measure a country's economic development (Wharton Magazine, 2007).

The GDP does not take into account environmental damages such as the consequences of CO_2 emissions, reduced biodiversity, and environmental accidents. On the contrary, an environmental disaster, like for example a major oil spill, will have a positive impact on GDP and render growth. The reason is that cleaning up such a spill increases the need for product and services which then add to the GDP. Continuous overfishing for example is good for the GDP—until the day there are no fish left. A sharing economy, where people do not purchase new products, but share with others, does not contribute to GDP. In addition, the fact that GDP does not measure well-being, happiness, level of equality, and so on is a key problem using GDP as an approach to measuring growth. Kuznets himself warned that the GDP was not developed to measure societal development.

3.5 Business Theory for Corporate Responsibility and Sustainability

So far in this chapter, I have described key economic theories which form the foundation of our current economic system, as well as examples of economists who during the last two centuries have been skeptical to the economic models of our society. The majority of these thoughts were developed before society developed a common awareness and agreement

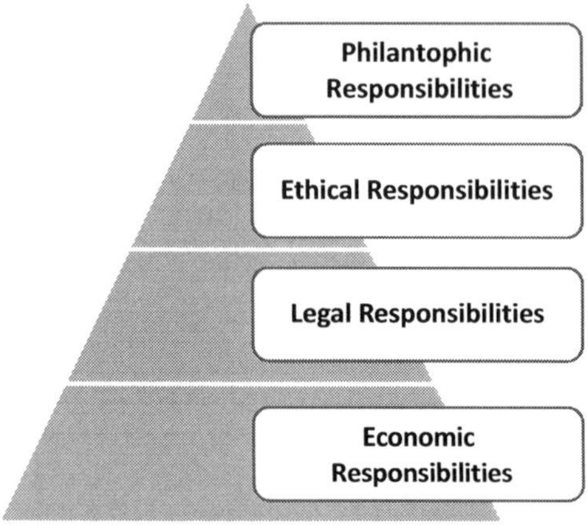

Fig. 3.1 Carroll CSR Pyramid

on the global environmental challenges we confront together. In the next section, I will put forward key theories on business models including the challenges and opportunities associated with sustainability and corporate responsibility.

The CSR Pyramid

Corporate responsibility is closely related to prioritizing. As addressed above, a key element in this discussion is the question for what the corporation is actually responsible. Archie B. Carroll, an American professor, developed the Pyramid of Corporate Social Responsibility (CSR), which illustrates a suggested priority list (Carroll, 1991). The model is presented in Fig. 3.1.

According to the model, corporate managers' key responsibility is to make money and then to fulfil legal requirements. Thereafter the company's responsibility is to behave ethically right. Finally, if there is any extra money available, the company should engage in philanthropic engagement and donations. Whether or not the priority for corporate operations is to make money and that operating according to law is second in priority have been discussed.

The approach to business responsibility reflected in this model is anchored in American corporate cultures. It suggests that philanthropic contributions, doing good for society, are something to be done if there is extra money available. As has already been mentioned, and will be an important element throughout this book, societal responsibility and sustainability have to be integrated in the company—not being an act of doing good when a surplus of money is available.

Furthermore, the order of the different elements in the pyramid varies depending on culture. In Africa for example, studies have found philanthropy is relatively more important and replaces Legal Responsibilities in Carroll's pyramid (Visser, 2005). Emerging markets will be further discussed in Chap. 8.

Stakeholder Theory

Corporate responsibility is closely related to which group or individuals that corporations should prioritize. Stakeholder theory differs from the CSR Pyramid in that the first model pinpoints different groups, whereas the latter focuses on areas of responsibility.

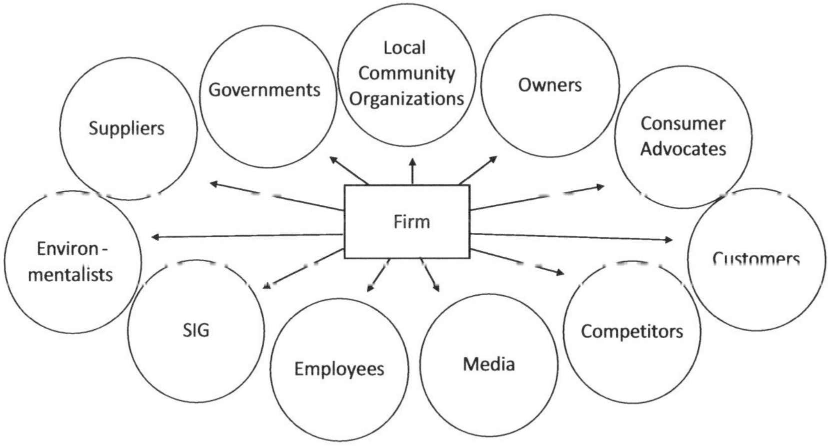

Fig. 3.2 The stakeholder model

Originally corporations had few stakeholders. In the beginning of the industrialization process, the key stakeholders of the corporation were the owners of the capital. Usually the managers, suppliers, customers, and employees had less power and therefore were less important. This latter group of stakeholders had very few rights, without any labor organizations, the owners decided wage and working conditions without any interference from employees. If competitors emerged, employees left the company for better wages. As industrialization went on, new stakeholders came along. Governments for example started having important impact on how corporations operated as did trade unions.

R. Edward Freeman, an American philosopher and business professor, is often put forward as the founder of stakeholder theory, who first visualized the model in his book *Strategic Management, A Stakeholder Approach* (Freeman, 1984). Still, many economists had addressed stakeholder theory prior to Freeman. The Swedish management theorist Eric Rhenman for example, suggested the idea already in 1968 (Rhenman, 1968).

Freeman's model is presented in Fig. 3.2 and consists of 11 different stakeholders. The model has been extensively revised over the years to include several more stakeholders that companies have today.

A sustainable company has to take different stakeholders into account and balance priorities. Some customers prioritize sustainable products (climate neutral, guaranteed no child labor, etc.) and other customers prioritize low price, so the company must decide which customer group to target and satisfy. More details on stakeholder management will be included in Chap. 8.

The Triple Bottom Line

The bottom line is usually referred to as the company's result, being profit or loss, reflecting total income less total expenses. Elkington's, a British author and entrepreneur, introduced The triple bottom line concept which extends corporate performance metrics beyond the financials. The model includes the economic bottom line, the environmental bottom line, and the social bottom line (Elkington, 1998).

Initially, the concept of corporate responsibility was associated with environmental issues, focusing on reducing emissions and more efficient use of resources. Societal issues did not receive the same attention. They were usually perceived as political issues and within the domain of the state, such as religious prosecution or racial discrimination. Even though human rights and working conditions for example were important elements of corporate performance, it was not incorporated in the responsibility setting in line with environmental issues. Human tragedies such as Bhopal and sweatshop labor among Nike's suppliers (see Chap. 5) brought attention to the social responsibility of corporations.

In his book *Cannibals with Forks*, Elkington describes the environmental bottom line as the extent to which the company's "natural capital" can be quantified and accounted for. He calls for more focus on measuring the environmental impact of corporations in terms of new metrics. The social bottom line addresses the importance of companies' social capital, both internally and externally. In the globalization process, issues such as treating workers well, human rights, indigenous people, community relations need attention. Manufacturing products that are safe to use and consume and employee training are also part of the social component of the triple bottom line. The economic bottom line addresses the long-term indicators of sustainability. He pinpoints that company value goes beyond assets minus liabilities and Elkington rebukes traditional accounting for not assessing the long-term sustainability of a company.

The triple bottom line is often referred to as the three "P"s; planet (environment), people (social), and profit (economic). Elkington claims that this interpretation of the model is incorrect. In 2018, he actually "recalls" the concept he coined in 1994, claiming that "business success or failure on sustainability goals cannot be measured only in terms of profit and loss. The wellbeing of billions of people and the health of our planet and the sustainability sector's record in moving the needle on those goals has been decidedly mixed." He clarifies that the "economic" element is not only financial profit, but contains a broader perspective as addressed above (Elkington, 2018).

Still, companies cannot survive if profit is not taken into account. So, what has to change is the manner in which profit is calculated. To do this, we need a different accounting approach where the true societal impact and cost of the different elements of the model are taken into account. This is often referred to as full cost pricing, which will be addressed in Chap. 6 on the circular economy.

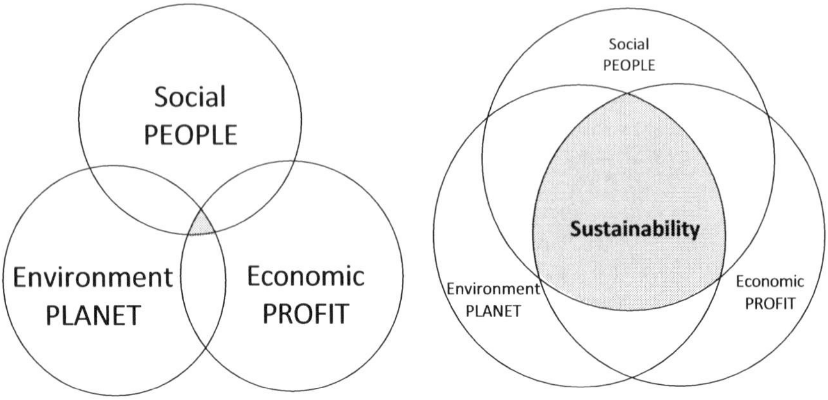

Fig. 3.3 The triple bottom line model—illustrating the move to sustainable development, integrating environmental, economic, and social issues in business operations

Corporations have to find a balance between the economic, environmental, and social bottom lines. The area in the middle, where the different impacts and results of business operations overlap, is where business is "sustainable". This concept is illustrated in Fig. 3.3.

Creating Shared Value

The concept of "shared value" is about doing good for society and business at the same time. "Shared value creating focuses on identifying and expanding the connections between societal and economic progress" (Porter & Kramer, 2011). The concept argues that for a long time companies have been perceived as the originators of our unsustainable development through poor working conditions, emissions, and inefficient use of resources. The argument is that companies in general will continue to behave in this unsustainable manner, even when being criticized by for example NGOs for their unsustainable conduct. In this "old model", companies are perceived as the source of the problem.

In the Shared Value Model, companies are identified as the *solution* for sustainable development, not as the problem. The argument is that in the long-term, sustainable behavior can increase profitability for corporations. However, in this setting, it is crucial to focus on the right issues associated with the company's impact.

In the United States, corporate philanthropy is very common. Actually, the median percentage of donations of the 250 world's largest companies was almost one percent of pre-tax net income (McClimon, 2020). Porter and Kramer claim that this is not sustainable. If for example the company is not doing well financially, donations are reduced for that year. Donations are often not an efficient way of improving the community, rather what makes the most impact is when corporations make sustainability part of doing business—and to increase profit. "Societal needs, not just conventional economic needs, define markets, and social harm can create internal costs for firms." Instead of donating money to NGOs and the local community, the company should collaborate with NGOs and integrate community challenges into its operations.

The 2011 ME Porter and MR Kramer's article presents the concept of "Creating Shared Value" (CSV) as the new concept relative to Corporate Social Responsibility (CSR). The article and the concept have received lots of attention and citations. That is one of the reasons I included it in this chapter. Even though the term CSV was new, the concept was not, when the article was published. It can be argued that the article "kicks up open doors". In Europe at least, corporate philanthropy has not been a central element in CSR as it is in the United States. The importance of collaboration with different stakeholders as part of business was already a key point in both stakeholder theory in 1984 and the triple bottom line concept in 1994.

3.6 Trends and Theories Capturing the Sustainability Issues in Business Models

Most of the economic theories our society is built on, as mentioned, do not consider environmental and social issues. The goal, economic growth, has been based on increasing production, consumption, and resource use. This has had considerable negative consequences on the environment through for example climate change, pollution, and loss of biodiversity. Economic growth based on overconsumption has also had negative consequences for human health through for example poor health, loneliness, inactivity, obesity, and so on. Since the turn of the century, economic theories acknowledging societies' sustainability challenges have come forward. This again influences business models.

The move from "brown growth", growth based on fossil fuel, to "green growth", growth based on renewable energy, is one example of changes in economic models—the purpose being creating wealth without harming the environment. The Green Economy is a central focus area of the European Commission (EC) . Bioeconomy, extending economic theories to include ecology, environmental => environment, energy, food supply, and natural resources, has also received more attention and is now part of the EU strategy.

Given the complexity of sustainable development, common for the pursuit and integration of new economic models is that different disciplines are included. Concepts such as the Caring Economy (Wenden, 2008) and the Doughnut economic model (Schokkaert, 2019) extend the concept of Green Growth and Bioeconomy to also include social issues as health, peace and justice, education, and so on. "Ecological economy" is an example of the inclusion of ecology in the economic model (Spash, 2013). Other examples of relevant fields to be included are psychology, sociology, philosophy, public policy, and so on. The Doughnut economic model presented among others in Kate Raworth's book *Doughnut Economics* is an attempt to provide a visualization of a sustainable society. The outer ring of doughnut represents the planetary limits, the inner ring represents the minimum living standards as set by the SDGs, whereas the hole in the middle, represents the proportion of people lacking access to basic essentials. To reach the goal that everybody should live in the edible part of the doughnut requires a substantial redistribution of consumption, away from today's situation where the richest one percent owns half of the world's wealth. Raworth is critical of many new growth concepts, including green growth, and in general challenges the focus on growth. Rather, she pinpoints a level of maturity at which the goal is that people are thriving.

Some of the elements in these new theories of growth and inclusion of different disciplines can be recognized in theories brought forward by scientists centuries and decades before the "world consensus" on sustainability global challenges that emerged in the 1970s. Aristotle, who is frequently referred to today with regard to (un)sustainable behavior, was involved in physics, zoology, psychology, economics, biology, and so on. Thomas Malthus who warned about unsustainable growth, was originally a priest, and Thorstein Veblen who warned about overconsumption, was a sociologist. Today, in line with what was the case when these scientists lived, the challenge is how to actually integrate these challenges and models in our growth concept.

Since the 1970s, when politicians, corporations, researchers, and people in general began explicitly recognizing society's sustainability challenges, revised and new business models including social and environmental elements have emerged. It is only a few decades ago that waste was dumped legally in the water, polluted emissions from factory pipes were not treated, and people were driving around in gas guzzlers. Realizing the cost of cleaning up such unsustainable ways of doing business has led to increases in resource prices and legislation to reduce the negative impacts. In Chap. 6 *Circular Economy*, I will look at a business model recognizing the sustainability challenges we are facing today.

Moving from "weak sustainability", substitution of natural capital with other types of capital, to "strong sustainability", not damaging natural resources, is also a growing field of research (Hankammer et al., 2021). Degrowth and downsizing economic throughput are examples of more expansive and challenging economic models. Even though full decoupling of economic growth and resource consumption might not be possible, we can come a long way by giving natural resources an economic value capturing external costs, that is, integrating externalities, along the lines of the Pigouvian tax. Degrowth, as in reduced consumption of natural resources, is good and achievable, but not without governments assigning value and pricing in external costs into resources that are currently used for free. To a large extent, the move from gas guzzling cars to small efficient cars can be credited with increases in gasoline prices. Taxes on cigarettes reduce the number of people smoking, resulting in prevention of diseases and also generating funding to treat smoking related health costs.

In Chap. 5 *The business case for sustainability*, I will look at different business approaches to sustainability and the move from a business model that accommodates sustainability to a business model that explicitly incorporates sustainability.

In Chap. 12, *The way forward*, I will reflect on what is necessary to transition to a more sustainable track for society.

References

Bowen, H. R. (1953). *Social responsibilities of the businessman*. Harper.

Carroll, A. B. (1991). The Pyramid of corporate social responsibility: Toward the moral management of organizational stakeholders. *Business Horizons, 34*(4), 39–48. http://search.ebscohost.com/login.aspx?direct=true&db=bth&AN=9707074820&site=ehost-live

Clark, J. M. (1916). The changing basis of economic responsibility. *The Journal of Political Economy, 24*(3), 209–229. https://doi.org/10.1086/252799

Elkington, J. (1998). *Cannibals with Forks: The triple bottom line of 21st century business*. John Wiley & Sons, Ltd.

Elkington, J. (2018). 25 years ago i coined the phrase "Triple Bottom Line." Here's why it's time to rethink it. *Harvard Business Review Digital Articles*, 2–5.

Freeman, R. E. (1984). *Strategic management: A stakeholder approach*. Pitman.

Friedman, M. (1970). A Friedman doctrine—The social responsibility of business is to increase its profits. *The New York Times*. https://www.nytimes.com/1970/09/13/archives/a-friedman-doctrine-the-social-responsibility-of-business-is-to.html

Hankammer, S., Kleer, R., Mühl, L., & Euler, J. (2021). Principles for organizations striving for sustainable degrowth: Framework development and application to four B Corps. *Journal of Cleaner Production, 300*, N.PAG-N.PAG. https://doi.org/10.1016/j.jclepro.2021.126818. https://login.ezproxy.library.bi.no/login?qurl=https://search.ebscohost.com/login.aspx?direct=true&db=bth&AN=150008795&site=ehost-live&scope=site

Hodak, M. (2007). Adam Smith's Folly. *Forbes*. https://www.forbes.com/2007/10/24/adam-smith-corporations-markets-marketsp07-cx_mh_1025hodak.html?sh=10d5a65e3c1b

Ingraham, C. (2017, December 6). The richest 1 percent now owns more of the country's wealth than at any time in the past 50 years. *The Washington Post*. https://www.washingtonpost.com/news/wonk/wp/2017/12/06/the-richest-1-percent-now-owns-more-of-the-countrys-wealth-than-at-any-time-in-the-past-50-years/

Keynes, J. M. (1930/2010). Economic possibilities for our grandchildren. In *Essays in Persuasion* (pp. 321–332). Palgrave Macmillan. https://doi.org/10.1007/978-1-349-59072-8_25

Kolbert, E. (2014). No time: How did we get so busy? *New Yorker*. https://www.newyorker.com/magazine/2014/05/26/no-time

McClimon, T. J. (2020). Corporate giving by the numbers. *Forbes*. https://www.forbes.com/sites/timothyjmcclimon/2020/01/16/corporate-giving-by-the-numbers/?sh=18375d1a6c51

Porter, M. E., & Kramer, M. R. (2011). Creating shared value: How to reinvent capitalism—and unleash a wave of innovation and growth. *Harvard Business Review, 89*(1–2), 62.

Rhenman, E. (1968). *Industrial democracy and industrial management*. Tavistock.

Schokkaert, E. (2019, Spring). Review of Kate Raworth's Doughnut economics. *Erasmus Journal for Philosophy & Economics, 12*(1), 125–132. https://doi.org/10.23941/ejpe.v12i1.412. https://search.ebscohost.com/login.aspx?direct=true&db=bth&AN=137859877&site=ehost-live&scope=site

Spash, C. L. (2013). The shallow or the deep ecological economics movement? *Ecological Economics, 93*, 351–362. https://doi.org/10.1016/j.ecolecon.2013.05.016. https://login.ezproxy.library.bi.no/login?qurl=https://search.ebscohost.com/login.aspx?direct=true&db=bth&AN=89436681&site=ehost-live&scope=site

Visser, W. (2005). Revisiting Carroll's CSR pyramid: An African perspective. In E. R. Pedersen & M. Huniche (Eds.), *Corporate citizenship in developing countries: New partnership perspectives* (pp. 29–56). Samfundslitteratur.

Wenden, A. (2008). Discourses on poverty: Emerging perspectives on a caring economy. *Third World Quarterly, 29*(6), 1051–1067. https://doi.org/10.1080/01436590802201030. https://search.ebscohost.com/login.aspx?direct=true&db=bth&AN=33158069&site=ehost-live&scope=site

Wharton Magazine. (2007, July 1). Inventor of GNP Measure: Simon Kuznets Hon56 Hon76. https://magazine.wharton.upenn.edu/issues/anniversary-issue/inventor-of-gross-national-product-measure-simon-kuznets-hon-56-hon-76-professor/

4

Key Tools for Social- and Environmental Performance, and the UN Sustainable Development Goals (SDGs)

Corporate responsibility related to sustainable development is a complex area as a number of confusing initiatives intended to help companies incorporate sustainability have emerged. From an international perspective, the international UN initiatives have had the most impact. I will give a short introduction to the history of key UN initiatives associated with environmental and social issues, but the main focus will be on the antecedents to the UN SDGs. Thereafter, I will present relevant initiatives and tools developed by corporations' and their tools and initiatives to approach environmental and social challenges. Well-known and widely applied certifications will be included.

4.1 UN Global Compact, 2000

The UN Global Compact (UNGC) is the UN organization for sustainable business. It was announced in 1999 at the annual World Economic Forum in Davos with the purpose to promote sustainable business. The UNGC (Box 4.1) initiative started with a call to business representatives

C. D. Ditlev-Simonsen, *A Guide to Sustainable Corporate Responsibility*,
https://doi.org/10.1007/978-3-030-88203-7_4

for around the world from UN Secretary-General to participate in setting up environmental and social cornerstones to support a global solution to global challenges. The development of the UNGC principles included UN labor organizations, the private sector, and civil society.

Box 4.1 The Ten Principles of the UN Global Compact

Human Rights

Principle 1: Businesses should support and respect the protection of internationally proclaimed human rights; and
Principle 2: make sure that they are not complicit in human rights abuses.

Labor

Principle 3: Businesses should uphold the freedom of association and the effective recognition of the right to collective bargaining;
Principle 4: the elimination of all forms of forced and compulsory labor;
Principle 5: the effective abolition of child labor; and
Principle 6: the elimination of discrimination in respect of employment and occupation.

Environment

Principle 7: Businesses should support a precautionary approach to environmental challenges;
Principle 8: undertake initiatives to promote greater environmental responsibility; and
Principle 9: encourage the development and diffusion of environmentally friendly technologies.

Anti-Corruption

Principle 10: Businesses should work against corruption in all its forms, including extortion and bribery.

The UN Global Compact (UNGC) aim is to "mobilize a global movement of sustainable companies and stakeholders to create the world we want". Aligning business with the ten principles and taking actions to advance the UN SDGs are ways that the UNGC supports companies' work.

Today, the UNGC has 12,452 member companies from 160 countries. The ten principles of the UNGC are mainly based on already existing declarations, principles, and conventions, like, for example, the UN Declaration of Human Rights, the ILO Declaration on Principles and Rights at Work, the Rio Declaration and the UN Convention Against Corruption.

Both companies and organizations can join the UNGC, regardless of their size, complexity, or location. These companies are divided in two types: Company; at least 250 full-time employees and SME (Small and Medium Enterprise), with less than 250 employees—but minimum one direct employee (prior to 2020, the minimum number of employees was ten). All companies can become members, except some limitations associated with production of antipersonnel, landmines, cluster bombs, and tobacco among others.

What is required to join the UNGC is that the CEO fills in the draft letter posted on the UNGC website that declares support for the ten principles and signs up for annual submission of a Communication on Progress (CoP). The CoP describes how the company works on implementing the ten principles. The application has to include the signature of the CEO/Managing Director and attached information about how the company has or plans to integrate the ten principles and expected outcomes. The UNGC is a voluntary initiative not a formal membership organization. Large corporations joining the UNGC have to contribute to support their engagement based on their annual gross sales/revenues (United Nations Global Compact, 2021).

The UNGC provides an encompassing library of information and tools on how to integrate sustainability in practice. Having signed up for annual reporting, Communication on Progress (CoP) serves as a good reminder on follow-up and sustainability integration. There are different levels of CoPs; Advanced, Active, and Learner (United Nations Global Compact, 2017).

Human Rights	Labour	Environment	Anti-corruption
All employees must go through a digital course annually on Human Rights.	For all new contracts we conduct a Due Diligence review to ensure no child labour.	In 2021 all our offices will go through an energy review. Plastic packaging will be reduced with 20% by 2025.	The company code-of-conduct includes a chapter on anti-corruption. All employees have to sign this Code of Conduct annually.

Fig. 4.1 Example of simple UNGC CoP for a small company

For a small, Learner, company the CoP with regard to the Ten principles can be very simple. In text below is an example of content in a Learner CoP (Fig. 4.1):

Why and How Is the UN Global Compact Relevant for Businesses in Practice?

The main contribution of the UNGC is a set of common issues for companies to reference. Many companies are struggling on deciding what sustainable development implies for their business. The ten principles pick up the key challenges regarding sustainable development and reflection on these as a checklist can be very useful. At the same time, not all ten principles are relevant for all companies.

For many companies applying the ten principles has helped advance sustainability within the company. A positive element in the UNGC, contrary to most UN initiatives, is that it is clear and concise. The UNGC has made positive contributions to many companies in terms of reputation and customer loyalty, employee loyalty, reducing costs, increasing innovation, and so on.

4.2 UN Millennium Development Goals, 2000

The UN Millennium Development Goals (MDGs) were developed by UN member states with the purpose of fighting poverty across the world, using different approaches. The goals were launched in 2000 and were set to be achieved by 2015. As for the UNGC, these principles were concrete and contributed with a common framework for global focus and work.

Whereas the UNGC principles focused on how and what corporations can contribute with both locally and internationally, the UN MDG's main focus was on activities related to issues in the developing word. Even though the UN MDG is not legally binding, the initiative has generated lots of positive changes. Furthermore, these achievements are measured and reported on. These are the eight UN MDGs and some examples of their respective contributions (United Nations, 2015):

Goal 1: Eradicate extreme poverty and hunger. *Extreme poverty has been reduced from 50% in the developing world in 1990 to 14% in 2015.*
Goal 2: Achieve universal primary education. *Primary school enrolment in developing countries from 83% in year 2000 to 91% in 2015.*
Goal 3: Promote gender equality and empower women. *Women working outside the agricultural sector have increased from 35% in 1990 to 41% in 2015.*
Goal 4: Reduce child mortality. *Under-five mortality has declined from 90 deaths per 1000 to 43.*
Goal 5: Improve maternal health. *Contraceptive prevalence increased from 55% in 1990 to 64% in 2015.*
Goal 6: Combat HIV/AIDS, malaria, and other diseases. *New HIV infections fell by 40% between 2000 and 2013.*
Goal 7: Ensure environmental sustainability. *1.9 billion people have gained access to piped drinking water since 1990.*
Goal 8: Global partnership for development. *In 2015, 95% of world population has access to a mobile-cellular signal.*

Why and How Are the Millennium Development Goals Relevant for Businesses in Practice?

First of all, the MDGs illustrate that setting worldwide, concrete goals have an effect—even though they are not legally binding. For corporations the eight goals pinpointed issues in the developing world that are key challenges. Even though the key purpose of the MDGs targeted nations to reduce poverty and hunger, it has been relevant for business as well. To companies operating in or that had supply chains involving developing countries, the goals were especially relevant. However, the key contribution of the MDGs is that it perhaps laid the foundation and inspired to the development of the UN Sustainable Development Goals (SDGs) which replaced the MDGs when they "expired" in 2015.

4.3 The UN Guiding Principles on Business and Human Rights, 2011

The UN Guiding Principles on Business and Human Rights (UNGP): Implementing the United Nations "Protect, Respect and Remedy" framework was endorsed by the Human Rights Council in 2011. The Guiding Principles were developed by the UN Special Representative of the Secretary-General on the issue of transnational corporations and other business enterprises through extensive consultations. The UNGPs define the responsibilities of governments and corporations with regards to human rights: the state duty to protect human rights, the corporate responsibility to respect human rights and access to remedy. The UNGPs contain 31 principles in the framework of the following three pillars, guiding how states and corporations should operate to fulfil their duties with respect to human rights (United Nations Human Rights, 2011):

1. States' existing obligations to respect, protect, and fulfil human rights and fundamental freedoms; *the state duty to protect human rights includes making and enforcing laws that protect against human rights abuse by third parties, including business enterprises.*
2. The role of business enterprises as specialized organs of society performing specialized functions required to comply with all applicable laws and to respect human rights; *companies must respect human rights—also when the states in which the company operates in do not enforce legislation relating to human rights. Companies are expected to carry out human rights with due diligence to identify, prevent, mitigate, and account for how they address their adverse human rights impacts.*

3. The need for rights and obligations to be matched to appropriate and effective remedies when breached. *This implies making it possible for, for example, employees experiencing poor working conditions to report this safely and to guarantee that they will not be subject to reprisals.*

The UN Guiding Principles are based on international human rights, including the International Covenant on Civil and Political Rights (1966); the International Covenant on Economic, Social, and Cultural Rights (1966); and the Core Conventions of the International Labor Organization. Human rights due diligence is gaining traction in business, not least due to investors' calls for more detailed information on companies' impact on human rights and legislation that is being adopted in several countries mandating human rights due diligence.

Why and How Are the UNGP Relevant for Businesses in Practice?

A key contribution of the UNGP has been to clarify the responsibilities of business enterprises when it comes to human rights, including their responsibilities with respect to their business relationships and value chains. Many companies use the UNGP to guide their operations and operations in emerging economies and as a framework for reporting. The UNGP are also relevant for small companies since they are not immune to being linked with adverse human rights impacts through their operations, products, or services.

Sometimes it can seem less relevant for a company in a well-regulated economy to focus on human rights. Many human rights issues such as forced labor and child labor are criminalized, and laws addressing human rights may be well enforced. Still, there are challenges in all countries, and in developed and rich countries, unacceptable working conditions and wages below national minimum level are uncovered. Modern slavery and poor working conditions are furthermore often widespread in global supply chains.

4.4 UN Sustainable Development Goals, 2015

The UN Millennium goals were launched in 2000 and set to be reached by 2015. The fact that the deadline for the Millennium goals was coming to an end called for a new set of goals and timeframe. The work on the SDGs started at the Sustainable Development conference in Rio in 2012. A 30-member Open Working Group was established to develop a proposal on the UN SDGs. During these three years a comprehensive job was done. In 2015, 193 UN Member States agreed upon the 17 goals in an historic new agenda: *Transforming Our World: The 2030 Agenda for Sustainable Development.*

Stakeholder engagement was a key element of the SDG development. Business and industry, children and youth, farmers, indigenous peoples, local authorities, NGOs, education and academia, and national and international authorities and politicians were consulted and involved (United Nations Sustainable Development, 2020). Seven million people were surveyed to find out what they thought were the planet's key challenges, 300 issues were raised, and 83 nations involved. Altogether, this was the largest consultation and involvement of different stakeholders in the UN history. Through a complex and comprehensive process, all this work was reduced to 17 goals (Fig. 4.2). The 169 targets associated with the goals make the goals more specific. To make measuring progress possible, 232 indicators were developed.

Each of the 17 goals generally has between 8 and 12 targets. Some of the targets are clearly defined, for example, SDG#3 Good health and well-being 3.1 "By 2030, reduce the global maternal mortality ratio to less than 70 per 100,000 live births", whereas others are more vague, like SDG#10 Reduce inequalities 10.4 "Adopt policies, especially fiscal, wage and social protection policies, and progressively achieve greater equality". The targets concretize the goals. Each target has between one and four indicators. The indicators are to be more specific on how to measure progress. With regards to target #10.4, the indicator, 10.4.1 "Labour share of GDP, comprising wages and social protection transfers" provide guidance on how target 10.4 is to be measured. This helps benchmarking achievements and in comparing countries and activities.

SUSTAINABLE DEVELOPMENT GOALS
1 NO POVERTY
2 ZERO HUNGER
3 GOOD HEALTH AND WELL-BEING
4 QUALITY EDUCATION
5 GENDER EQUALITY
6 CLEAN WATER AND SANITATION
7 AFFORDABLE AND CLEAN ENERGY
8 DECENT WORK AND ECONOMIC GROWTH
9 INDUSTRY, INNOVATION AND INFRASTRUCTURE
10 REDUCED INEQUALITIES
11 SUSTAINABLE CITIES AND COMMUNITIES
12 RESPONSIBLE CONSUMPTION AND PRODUCTION
13 CLIMATE ACTION
14 LIFE BELOW WATER
15 LIFE ON LAND
16 PEACE, JUSTICE AND STRONG INSTITUTIONS
17 PARTNERSHIPS FOR THE GOALS

Fig. 4.2 The UN Sustainable Development Goals (SDGs)

There are different ways to categorize the SDGs. The Stockholm Resilience Centre, a recognized institution in sustainable research, uses three categories: Biosphere (SDG#6, 13,15 and 14), Society (SDG#1, 2, 3, 4, 5, 7, 11 and 16) and Economy (SDG#8, 9, 10 and 12). Partnership for the Goals, brings the goals and categories together.

Different goals have different degrees of specialization and concreteness—same with the indicators. Furthermore, the indicators can be revised. In 2020, 36 changes in the global indicator framework were approved (Pandey, 2020). Making the indicators more dynamic is a good approach to ensure that the indicators are applicable and actually measure what they are supposed to. However, changing indicators make it more complicated to measure progress.

While the ten MDGs were mainly aimed at poorer countries and nations, the 17 SDGs also addressed the developed world and rich countries. Calling for collaboration with corporations and that rich countries were no longer only to donate money to poor countries, but actually had to shift to come on a sustainable track, was new. Reduced consumption, less negative impact on the environment, and so on are much more demanding for people in rich countries than donating money to poor countries.

As people were skeptical to the MDGs, of which many were achieved, there is even more skepticism to the SDGs. This is not surprising since the SDGs are more encompassing and involving many more stakeholders. One can be pretty sure that not all of these goals will be achieved by 2030. However, the world agreeing on a common agenda is a great step forward.

The most substantial critique of the SDGs is that the endeavor will be too expensive to achieve, and that there is not enough money put aside to finance these goals. The UN suggests that achievement will need trillions of dollars, and specifically investment in developing countries will require the most financing (UN Sustainable Development Goals, 2016). The World Bank estimates it will take $ 4 TN annual investment to create the infrastructure necessary to achieve the SDGs, other UN bodies estimate the budget to be $5–7 TN each annually (Gillian, 2019). At the same time, it is estimated that following up the SDGs could render 380 million jobs and it is a great opportunity for the private sector (Blyth, 2020; Business Call to Action, n.d.)

In addition to being expensive to implement, the SDGs are also put forward as a "fairy tales, dressed in the bureaucratese of intergovernmental narcissism, adorned with the robes of multilateral paralysis, and poisoned by the acid of nation-state failure". In addition to being critical to the SDGs, this article in Lancet, a very recognized publication, concludes that the SDGs "have broad legitimacy among all parties—which is a big deal" (Horton, 2014).

The fact that so many stakeholders were invited to participate in deciding on what the SDGs should focus on lent the SDGs process and decisions support from many and important stakeholders on a worldwide basis. On the other hand, involving stakeholders in the process has also been criticized. It is argued that these actors will only set goals which they will be comfortable to reach and not demanding enough.

Several of the goals are contradictory as well. For example, Goal #13 Climate Action, "Take urgent action to combat climate changes and its impacts" is not possible to reach if Goal #8—Target 8.1 calls for at least seven percent gross domestic product growth per annum. Initially at least, such a growth will to a large extent be based on fossil fuels.

The SDGs are not legally binding, which means that countries as well as companies can withdraw and are not obligated to reach the goals. Still, if the goals were legally binding, the process would have certainly been much longer and not all the countries would have supported the initiative. Having an "intentional" agreement like this sets a good framework for further work and implementation. Some of the goals, like SDG # 13 Climate action, are however already addressed in the Paris Agreement. The Paris Agreement is a legally binding international treaty on climate change which entered into force in 2016 and will be addressed later in the chapter.

So, to sum up, the SDGs are challenging, maybe not realistic, but a necessity for a sustainable future and a good framework to organize the work on sustainability—from the point of view of nations, companies, organizations, and individuals (Fig. 4.2).

What Do the 17 Goals Contain?

In this section, I will introduce the key issues and challenges associated with 17 SDGs and targets. Some of the targets are measurable, whereas many are more general. I will provide examples of both. I will first describe what each SDG contains, and then I will alternatively, and when relevant, relate the content to specific examples. I will include examples from the developed world illustrating the relevance of the SDGs in these parts of the world as well. A key challenge with the SDGs is that some of the goals are mutually exclusive. Many developed countries which have full score ("green" according the SDG index) score "red" on climate action. The key issue is how to score "green" on all the 17 indexes. No country has managed that so far.

The first four goals are closely related to the millennium goals, with focus on poverty, hunger, education, gender equality, and health focused on children, maternal health, and combat of HIV/AIDS.

#1 NO POVERTY: In 2011 one billion, that is more than 12 percent of the population, lived in extreme poverty (on less than $ 1.25 a day[1]). The share of the world population below the poverty line has been declining, and prior to COVID-19, less than 10 percent of the population lived in extreme poverty. COVID-19 has led to increases in extreme poverty, which is a major setback in eradicating it by 2030. To reach this goal increased support from rich countries to support countries struggling

[1] The poverty line was raised to $ 1.90 in 2011.

with poverty is essential. In Chap. 11, I will look closer at what are key issues to render sustainable development in developing countries. It is a paradox that during the last few decades the poor countries have become poorer, whereas the rich countries have become richer. The gap between the two has increased at the same time as the discussion about how to close the gap has increased.

In the industrialized world, there is no extreme poverty, but still many live below the poverty threshold. In the EU, this is 60 percent below the media income. For people living in a country where there is so much available and many people living an affluent lifestyle, it is especially hard to only be able to cover housing and inexpensive food. For some this can be more challenging than living in a country where everyone has a similar situation, yet low standard of living. For children this is especially challenging. When all your friends can afford access to playground, sports, movies, and travel whereas you cannot, it can be devastating.

#2 ZERO HUNGER: Since 2014 to 2018, the percentage of the population affected by moderate or severe food insecurity increased from 23 to 26 percent. COVID-19 has led to an increase in the threat to the food systems. The goal is particularly focused on the poor and people in vulnerable situations, like infants and children. It is not only lack of food that is the problem, but malnutrition, especially the lack of key vitamins and minerals. To eradicate hunger, better conditions for small farmers are crucial.

Even though SDG #2 addressed hunger, many developed countries score low on these goals. The reason being the level of obesity. Obesity is related to the opposite of food shortage. In the United States, more than a third of the population is obese, scoring "red" on the country index. Obesity is often associated with poor health and had negative impact on well-being.

It is paradox that when more almost 11 percent of the world population is chronic undernourished, it is estimated that one third of all food produced globally is lost or goes to waste (Food & Agriculture Organization of the United).

#3 GOOD HEALTH AND WELL-BEING: There has been much progress in many health areas; however, again COVID-19 has imposed many healthcare disruptions. Less than half of the world population in

2017 had access to essential health services. Key goals for SDG #3 are to reduce maternal mortality and prevent death among newborns and children. Epidemics of AIDS, tuberculosis, malaria, and so on are also key issues. This SDG provides concrete indicator for how to measure improvements. Number of incidents by 1.000 people is a distinct way to measure changes.

In the developed world, material mortality is low with relatively few HIV infections and prevalent access to healthcare. Still, the fact that there are many people in poor physical condition is a problem which is not fully taken into account as an SDG indicator. Too little physical activity and obesity have a negative impact on well-being and happiness and need more attention in most developed countries.

#4 QUALITY EDUCATION: A key target for SDG#4 is to ensure that all girls and boys complete free, equitable, and quality primary and secondary education. More access to education for women is also a relevant with respect to this goal. There have been improvements in education among children the last two decades. Primary school completion in 2000 was 70 percent, whereas in 2018 it had raised to 84 percent.

There is great potential in digital and remote learning, however, access to the internet and digital tools is necessary to get take advantage of these resources. COVID-19 has reduced access to schools for children both in developing and developed countries.

Both in developing and developed countries, school drop-outs are a challenge. In the developed world, providing education that also addresses the SDGs is important. Business students for example need to be more aware of the SDG challenges and how to address these. Knowledge about sustainable development needs to be included in all levels and fields of education.

Increased awareness and knowledge in the field of sustainability is also crucial for sustainable development. Therefor integrating sustainability in curriculum at all levels and all fields of education is important—from kindergarten to universities.

#5 GENDER EQUALITY: This goal focuses on achieving gender equality and empowering all women and girls. The fact that women spend about three times as much time as men in unpaid domestic and care work is unfair. Unpaid domestic work for women has increased as a result of COVID-19. Today women account for 70 percent of health and social workers, maybe the most important work in today's society. Yet their average income is much lower than men. Still, there has been some achievements, there has been a decline in forced early marriage for girls, and more women are in leadership roles. Giving women better access to resources is good for society. If women farmers had the same access to resources as men, it is estimated that the number of hungry people could be reduced by 150 million (Food and Agriculture Organization of the United Nations, 2016). Gender inequality is still a large challenge in developed countries as well.

#6 CLEAN WATER AND SANITATION: Ensuring availability and sustainable management of water and sanitation for all is the goal by 2030. In 2019, one in three people globally did not have access to safe drinking water and 4.2 billion did not have safe sanitation (World Health Organization, 2019). These are both key services to prevent spreading of COVID-19. The main challenge to achieve SDG#6 is lack of money and funding. Providing water to people with little or no money to finance the service requires support by the government. When the government has limited resources as well, clean water and good sanitation are hard to achieve.

Innovation can be a great contribution to clean water and sanitation. Eighty percent of the world's wastewater is released into the environment without adequate treatment. Yet, wastewater is a valuable resource and has a great potential from which clean water, energy, nutrients, and other resources can be recovered (World Bank Group, 2020).

There are several initiatives to taken to recover the value in sewage. One example is the Nano Membrane Toilet which can treat human waste on-site without external energy or water (The Nano Membrane Toilet Project, n.d.). In the developed countries, increasing efficiency of the sewage system has great potential in reducing the use of clean water. Still, it is not enough to only provide the service; information and trust need to develop so that people do not refuse to use the water due to perceived lack of quality. A concrete example in Arusha, Tanzania, illustrates this. What was converted from sewage to safe drinking water is used for irrigation.

#7 AFFORDABLE AND CLEAR ENERGY: Increased share of renewable energy and improved energy efficiency are key actions to achieve this goal. Eight hundred million people lack access to electricity and three billion are still relying on wood, coal, and charcoal for cooking. Even though energy sources like wood are renewable, it takes several years for trees to be re-grown after harvesting. In Uganda, almost three percent of the forest is cut down for cooking among others (Tyson, 2020). If this continues, the country's entire forest will be lost in less than 25 years. Countries in the Equator area have more exposure to sunlight and more stable seasons, and therefore also have great potential for alternative energy sources, like solar panels.

In the developed world, increased energy efficiency can be an important contribution. Also, new energy sources like wind and wave power have potential. These sustainable energy alternatives are starting to compete with more conventional energy sources also when it comes to price. Still, many of these more sustainable energy sources require large areas of land and impact biodiversity.

#8 DECENT WORK AND ECONOMIC GROWTH: Maybe the biggest challenge associated with SDG#8 is poor working conditions in emerging markets and that currently about 40 million people are enslaved worldwide (Hodal, 2019). Focus on supply chain management can contribute to eliminate this.

In poor countries, more than two thirds of the population work in agriculture, whereas the number for rich countries is less than five percent (Roser, 2013). In several countries, being a farmer is not perceived as a goal, and work in industry and factories are kind of at a "higher level". I think we need to discuss this attitude, and maybe give the role of the farmer, even though the farm is not large and driven by machinery, more credit. A life on a farm is not necessarily a less valuable standard of living than spending a full day in a factory or an office. For farmers in poor countries however, more knowledge about good and efficient farming is required, as well as nutrition. To achieve sustainable development, economic growth in the right business areas is crucial, avoiding mass production of unnecessary and polluting products.

#9 INDUSTRY, INNOVATION, AND INFRASTRUCTURE: A good infrastructure is a prerequisite for sustainable development. Clean water and good sewage systems as well as roads and public transportation are important for both health and efficient ways of moving goods and services. Every year much food and resources are lost due to poor infrastructure.

A good infrastructure is not only getting resources to people, but also to return resources for remanufacturing and resale for a circular economy (see Chap. 6). Increased public transportation, transportation based on renewable energy and increased energy efficiency, and a society increasingly based on a shared economy are key issues to address in Goal #9.

#10 REDUCED INEQUALITIES: The GINI index (The World Bank, n.d.) measures income inequality. The GINI coefficient can be between 1 and 0. The 1 implies that one person owns all income and capital, whereas 0 indicates that the populations share income and capital equally. The Nordic countries are the ones with the lowest GINI coefficient, implying more equality. Poor countries, however, seem to have more inequality than rich countries, and the COVID-19 had the most disproportionate impact on the poor and most vulnerable groups. That almost half of the world's wealth is owned by the richest one percent is in itself a paradox (Neate, 2017). As will be addressed in the last chapter, increased wealth and income is not necessarily correlated with happiness.

#11 SUSTAINABLE CITIES AND COMMUNITIES: About one million people live in slums, and the share of urban population living in slums worldwide rose to 24 percent in 2018. As people live close to each other in urban areas, COVID-19 has been relatively more contagious there. Over 90 percent of COVID cases have been in urban areas. In developing countries, where people are leaving farming and moving to cities searching for work, the rural to urban migration is a great challenge and is the key cause of the growing number and size of slums. Providing work outside cities and improving the framework to attract farmers is an alternative to more slums (Broom, 2019). The challenge of the poor image of being a farmer in for example in Africa will be addressed in Chap. 11.

In rich countries, population leaving rural areas and moving into the cities is a well-known challenge. Houses and farms are being abandoned and falling into disrepair. In many "peripheral" areas only retired people or unemployed people remain. Some governments have taken actions to reverse this dynamic by reducing tax for people living in rural areas as well as moving government offices into rural areas. Work attracts young people.

#12 RESPONSIBLE CONSUMPTION AND PRODUCTION: Overconsumption in developed countries is the main challenge to sustainable development. On average the ecological footprint, the metric that measure how much nature people use (Global Footprint Network, n.d.), was 2.75 planets per person in 2016. The planets biocapacity is 1.63 global hectares per person. This implies that we already over consuming and living on deficit. People in the developed part of the world consume many times their "allowance". If everybody lived like people in South-East Asia and East Africa, we would be within the one planet limit (Guinness World Records, 2016).

Even though we have been aware of the problems associated with overconsumption for several decades, our consumption increased in the same period. In Norway for example, the import of textiles, which is something there is good data for, has almost quadrupled from 1990 to 2010.

A reduction in the ecological footprint can be achieved by reducing consumption of the more damaging products, like meat, throwing away less food, changing from incandescent to LED lightbulbs, car-sharing, nudging, reusing, and recycling. However, to become sustainable, with a footprint in line with the one-plant limit, a total shift of consumption is necessary. This fact is uncomfortable for the industrialized world but need more attention.

#13 CLIMATE ACTION: Due to greenhouse gas emissions, the global average temperature is increasing. More frequency of wildfires, long drought, and increase in the number and duration of tropical storms are related to climate change. 2019 was the second warmest year of all times. Even though the key SDG#13 goal is to reduce missions that cause the extreme weather, many countries and companies are moving toward *adaption* to the negative consequences. That is not reducing the problem (emissions) but adapting to the changes. Many poor countries cannot afford such adaptions. Reduced rainfall, which is one consequence of climate change, leads to poor harvests and food shortages in developing countries. In the United States, the loss associated with the 22 weather and climate disasters in 2020 exceeded one billion dollar (National Centers for Environmental Infomation, n.d.).

Since emissions from burning fossil fuels are the major source of the increase in greenhouse gas emissions, major steps are being taken to them. In many places, renewable energy is available and prices per unit of energy (kWh) are becoming competitive. Still, fossil fuel is currently our main energy source and 84 percent of total primary energy consumption in 2019 (BP, 2020). It will take time before we can switch to more sustainable sources of energy.

COVID-19 is likely to result in a six percent reduction of GHG in 2020, still 7.6 percent reduction is required to limit global warming to 1.5 °C (United Nations Sustainable Development, n.d.). On average Norwegians emit 8.4 tons of CO_2 annually, whereas the world average is five tons.

It is the Paris Agreement that acts on the UN SDG#13. This is an international legally binding agreement aimed at reducing climate gases (reduce temperature increase to well below 2 °C relative to pre-industrial levels), increasing climate adaption, and providing a financing system for a low-carbon future. The agreement was signed by 175 countries in 2015 in Paris and has been ratified by 192 countries. United States, a major emitter of climate gases, withdrew from the agreement in 2017 and was not part of the agreement from 2020 to 2021. The United States joined the Paris Agreement in 2021. Achieving the goals of the Paris Agreement is very ambitious, and will be very demanding, if possible, to achieve. Many argue that it will require an economic and social transformation and others that sanctions are necessary to achieve the ambitions of the Paris Agreement.

#14 LIFE BELOW WATER: The ocean system is threatened by pollution, overfishing, and climate change. Human waste and emissions represent a major challenge, and it will not be easy to clean up. A plastic bottle left in the water, for example, will last around 450 years. On average 13,000 pieces of plastic litter can be found on every m^2 of the world's oceans. Forty percent of the world's population depends on the ocean economy (Willige, 2020). As ocean temperature rise, marine wildlife habitats have to relocate. This can remove the livelihood for example fishermen—especially in poor countries. As the global temperature increases, icebergs at the poles melt, and water rises. This has a severe impact on the lives of people living in the coastal area. In the Netherlands, nearly fifty percent of its landmass is already at or below sea level (Glick, n.d.). The worst-case scenario of high climate emissions can imply an ocean rise of 2.5 meters (Lindsey, 2021).

#15 LIFE ON LAND: Forests are one of the main sources of capturing CO_2 emissions. However, every year we are experiencing deforestation. In 2016, for example, forest areas almost the same size as Italy disappeared. An example of the chain effect of land changes is the tundra. As temperature rises, permafrost tundra thaws resulting in increased greenhouse gas emissions in the form of methane. Methane is a much more powerful greenhouse gas than CO_2 (over a 20-year period about 84 times more potent) (UNECE Sustainable Development Goals, n.d.).

Changes in temperature also impact biodiversity. Of the 8300 animal breeds known, 22 percent are at risk of extinction and eight percent are already extinct (UNDP Seoul Policy Centre for Knowledge Exchange through SDG Partnerships, n.d.). The excessive use of fertilizers is a main source of soil degradation. There is a great potential for better and more efficient management of land in developed and undeveloped countries—both in terms of better yield and more sustainable management.

#16 PEACE, JUSTICE AND INSTITUTIONS: Wars, violence, abuse, exploitation, trafficking is continuously going on around the world. After the World War II, the number of deaths associated with war has declined continuously. Still civil wars in Yemen, Syria, and the Tigray have caused death, hunger, and terrible situations for many people. Terrorism has grown, and number of death tolls from terrorism has more than four folded from 2010 to 2014 (Ritchie et al., 2019).

For business, reduction of corruption and bribery might be one of the key challenges related to SDG#16. The global cost of corruption is five percent of global gross domestic products (United Nations Secretary-General, 2018). Corruption will be addressed in greater detail in Chap. 10.

#17 PARTNERSHIP FOR THE GOALS: This goal is about ensuring implementation of the rest of the goals. A prerequisite for achieving the goals is collaboration among different stakeholder beyond nations. Cooperation between corporations, governments, NGOs, and more is crucial. One of the main reasons for the success of the SDGs is that they are based on collaboration among different stakeholders. Involvement renders ownership among stakeholders, and a common agreement and dedication to reach the goals.

Funding is another crucial element to achieve the goals. In the long term, the SDGs form the basis of reduced costs. Reductions in emissions, pollution, better health are all good for economies. To achieve these positive economic effects in the long term, funding is necessary to get started. Target 17.2 is for developed countries to contribute with 0.7 percent of ODA/GNI (Official Development Assistance/Gross National Income). This goal was proposed already in 1970, but as of now, only five countries in the world meet this target.

To measure progress, the country profiles are available from the Sustainable Development Report Dashboard—Country Profiles (Sustainable Development Report, 2020), tracking progress and trends in achieving the SDGs for all the 193 member states. This is an excellent basis for benchmarking countries and business focus.

4.5 Why and How Are the SDGs Relevant for Business?

A majority of large multinational corporations address one or more of the SDGs. Two years after the SDGs were launched, 40 percent of the world's largest 250 companies acknowledged the SDGs in their reporting (KPMG, 2018). As the targets and indicators are useful for benchmarking and comparing for countries, it is so for companies as well. I will now go through examples of how four well-known companies: Coca Cola, H&M, Huawei, and Phillip Morris, are applying the SDGs in practice. These companies are selected for several reasons. First of all, they produce consumer goods. In that way, they are operating in the ends-use marked, even though their products are very different. Second, the companies are originally anchored in different countries, H&M in Sweden, Coca Cola and Philip Morris in America, and Huawei in China. The companies' products are often criticized for being non-sustainable, H&M for mass production of garments that people do not need, Coca Cola for selling sugar drinks and Philip Morris for producing and selling a very unhealthy product, cigarettes, and Huawei for causing security risks.

These companies have sustainability reports from 70 pages to almost 200 pages, and to make this manageable I will only focus on one SDG. Goal #12 Responsible Consumption and Production is very relevant for consumer products manufacturers, and I have therefore chosen to focus on that and associated targets.

Coca Cola is an US-based company and the world's largest beverage company. It is a major provider of soft drinks, juice, and tea and coffee. The company's 2019 Business & Sustainability report is 73 pages long.

12.2 By 2030, achieve the sustainable management and efficient use of natural resources. *In 2018 the company launched World Without Waste with three fundamental goals; 1. Design—Make 100 percent of the package recyclable globally by 2025 and use at least 50 percent recycled material in the packaging by 2030, 2. collect and recycle a bottle or can for each one sold by 2030, and 3. partner with multi stakeholders to create platforms for collaboration.*

12.5 By 2030, substantially reduce waste generation through prevention, reduction, recycling, and reuse. *Coca Cola is one of the founding members of the PET Recycling Company (PETCO) which has led to an increased recycling rate in several African countries and is still expanding.*

12.6 Encourage companies, especially large and transnational companies, to adopt sustainable practices and to integrate sustainability information into their reporting cycle. *Through its sustainability report, the company addresses this issue.*

12.8 By 2030, ensure that people everywhere have the relevant information and awareness for sustainable development and lifestyles in harmony with nature. *Coca Cola works on pursuing water security and 160 percent of water used in finished beverages and their production was in 2019 replenished in nature and communities. Since 2010, 10.6 million people have been reached through the company's water and sanitation program.*

12.a Support developing countries to strengthen their scientific and technological capacity to move toward more sustainable patterns of consumption and production. *In 2019, the company produced the first sample bottle using recovered and recycled marine plastics. Twenty-five percent of the bottles were from the Mediterranean Sea and beaches.*

The company's report sounds convincing, but there are still many negative issues that have not been properly addressed. For example, for three straight years Coca Cola has been named the world's worst plastic polluter. From plastic waste found on beaches, in parks, and near rivers etc., Coca Cola bottles were the most common (Embury-Dennis, 2020). With regards to health effects, there are numerous medical studies showing a correlation that consuming Coca Cola beverages, both regular and diet, can lead to obesity, type 2 diabetes and tooth decay.

H&M is a Swedish company "making fashion and design accessible to everyone in a sustainable way". The company had over 5000 stores and about 180,000 employees. The H&M Group Sustainability Performance Report of 2019 is 85 pages.

SDG #12 is covered in the two chapters "Leading the Change" and "Circular & Climate Positive". The company does not respond directly to the SDG targets and has a more general approach to the SDG goals.

With regards to "Leading the Change", Innovation; for solutions to complex social and environmental challenges. Through a circular innovation lab, the company works on recycled and other sustainably sourced materials.

Transparency, openness about business, performance, challenges, and product details to customers. In 2019, the company launched the Product Transparency Solution which makes it possible for online customers to see information about product materials, factory and garment care, or recycling options.

Rewarding sustainable action, H&M collaborates with different stakeholders to incentivize more sustainable behaviors. Sustainability goals are set at the executive level and part of management's evaluations, customers are urged to sustainable actions by the garment collection schemes and suppliers receive sustainability training.

With regards to Circular & Climate Positive, the goal is to achieve full circularity and becoming climate positive by 2040. The approach is to decouple emissions from business growth through energy efficiency, 100 percent renewable energy, circular approach, and carbon sinks. From 2016–2018 the company has reduced its CO_2 emissions; however, in 2019, they increased by 8 percent.

All of this seems quite convincing from a sustainability point of view, but the fact that H&M has factories in Myanmar which employ 14-year old children and they market to people to buy new clothes with a 15 percent rebate in exchange for used clothes is not sustainable. In fact, a company that has a business model based on low cost and fast fashion cannot be considered sustainable.

Huawei is a Chinese company and a "leading global provider of information and communication technology (ICT) infrastructure and smart devices". The company has 194,000 employees and operates in more than 170 countries and regions. The 2019 Sustainability Report contains 110 pages.

SDGs are part of the company's Sustainability Strategy covering several SDGs. SDG #12 is associated with Security and Trustworthiness and Environmental Protection.

Cybersecurity and privacy protection are among the company's top priorities. Major progress in 2019 included: "Guaranteed network availability during more than 200 major events and natural disasters, Published an AI security and privacy protection white paper, obtained more than 20 cyber security and privacy certifications for our main products; and Saw multiple Huawei entities obtain ISO 22301 (business continuity management) certification".

Contributing to a clean, efficient, low-carbon, and circular economy are key elements in the company's Environmental protection strategy. Huawei increased the energy efficiency of their main products by up to 22 percent, cut CO_2 emissions intensity by 32.7 percent compared with the base year, recycled 86 percent of returned products, and used 1.25 billion kWh of clean energy, thereby reducing the emissions by 570,000 tons.

The Huawei report on Consumption and Production also seems convincing. However, the fact that Huawei has been allegedly involved in state sponsored and industrial espionage as well as human right violations is not addressed in the report. These omissions diminish its trustworthiness and it detracts from the positive contributions the company presented in its sustainability report.

Philip Morris International (PMI) is the world's largest tobacco company based in the United States, with about 73,500 employees and 38 production facilities worldwide. The company's Integrated Report 2019 is 187 pages.

SDG # 12 is one of several SDGs PMI recognizes that it can contribute to. Improving lifecycle impact of products can be attained through reducing environmental impact of tobacco growing. Efficient low-carbon manufacturing, litter prevention, product eco-design, and recycling programs are primary contributions. The company is committed to finding alternatives to cigarettes "as quickly as possible".

The company target is to become carbon neutral by 2030 as a company and by 2050 through the whole value chain. The plan is furthermore to achieve a 50 percent reduction of plastic litter from the production by 2025.

Philip Morris pays attention to reducing its environmental impact, but the company's key challenge is that it is in the business of producting an unhealthy product. According to the WHO, tobacco kills up to half of its users and more than eight million people annually. Even though the company works on providing alternatives to its consumers, they are still expanding production in Africa for example, where the use of tobacco is increasing.

So, yes, companies are pursuing sustainability, but self-reporting on good performance is not always credible. There is growth in the market for sustainable and "green" products, and many companies market their products as such without data to support their claims. This gives a false impression that the products and companies are operating in a sustainable way, when it is in fact greenwashing.

From a more comprehensive perspective, can producing detrimental products such as tobacco and fast fashion ever become sustainable? Criticizing companies and sectors for behaving in a non-sustainable way is common—it happens all the time. But, companies are not the only ones that should be targeted with criticism. If we as consumers stopped purchasing such products demand would plummet and the production of such items would end.

SDGs in Practice: A Case

This case is based on an interview with a VP in one of the largest aluminum companies worldwide.

Involved in a resource intensive industry, the company has been actively involved in fulfilling their environmental and social responsibilities for several decades. When the Millennium goals were launched in 2000, the company was keen to implement and contribute to achievement of these. However, the Millennium goals were aimed at nations, not at corporations and it was therefore unclear how companies could contribute in their operations and practice.

The Sustainable Development Goals however were much more business oriented. Already when the SDGs were launched in 2015, the company started benchmarking itself relative to each of the 17 goals. Current status on performance with regards to each goal, and to which extent the company contributed positively or negatively to the goal, was mapped. Except for Goal #13 Climate Action, the analysis was not quantitative but qualitative. Even though there is no common, or official, approach to self-benchmarking with regards to SDGs, the process still resulted in awareness and made it easier to decide how to proceed on the sustainability journey.

A team representing employees across the company then started worked on identifying which of the goals were most relevant and where the company could contribute the most. In this process, it became evident that the most relevant goals could be divided into three groups:

1. Improving our footprint (Goal #13, #14, and #15)
2. Making a Positive Difference (Goal #8, #8, and #16)
3. Driving Innovation (#9, #12, and #13)

Most of the goals chosen are self-explanatory, relevant to the company sector. Other goals like for example *#4 Quality Education, "Ensure inclusive and equitable quality education and promote lifelong learning opportunities for all"* is less obvious for an aluminum company. It is therefore a good example of how company impact comes forward when all the SDGs are reviewed, one by one.

As the company is operating in developing countries, the local workforce needs education to work at the facilities. In a long-term perspective, enhancing primary education for the local society will form a good basis for employees in the future. It is an advantage for everyone that local people, with their families close, can operate the facilities in a longer perspective, instead of importing the workforce from company HQ far away. The primary school contribution is done in cooperation with local schools and education authorities. The company also supports technical training and university level degrees in fields relevant to the company operation. In that sense, the company is working along the lines of the Triple-Bottom-Line, doing good for people, planet, and profit.

4.6 Additional Relevant Initiatives and Tools for Sustainable Performance

There are hundreds of initiatives and standards for how companies can address environmental, social, and sustainability issues.

I will give a brief overview and introduction to the initiatives which are most applied, accredited, and relevant. Such initiatives have different forms. Some provide frameworks that companies have to fulfill in order to get approved or certified. Such approvement can be a requirement for eco-labels and for being approved as a supplier for a company. Other initiatives are frameworks that companies can use for organizing and reporting on sustainability related issues. Other initiatives provide platforms where ESG data, especially on climate issues, can be posted for analysists and investors. Finally, there are laws and regulations on an international level which it is important to be aware of—also relevant for small companies.

Initiatives for Certifications

There are close to 500 different ecolabels. These are certification schemes that companies apply to meet compliance and demand from customers, but also to promote their own brand. The choice between the many different certification schemes depends upon among others the sector and type of business. These are three well recognized certification initiatives.

Forest Stewardship Council (FSC). If a product made of wood, including paper, chairs, flooring, and so on has a FSC label, you know that the forest the product is from is managed in an environmentally responsible way.

Fair Trade Certified. If you purchase a product with a Fair Trade label, you know that the farmers involved in the production among others have received fair wage, healthcare, housing, and education. Coffee and tea are typical products with the Fair Trade label.

Marine Stewardship Council (MSC). If you purchase a seafood product with a MSC label, you know that the products are from a fishery that is sustainably managed (no overfishing), minimizing environmental impact and run effectively.

Having these certification labels can make products preferred by customers. It can also be a good yardstick for the producer to ensure good sustainable production. On the other hand, becoming certified requires fulfilling a long list of criteria which can be costly to implement. It can be expensive to manage production according to the criteria set, especially if the company needs third-party certification bodies to approve the production site. For some labels, the companies have to pay a premium, which increases the price of the products. Still, being certified can also be a requirement for getting contracts for products and customers can be willing to pay a higher price for the products.

ISO 14001: Environmental Management System (EMS) is the most well-known and applied environmental certification for business-to-business (B2B). ISO 14001 was launched in 1996 as a follow-up of the Rio conference. It has gone through three revisions after that, the latest in 2015. The purpose of the standard is to enhance the company's environmental performance, fulfill compliance obligations, and achieve environmental objectives. ISO 14001 EMS covers the context of the organization, Leadership, Planning, Support, Operation, performance evaluation, and Improvement. It can be used by all types of organizations and corporations. Benefits of an ISO 14001 certification is improved resource efficiency, reduction of waste, reduced costs, and so on. Studies have shown that even though certification is associated with direct and indirect costs to fulfilling requirements, companies that are certified are more competitive, more efficient, and win more contracts (Gonçalves, 2018). The main motivation for most companies becoming certified is that it is a requirement for becoming a supplier in the value chain. For companies wanting to ensure that all is in order with regard to environmental issues in the supply chain, to require certification is a simple solution. By 2017 there were more than 300,000 ISO 14001 certifications. For discussing one ISO product related to environment, it is relevant to touch upon an additional ISO initiative, ISO 26000, on social responsibility, even though this is not associated with certification.

ISO 26000 Guidance on social responsibility was launched in 2010. Being a "Guidance", ISO 26000 is not for certification. ISO 26000 is a framework for how to become a sustainable company or organization. The concept of social responsibility in this ISO standard has seven core subjects: human rights, labor practices, the environment, fair operating practices, consumer issues, and community involvement and development.

The Guidance manual is of 106 pages and can be purchased and downloaded online. The content is however rather vague. Given that there are so many new tools which attempt to contribute with the same assistance as ISO 26000, there might be other and more efficient tools that are more applicable.

There are several organizations and frameworks for guiding *reporting* on sustainability and it can be confusing with so many different initiatives. Given that companies measure and report in different formats, it is difficult to compare performance. Merging these initiatives is on its way, but it will take some time before it is ready. Next, I will provide a short list of different tools, including purpose, usefulness, and application. I will start with initiatives related to climate issues.

Greenhouse and Climate Reporting

The Greenhouse Gas (GHG) Protocol Corporate Accounting and Reporting Standard is a comprehensive global standardized framework to measure and manage GHG emissions. It helps countries and companies to account for, report and mitigate emissions, and provide a standardized measurement of GHG as well as accounting and reporting standards. The framework is developed through a partnership between World Resource Institute (WRI) and the World Business Council for Sustainable Development (WBCSD) and the first edition of the standard was published in 2001. The GHG Protocol was initiated with large multinational corporations like BP and GM, and eventually additional multinational corporations like Norsk Hydro, Tokyo Electric, Royal Dutch Shell as well as NGOs like WWF and The Energy Research Institute collaborated on developing the framework. This framework is the most widely used accounting standard for GHG and can be used to report in the Paris Agreement setting.

Emission factors convert corporate activity data to GHG emissions. Calculating GHG emissions based on kilometers driven by a company car and kilos of natural gas used are examples of company activities which can be converted to GHG equivalents. National environmental agency often provides simple tools for this type of assessment.

GHG emissions include CO_2, CH_4, N_2O, HFCs, PFCs, SF_6, and NF_3 (Environmental Protection Agency, 2020). The approach is based on three "scopes".

- Scope 1 Covers direct GHG emissions. That includes emissions from sources that are owned or controlled by the company. For an SME that could be fossil fuel used to run its own machinery and gasoline used by its own cars.
- Scope 2 Covers indirect GHG emissions from energy consumption. This includes for example electricity or district heating consumed. It is based on the mix of fossil and renewable sources of energy either by location and production or by market mechanisms like renewable energy certificates.
- Scope 3 Covers all other indirect GHG emissions the company is indirectly responsible for along its entire value chain, both upstream and downstream. This includes, for example, emissions from buying products from suppliers and from its products when customers use them. Scope 3 emissions constitute the greater majority of a company's GHG emissions.

The GHG protocol is the most widely recognized framework used for companies today.

CDP runs a global disclosure system and ranking system, Disclosure Insight Action, for investors, companies, and cities to manage their environmental impacts. For the last 20 years, this has been the key platform for institutional investors to collect data on corporations. Over 8400 companies with over 50 percent of global market capitalization have used the CDP as a channel for disclosing their environmental data in 2019.

Climate Disclosure Standard Board (CDSB), formed in 2011, offers companies a framework for reporting environmental information with the same format as financial information. CDSB is committed to advancing and aligning the global mainstream corporate reporting model to equate natural capital with financial capital. The Board is a consortium of business and environmental NGOs.

Task Force on Climate-Related Financial Disclosures (TCFD) was initiated by the Group of 20 Finance Ministers and Central Bank Governors and launched at the end of 2015 by the Financial Stability Board (FSB), an international body monitoring and making recommendations about the global financial system, under the chairmanship of Michael Bloomberg, founder of the world's largest finance software companies. The purpose was to create a financial disclosure framework to provide investors, banks, and insurance underwriters better transparency regarding climate-related risks and opportunities that may impact disclosing company. TCFD is quickly gaining traction among regulators and the largest companies in the world; 60 percent of the 100 largest companies support TFCD, particularly in Asia and Europe. It consists of 11 different questions in 4 topic areas: governance, strategy, risk management, and metrics and targets. Since it is voluntary, companies generally selectively disclose information and generally include them in their sustainability reports.

As is evident there are a myriad of slightly different initiatives for keeping track of corporate disclosure on environmental issues. This is confusing and inefficient. It is positive and also necessary that many of these are starting to cooperate and merge. In the next section, I will give an overview over different frameworks for general sustainability reporting.

Sustainability Reporting Frameworks

The Global Reporting Initiative (GRI): Since companies started reporting on social and environmental issues, the issues addressed and way of reporting had no common framework and the content was therefore, or even, impossible to compare. In response to this, the Global Reporting Initiative (GRI) was developed by a network with representatives from companies and organizations founded in 1997 and the first version of GRI Guidelines was launched in year 2000. The GRI has later been revised and new and more encompassing versions were later launched. The latest version is GRI G4. Today the GRI is the world's most widely used standard for sustainability reporting. It starts with an environmental focus, later on economic, environmental, and social performance, and lastly how the SDGs are part of the framework for reporting.

Today, out of the largest 100 companies in 52 countries, 80 percent report according to the GRI framework (Global Reporting Initiative, 2020).The GRI framework has developed both in size and specialization related to sectors and operations. Even though the framework and guidelines are available for download at the GRI website, they are too encompassing for most SMEs. Still, the general framework as well as framework can assist SMEs by inspiring to action as well as a checklist for activities.

The International Integrated Reporting Council (IIRC), launched in 2010, is an international initiative by a group of stakeholders, regulators, investors, companies, standard setters, the accounting profession, and NGOs. The purpose is to integrate the annual and sustainability reporting. As the goal is to integrate sustainability in daily business, the reporting also has to be integrated. The initiative contributes with guidance and training on integrated reporting (Integrated Reporting, n.d.). In 2019, 58 percent of top 40 French listed companies produced integrated reports (Sweet, 2019). In 2021 IIRC merged with SASB (The Sustainable Accounting Standards Board) to form the Value Reporting Foundation (VRF). The merger of different reporting initiatives makes it less confusing both for companies as well as investors to evaluate companies. The EU taxonomy addressed in Chap. 9 will be a major step in the direction of a more coherent reporting system.

The Sustainability Accounting Standards Board (SASB) was formed in 2011 with the purpose of developing sustainability accounting standards. SASB contributes to facilitating the comparison of corporate data and communications between companies. In 2021, IIRC and SASB merged to form the **Value Reporting Foundation (VRF)**. Key resources from the VRF framework include Integrated Thinking Principles,

Integrated Reporting Framework and SASB standards to contribute to more coherent international corporate reporting. This merger between the IIRC and SASB makes it easier for companies to report and, together, this will make it attractive and realistic for more companies to report.

International Sustainability Standards Board (ISSB)—the formation of the ISSB, announced in November 2021, is an initiative to consolidate sustainability reporting and disclosure frameworks from CDP, CDSB, the GRI, and VRF. The ISSB will create one common comprehensive corporate reporting framework. New regulatory frameworks for reporting, like the EU taxonomy (Chap. 9), are often based on experiences from voluntary corporate initiatives through foundations and organizations like the ones mentioned above. In this way the "soft laws" based on corporate self-reporting norms make new "hard laws" more likely to work.

The European Union (EU) has with the *European Green Deal* policy initiative of 2019, committed to make Europe climate neutral in 2050. The United States has pledged to become carbon neutral by 2050 and China by 2060. The Green Deal includes ambitious action plans for among others the circular economy and a revision of energy taxation. It can be argued that EU is ahead of other countries, and I will therefore include two regulations associated with EU reporting requirements which will have an impact on companies from outside the EU that are doing business within the EU such as importing manufacturing products.

EU Directive 2014/95/EU, the non-financial reporting directive (NFRD), requires large companies to disclose information on how they operate and manage social and environmental challenges. A key goal is to make companies more aware of their societal impact and provide relevant and comparable information to stakeholders, like investors, NGOs, customers, and the media. Companies are required to include non-financial statements in their annual reports. Issues to be covered in the report include policies on environmental protection, social responsibility and treatment of employees, respect for human rights, anti-corruption and bribery, and diversity on corporate boards. The EU has developed more detailed guidelines for reporting, which make reference to the UN Global Compact, the OECD Guidelines for Multinational Enterprises and ISO

26000. The EU directive applies to listed companies with more than 500 employees and covers about 11,700 companies (European Commission, n.d.-a). In 2019, the EC published new guidelines on reporting climate-related information to accompany the NFRD and is based on recommended disclosures of the TCFD.

Corporate Sustainability Reporting Directive (CSRD): The EC in April 2021(European Commission, n.d.-b) adopted a proposal to amend the NFRD. The proposal will, among others, extend the scope to all large companies (about 50.000), would require more detailed reporting as well as auditing. Even though the reporting requirements will be more comprehensive, the uniform standards will make the reporting easier for companies to produce and easier to read and compare for external stakeholders like investors and NGOs. It is anticipated that the CSRD standards will be adopted in 2022.

Supply Chain Guidance, Transparency, and Mandatory Due Diligence

The OECD Guidelines for Multinational Enterprises are recommendations from governments to multinational enterprises operating in or from their territories. They were adopted in 1976 as part of the Declaration on International Investment and Multinational Enterprises and have later been updated several times to be in line with developments in the landscape for international investment and multinational enterprises. The most recent update was in 2011, which included a new human rights chapter and a new and comprehensive approach to due diligence. Updates are made with the active participation of business, labor, NGOs, non-adhering countries, and international organizations (OECD, 2011). The Guidelines are non-binding, but still, as a multilaterally agreed code of responsible business conduct, they are widely recognized and used. The Guidelines cover disclosure, human rights, employment and industrial relations, environment, combating bribery and bribe solicitation and extortion, consumer interests, science and technology, competition and taxation (OECD, 2011).

Even though the guidelines are aimed at multinational enterprises, they are relevant for all enterprises. These Guidelines are also relevant for organizations outside the company to evaluate corporate performance with regards to sustainability. Interested parties may file complaints with allegations of non-observance of the Guidelines to National Contact Points (NCPs), which are established to promote the Guidelines and handle complaints in OECD countries and other countries adhering to the Guidelines.

Individual organizations, often trade unions and NGOs, may submit complaints where they allege that corporations are not observing the OECD Guidelines. The NCP determines whether to accept the complaint based on the procedural guidance of the OECD Guidelines. From 2000 to 2020, 500 specific instances were handled by the NCP internationally. After a complaint is submitted, it goes through a process of initial assessment by the NCP. If the complaint is accepted, the NCP offers its good offices to the parties (dialogue and/or mediation). This may result in a joint statement from the parties, or, if the parties do not agree on one, the NCP will issue its final statement. Sometimes companies admit not operating in line with the Guidelines and agree to change policies and/or practices. Other times they do not agree with the allegations and are not willing to change.

In a complaint submitted to the NCP in Norway in 2020, organizations claimed that a group of corporations, including Samsung Heavy Industries, Total, and Equinor, failed to exercise due diligence and operate in line with the OECD Guidelines when it comes to transparency and human rights in conjunction with an accident during the construction of an oil platform on Norwegian territory. A labor association in Yemen has submitted complaints against DNO, a Norwegian company operating in Yemen, for firing employees and closing down facilities. DNO was not found to be in violation of the OECD Guidelines in the specific instance that was closed in 2020. Another example illustrating the variation in complaints was submitted by Jinjevaerje Sameby in Sweden. The complainants alleged that Statkraft AS planned to set up windfarms in the area without consulting the local population involved in reindeer herding in the area. The parties did not reach an agreement, and the NCP concluded in its Final Statement that Statkraft had failed to comply with the OECD Guidelines. Even though the complaint mechanism does not entail fines or punishment, the complaints make companies aware of the OECD Guidelines and participation may prompt them to act in accordance with them. Avoidance of negative media coverage can also be an important motivator for observing the OECD Guidelines.

Transparency Acts An important focus in the field of responsible business conduct in recent years has had an adverse impact on human rights by business relationships in global supply chains. Of the estimated 40 million people working in slavery-like conditions, one in four are children. Women and girls are especially affected by forced labor in the commercial sex industry. Given these challenges and the demand for information on working conditions and human rights among stakeholders like non-governmental organizations, media, and customers, several countries are adopting legislation that extends transparency requirements and due diligence to business relationships and supply chains.

In addition, investors call for stronger requirements when it comes to environmental social and governance issues (ESG). The Investor Alliance for Human Rights (IAHR) represents 160 institutional investors which manage more than $1.9 trillion assets under management. They call on the EU and the US Congress to adopt regulations mandating due diligence with regard to ESG issues (Investor Alliance for Human Rights, n.d.). New laws on transparency pertaining human rights and working conditions in supply chains have been developed and adopted in recent years.

The first law on transparency in the supply chain, the **California Transparency in Supply Chains Act—TISC**, was passed in 2010. The law requires companies to report on efforts to combat slavery and human trafficking. The TISC was a frontrunner for the UK Modern Slavery Act of 2015 addressing slavery, compulsory labor, and human trafficking Section 54 on Transparency in Supply Chains (TISC) requires companies to report on risks of, and efforts to eradicate, modern slavery. If there are no such risks, the company may report this.

The **French Corporate Duty of Vigilance Law** was passed in 2017. The initiative for the law came in the aftermath of the Rana Plaza accident in Bangladesh in 2013. Mandatory due diligence is a key element in the law. This law makes it legally binding for large companies to identify and prevent adverse human rights and environmental impacts resulting from their own activities, from activities of companies they control, and from activities of their subcontractors and suppliers, with whom they have an established commercial relationship. (European Coalition for Corporate Justice, 2017) Liabilities apply when companies do not fulfill their obligations, by for example not having a plan for the above issues or when they do not follow up the plan.

The law is related to the UN Guiding Principles on Business and Human Rights (UNGP). Other laws, inspired to varying degrees by the UNGPs, have been initiated and passed in other countries, like the UK Modern Slavery Act of 2015 and the Dutch Child Labour (Duty of Care) Act of 2019.

Along the above lines, the **"Transparency Act" (Åpenhetsloven)** was passed in Norway in June 2021 and will enter into force July 1st 2022. This law is argued to go the furthest with regards to ensuring basic human rights and decent working conditions associated products and services. The act applies to companies which meet at least two of the following three conditions: over 70 MNOK in sales revenue, over 35 MNOK on its balance sheet and a minimum of an aggregate of 50 full-time employees. So, effectively, this will apply to about 9000 companies in Norway. As a member of the committee which drafted this law, I would like to emphasize that it is significant considering Norway's relatively small size in terms of population. The laws apply to a relatively large proportion of Norwegian companies in comparison to similar transparency laws in other countries. The Act includes three key obligations: duty to carry out due diligence, duty to account for due diligence and the right to information. A company covered by this Act is required to conduct a due diligence assessment, reporting, and provide transparency throughout its supply chain with regards to human rights and working conditions. The right to information implies that a company is obliged to respond to any written request regarding the actual and potential adverse impact of its operations and products on human rights. The law is based on international obligations, specifically the UN Guiding Principles on Business and Human Rights (UNGP), the OECD Guidelines for Multinational

Enterprises and the UN SDGs. So far we do not know the effect of the law. Many requests from external stakeholders can be expensive for companies, but on the positive side increases in corporate awareness should improve human rights performance in supply chains. The act is available in English through Lovdata. Several countries as well as the EU are working at similar actions to increase transparence and improve working conditions in the supply chain.

References

Blyth, N. (2020). Sustainable development goals and the business community. *DailyFT*. http://www.ft.lk/opinion/Sustainable-development-goals-and-the-business-community/14-695549

BP. (2020). *Statistical review of world energy 2020* (69th edition). https://www.bp.com/content/dam/bp/business-sites/en/global/corporate/pdfs/energy-economics/statistical-review/bp-stats-review-2020-full-report.pdf

Broom, D. (2019). Millennials are transforming African farming. https://www.weforum.org/agenda/2019/06/the-millennials-giving-african-farming-an-image-boost/

Business Call to Action. (n.d.). *More than philanthropy: SDGs present an estimated US$12 trillion in market opportunities for private sector through inclusive business*. https://www.businesscalltoaction.org/resources/more-philanthropy-sdgs-present-estimated-us12-trillion-market-opportunities-private-sector

Embury-Dennis. (2020). Coca-Cola named world's worst plastic polluter for third straight year. *Independent*. Monday December 7th

Environmental Protection Agency. (2020). *Guide to greenhouse gas management for small business & low emitters* (August). https://www.epa.gov/sites/production/files/2017-01/documents/guide_to_greenhouse_gas_management_for_small_business_low_emitters.pdf

European Coalition for Corporate Justice. (2017, February 23). *French corporate duty of vigilance law: FAQs*. https://corporatejustice.org/publications/faqs-french-duty-of-vigilance-law/

European Commission. (n.d.-a). *Corporate sustainability reporting*. https://ec.europa.eu/info/business-economy-euro/company-reporting-and-auditing/company-reporting/corporate-sustainability-reporting_en

European Commission. (n.d.-b). *Proposal for a Corporate Sustainability Reporting Directive (CSRD)*. https://ec.europa.eu/info/business-economy-euro/company-reporting-and-auditing/company-reporting/corporate-sustainability-reporting_en#review

Food and Agriculture Organization of the United Nations. (2016, December 16). *Women hold the key to building a world free from hunger and poverty*. http://www.fao.org/news/story/en/item/460267/icode/

Gillian, T. (2019). Governments won't fund sustainable development. Will private finance step in? *Financial Times*. https://www.ft.com/content/82ef5e8e-1ea1-11e9-b126-46fc3ad87c65

Glick, D. (n.d.). The big thaw. *National Geographic,*. https://www.nationalgeographic.com/environment/article/big-thaw

Global Footprint Network. (n.d.-b). *Ecological footprint*. https://www.footprintnetwork.org/our-work/ecological-footprint/

Global Reporting Initiative. (2020, December 1). Sustainability reporting is growing, with GRI the global common language. https://www.globalreporting.org/about-gri/news-center/2020-12-01-sustainability-reporting-is-growing-with-gri-the-global-common-language

Gonçalves, A. (2018, October 26). Are ISO 14001 certified companies more competitive, efficient & sustainable? *Youmatter*. https://youmatter.world/en/are-iso-14001-certified-companies-are-more-competitive-and-efficient/

Guinness World Records. (2016). *Smallest ecological footprint (per capita, country)*. https://www.guinnessworldrecords.com/world-records/637715-smallest-ecological-footprint-per-capita-country

Hodal, K. (2019, February 25). One in 200 people is a slave. Why? *The Guardian*. https://www.theguardian.com/news/2019/feb/25/modern-slavery-trafficking-persons-one-in-200

Horton, R. (2014). Offline: Why the sustainable development goals will fail. *The Lancet, 383*(9936). https://www.thelancet.com/journals/lancet/article/PIIS0140-6736(14)61046-1/fulltext

Integrated Reporting. (n.d.). Frequently asked questions. https://integratedreporting.org/FAQS/#what-is-the-international-integrated-reporting-council-iirc

Investor Alliance for Human Rights. (n.d.). *About the investor alliance for human rights*. https://investorsforhumanrights.org/about

KPMG. (2018). *How to report on the SDGs: What good looks like and why it matters*. https://home.kpmg/xx/en/home/insights/2018/02/how-to-report-on-the-sdgs.html

Lindsey, R. (2021). Climate change: Global sea level. *Climate.gov*. https://www.climate.gov/news-features/understanding-climate/climate-change-global-sea-level

National Centers for Environmental Information. (n.d.). Billion-Dollar weather and climate disasters: Overview. *National Centers for Environmental Information*. https://www.ncdc.noaa.gov/billions/

Neate, R. (2017, November 14). Richest 1% own half the world's wealth, study finds. *The Guardian*. https://www.theguardian.com/inequality/2017/nov/14/worlds-richest-wealth-credit-suisse

OECD. (2011). *OECD guidelines for multinational enterprises*. https://www.oecd.org/daf/inv/mne/48004323.pdf

Pandey, K. (2020). Sustainable development goals: 36 changes in global indicator framework. *Down to Earth*. https://www.downtoearth.org.in/news/climate-change/sustainable-development-goals-36-changes-in-global-indicator-framework-69716

Ritchie, H., Hasell, J., Appel, C., & Roser, M. (2019, November). Terrorism. *Our World in Data*. https://ourworldindata.org/terrorism

Roser, M. (2013). Employment in agriculture. *Our World in Data*. https://ourworldindata.org/employment-in-agriculture

Sustainable Development Report. (2020). *Country profiles*. https://dashboards.sdgindex.org/profiles

Sweet, P. (2019, September 23). Listed companies increase use of integrated reporting, says IIRC. *Accountancy Daily*. https://www.accountancydaily.co/listed-companies-increase-use-integrated-reporting-says-iirc

The Nano Membrane Toilet Project. (n.d.). The nano membrane toilet. http://www.nanomembranetoilet.org/

The World Bank. (n.d.). Metadata glossary. *Databank*. https://databank.worldbank.org/metadataglossary/gender-statistics/series/SI.POV.GINI

Tyson, J. (2020). Cooking up a solution to Uganda's deforestation crisis with mud stoves. *The Guardian*. https://www.theguardian.com/global development/2020/jun/29/cooking-up-a-solution-to-ugandas-deforestation-crisis-with-mud-stoves

UN Sustainable Development Goals. (2016). The sustainable development agenda. https://www.un.org/sustainabledevelopment/development-agenda-retired/

UNDP Seoul Policy Centre for Knowledge Exchange through SDG Partnerships. (n.d.). *Goal 15: Life on land.* https://www1.undp.org/content/seoul_policy_center/en/home/sustainable-development-goals/goal-15-life-on-land.html

UNECE Sustainable Development Goals. (n.d.). Methane management: The challenge. https://unece.org/challenge

United Nations. (2015). *The millennium development goals report 2015.* https://www.un.org/millenniumgoals/2015_MDG_Report/pdf/MDG%202015%20rev%20(July%201).pdf

United Nations Global Compact. (2017, December 5). *Enact: What, how and why?*https://www.sa.is/media/2864/erika.pdf

United Nations Global Compact. (2021). *Our finances.* https://www.unglobalcompact.org/about/finances

United Nations Human Rights. (2011). *Guiding principles on business and human rights.* https://www.ohchr.org/documents/publications/guidingprinciplesbusinesshr_en.pdf

United Nations Secretary-General. (2018, December 5). *Cost of corruption at least 5 per cent of global gross domestic product, secretary-general says in International Day message* [Press Release]. https://www.un.org/press/en/2018/sgsm19392.doc.htm

United Nations Sustainable Development. (2020). *About major groups and other stakeholders.* Division for Sustainable Development Goals. https://sustainabledevelopment.un.org/mgos

United Nations Sustainable Development. (n.d.). *Goals.13: Take urgent action to combat climate change and its impacts.* https://sdgs.un.org/goals/goal13

Willige, A. (2020). 4 challenges we need to solve to protect our ocean. *World Economic Forum.* https://www.weforum.org/agenda/2020/09/oceans-coral-reefs-climate-change-pollution-overfishing/

World Bank Group. (2020, March 19). *Wastewater a resource that can pay dividends for people, the environment, and economies, says World Bank* [Press release]. https://www.worldbank.org/en/news/press-release/2020/03/19/wastewater-a-resource-that-can-pay-dividends-for-people-the-environment-and-economies-says-world-bank

World Health Organization. (2019, June 18). 1 in 3 people globally do not have access to safe drinking water—UNICEF, WHO. https://www.who.int/news/item/18-06-2019-1-in-3-people-globally-do-not-have-access-to-safe-drinking-water-unicef-who

5

The Business Case for Sustainability

In this chapter, I will discuss how companies actually address sustainability challenges. First, the chapter will begin with examples of different corporate approaches to taking responsibility for sustainability. Second, I will explore how companies are viewed from the stakeholder point of view, so how others outside the company view the managers' motivation for engaging in corporate responsibility. Although the majority of companies are still motivated by risk reduction and/or branding in their sustainability work, this chapter will reframe the motivation into something more positive—a business opportunity.

The chapter will analyze four key happenings which triggered focus on sustainability and changed the environment: the Nike sweatshop case; the Arthur Andersen corruption case; the VW case on incorrect emission reporting and, finally, the Rana Plaza building collapse case. The model of sustainability and change, from ignoring that there is a corporate challenge, to reacting, defending, accommodating, and finally moving to a proactive approach to sustainability will be used as a framework for business development and evaluation through the four cases. In essence, the journey will be on the transition from reducing unsustainability to a focus on creating sustainability (Hoffmann, 2018).

C. D. Ditlev-Simonsen, *A Guide to Sustainable Corporate Responsibility*,
https://doi.org/10.1007/978-3-030-88203-7_5

5.1 Who Initiates Sustainability Focus in Companies: And What Is the Outcome?

There are a multitude of drivers motivating leaders and companies to pursue sustainability and address the company's responsibilities. The position and role of the person within the corporate hierarchy initiating such engagements is an important antecedent of how the company will proceed on sustainability and where it will end up—that is, what will be the result. The importance to individual preferences in the sustainability process is often overlooked and I will therefore include it in this chapter.

In a study following four companies after the concept of corporate responsibility and addressing sustainability issues was introduced, the impact of individuals in the sustainability process comes forward. The person in charge of introducing the concept, the "translators", had chosen very different approaches to apply and follow up the corporate responsibility process. One way to explain the difference in strategies and outcomes is that each of the four employees had different power and impact within their respective organizations. Another is that the employees had different ways of working—different personalities (Ditlev-Simonsen, 2010).

Starting with the impact of position, assume the person introducing the corporate responsibility and sustainability focus into the company is part of the top management team. This person does not necessarily have to consult with other employees. This manager can make his/her own interpretation of the company's responsibilities with regards to sustainability and implement it as he/she deems appropriate. If the "translator" is the Director of Public Relations/Communication, the initiatives are likely to be closely related to communicating the company's sustainability focus, even though this might not necessarily be part of the company culture. There are many examples of company responsibility and sustainability reports containing great presentations of the company's sustainability engagement, but if you asked a random employee, they would not know anything about it. It is also common to find companies, which issue non-/extra-financial reports full of great sustainability stories and printed on recycled paper. However, these same companies' corporate annual reports do not mention social responsibility or sustainability at all. This signals that the issues are most likely not integrated in the company's day-to-day operations.

So, we see that the role, position, and even personality of the person who starts the sustainability focus process impacts the degree of a company's engagement and focus on this field. If the Head of Investor Relations as opposed to the Director of Communications initiates a company's sustainability engagement, there tends to be a much larger investor focus.

We also see that if the person in charge of the company's sustainability engagement is at the bottom of the company's hierarchy, driven by for example personal interest and/or delegated the responsibility to a senior manager, initiatives rarely succeed without greater awareness, support, and buy-in from colleagues. So, if an employee at the lower echelons of the organization manages to make sustainable changes in the company, it is likely to have a more encompassing effect. Still, as will be discussed in Chap. 7, that sustainability is anchored in top management is a prerequisite for a successful sustainability process.

5.2 Perception of Management Motivation for Social Responsibility

In addition to responsibility and sustainability drivers anchored in position and personality, managers/companies are motivated by different goals. Asking board members, employees at two NGOs, World Wide Fund for Nature (WWF) and Amnesty International, and master students what they assumed motivated senior managers in the 20 largest companies in Norway to pursue corporate responsibility, the answers were surprisingly aligned. One would have thought that critical NGOs were likely to be more skeptical about managers' motivations, than for example corporate board members (Ditlev-Simonsen & Midttun, 2011).

The respondents, the board members, NGO employees, and students were asked to rate ten different motivation factors why managers pursue corporate responsibility. These include: Profit (short-term revenue) (Friedman, 1970), Value maxim (long-term profit) (Jensen, 2001), Stakeholdership (pressure from out or inside) (Freeman, 1984), Cluster building (that companies in the same sector "push" each other) (Porter, 1998), Branding (to improve reputation) (Fombrun, 2005), Innovation (competitive advantage through better products) (Kanter, 1999),

Copying and imitating (pursuing sustainability because everybody else does so) (DiMaggio & Powell, 1983), Ethics and morals (more deeply motivated to do and behave "good") (Hursthouse, 1999), Managerial discretion (the discrete individual motivation) (Bhattacharya et al., 2008; Williamson, 1964) and, finally, Sustainability (World Commission on Environment and Development, 1987) (motivated by not compromising the future for the next generations).

The results show that the three groups of respondents assume the key motivator for sustainability among senior managers was Branding, so to look good. The respondents in general did not think ethics and morals were key drivers for responsibility or sustainability—except among students. Business graduate students thought managers' motivation was more driven by sustainability than the board members and NGOs. Asking the same three groups, what they thought *should* be the key drivers for sustainability the three groups yet again agreed; Sustainability and Ethics and morals should be the key drivers for behaving socially responsible.

This shows that together students, leaders, and NGOs in general are rather skeptical to senior leadership. It can seem like making money in itself is against morality and sustainability. But as addressed in earlier chapters, this is not necessarily true. The goal should be to satisfy economic, environment, and social issues at the same time—the Triple Bottom Line.

Many companies still use sustainability engagement as a marketing tool to develop their brand. Companies want to differentiate their products as those that are better to the environment and really care about the society around. Some companies use the sustainability "element" in their marketing program, without the concept being part of the company as such, but as more of a superficial effect. If something happens revealing that the sustainability engagement is barely a thin layer of fluffy words outside the company, the loss of brand value can be significant. A good example that will be addressed later is VW's deceiving emission testers in 2015, which led to a drop in brand value from US$31 billion to US$21 billion (Brand Finance, 2015).

For many leaders approaching sustainability is motivated by reducing risk, not to capture the opportunities. When reflecting over the last four decades' scandals and tragedies, they are almost all associated with responsibility and sustainability issues—environment damage, poor treatment of people, bad working conditions, child labor, and behaving irresponsibly through bribing and corruption. However, the positive effect, the opportunities of supporting the company brand and reputation, also has great potential.

5.3 The Value of Corporate Responsibility in a Sustainable Setting

Up to 1990s a large part of a company's value was in "tangible" assets. Tangible assets are something that can be touched, like machinery, cars, products, and so on. As business developed and new companies and products like Facebook, Amazon, Twitter, Google, and so on emerged, factories with traditional machinery are to a lesser degree necessary to make business. The companies mentioned are now among the worlds' largest companies and their value is based on "intangible" assets. Intangible assets are business concepts, goodwill, intellectual capital, patents, brands, reputation, and so on. Figure 5.1 illustrates the shift from tangible to intangible elements as part of the company's market value.

Today intangible assets contribute to more than 88 percent of the average business' value (Juetten, 2014). Reputation is a substantial part of this intangible value. For the S&P 500, it is estimated that reputation is more than 20 percent of the gross market capitalization (Sustainable Brands, 2019), ten percent of that is linked to the company's Corporate Responsibility engagement.

In contrast to tangible assets, intangible assets can be damaged resulting in a significant drop in the value of the company, if the company is associated with negative events. Such events are usually associated with sustainability issues like revealing poor working conditions among suppliers in low cost countries, environmental damage, and corruption.

Some companies are good at presenting themselves as sustainable, establishing a brand reflecting sustainability. Still, and as I will show in the cases below, companies which have presented themselves as responsible are not necessarily so. Other companies behaving sustainably are not given credit for that as they have not been marketing their engagements in societal and environmental issues.

Before the "digital age" companies' operations, typically in poor countries, could entail unacceptable conditions like low wages, bad working conditions, tragedies, and environmental damage. Situations like this was

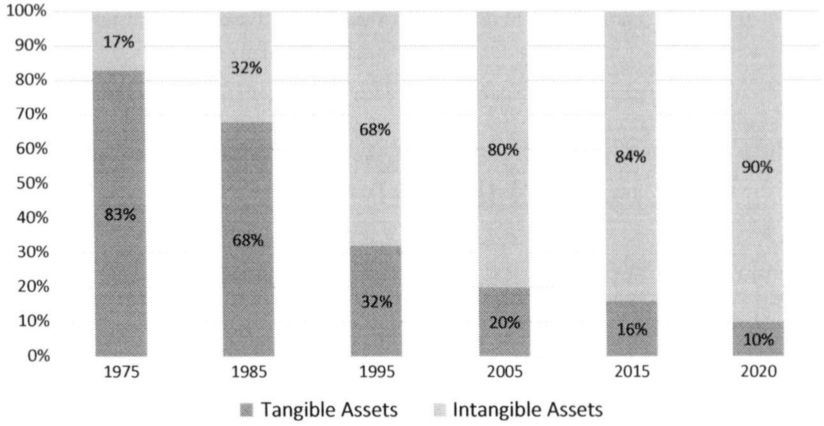

Fig. 5.1 Components of S&P market value

hard to detect and less likely to be followed up. With today's digital tools, such conditions can instantly be made public through photos taken by phones and distributed all over the world through social media like Twitter, Instagram, and Facebook. The risk of such scandals happening to companies is a great motivation factor for ensuring good conditions in the supply chain. It takes many good initiatives and activities to build a good reputation, and only one bad one happening to lose it.

5.4 Stages and Strategies Toward Responsible Sustainable Business

Maybe the key motivator for companies today to pursue sustainability and responsible behavior is avoidance of tragedies, accidents, and scandals associated with irresponsible behavior. Naturally, most companies which face such situations have to act in one way or the other. But, maybe more important is the impact such tragedies and scandals have on the majority of *other* companies. Very many of these investigate their *own* operations when scandals and tragedies come forward and take actions so that they will not end up in similar situations.

Already in 1974, Ian Wilson argued for taking a proactive strategy, not to try to stop societal pressure for change, but rather "moving quickly beyond mere compliance to develop imaginative solutions that have the effect of internalizing the new societal expectations in the day-today operations of the corporate system" (Wilson, 1975). He suggested the following four possible business strategies, arguing that the last one, Proaction, should be the key focus.

1. Reaction
2. Defense
3. Accommodation
4. Proaction

These strategies are equally relevant today, almost half a decade later. Applying the four categories to evaluate the level of maturity of corporate approach to sustainability and corporate responsibility can be very useful. Several similar approaches to benchmark and evaluate corporate performance relative to different stages have been suggested. The following five stages of organizational learning are suggested by Simon Zadek.

1. Defensive (Deny practices, outcomes, or responsibilities),
2. Compliance (Adopt a policy-based compliance approach as a cost of doing business),
3. Managerial (Embed the societal issues in their core management process),
4. Strategic (Integrate the societal issues into their core business strategies), and
5. Civil (Promote broad industry participation in corporate responsibility) (Zadek, 2004).

Neither of these models include the "Ignore" phase where the company simply ignores the challenges at stage (Ditlev-Simonsen, 2014). On top of Zadek's model is "Civil" related to "long-term economic value by overcoming any first-mover disadvantages and to realize gains through collective action". This stage as formulated does not explicitly involve innovation, being ahead of the market and creating new products. Furthermore, none

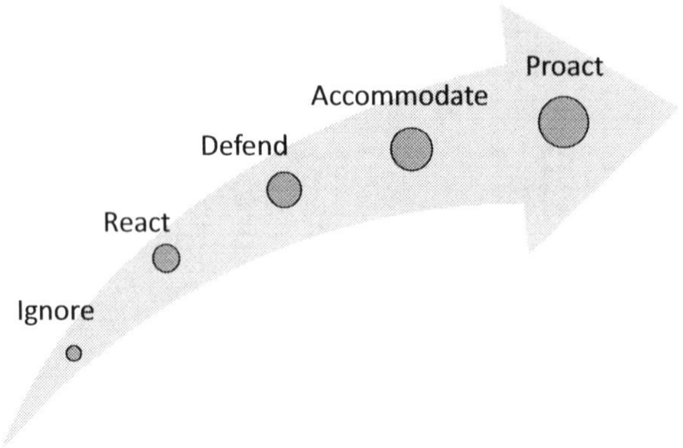

Fig. 5.2 The stage model—Stages in sustainability approaches and change

of the models are directly aimed at responsibility and sustainability. A revised model combining the Wilson and Zadek model to explicitly focus on sustainability is based on the following five steps and Fig. 5.2.

Revised stage model for sustainability strategy and examples of claims

1. **Ignore**—not being aware of or overlook the social and environmental issues faced.
2. **React**—recognizing the issues and reacting—*"There is something called sustainability and responsibility 'out there'—but not relevant for us".*
3. **Defend**—conveying that the issue is not part of the company responsibility. *"This is not our problem. Environmentalists and human right organizations are wrong. It is other actors to clean up the problem."*
4. **Accommodate**—agree to clean up what the company is criticized for. *"Have a look at our newly released sustainability report, it is attached to our annual report. We are thinking responsibility and have installed all LED light bulbs and contract on acceptable working conditions with our suppliers", "We only purchase from environmentally certified companies", and "We are sorting our waste".*
5. **Proact**—change attitude and foresee challenges and perceive these as innovative opportunities to position the company. *"We are no longer focusing on reducing negative impact on society but see sustainability as a business opportunity". "We are applying a new sustainable business model providing system change", "We are designing for a circular economy", and "We word with different stakeholders to be part of a circular economy."*

Awareness of the different stages and through benchmarking itself, a company facilitates the process of improving sustainability operations. This is a good tool for that. I will illustrate and analyze the Stage model and strategies with four cases which are to a certain degree considered "game changers" with regards to environmental and social issues.

I begin with the Nike sweatshop case on poor working conditions in poor countries. The second case is about Arthur Andersen's, one of the world's largest accounting firms, involvement in corruption. The third case is the VW case on tampering emission technology and the fourth and final case is the Rana Plaza Bangladesh case where the factory where people were working under unacceptable conditions collapsed killing many employees.

First, I will present the cases; thereafter I will apply them according to the model and the five stages. It is important to note these five stages are not associated to any particular timeframe. Although companies a few decades ago were more likely to be at the first stage, *ignoring* any sustainability challenges, there are still many companies employing this strategy. Other companies have gone through all the five stages and are now continuing in the *Proaction* phase in one part of their operations, whereas the company is at level one, Ignore, in other parts of its operations.

5.5 Four Cases: Nike, Arthur Anders, Volkswagen, and Rana Plaza

This is a presentation of four cases and the process the companies went through after the misbehavior was detected, through the process of response and the final result.

Nike—from underperformance to leading sustainability change

In the 1960s, Nike's business model focused on selling innovative, quality, and affordable product running shoes. They outsourced all production to Asia, while their competitors were still using high wage European labor. In the 1980s, Nike discovered the importance of marketing. It started building

(*continued*)

(continued)

a brand to create a long-lasting emotional tie with the consumer, while the product became the most important marketing tool (Willigan, 1992).[1]

Then in the 1990s, Nike was barged into by media stories and vivid imagery from major news outlets and human rights groups of exploitation in their suppliers' factories in Indonesia, Vietnam, and Pakistan.[2] Allegations of refusing to pay minimum wages, forcing overtime, using child labor, corporal punishment, and poor working conditions filled the headlines.[3] For years, Nike strongly denied allegations.[4] They maintained it was not the company's responsibility to investigate working conditions of its suppliers' factories. To quell its critics, Nike introduced a code of conduct for suppliers with expectations for suppliers to abide, but implementation and monitoring was flawed.[5] It was also unconvincing for investors and the public. A Nike employee even leaked an internal audit by Ernst & Young, documenting unsafe conditions for workers, undermining Nike's claims.[6]

Coincidently facing falling stock prices and weak sales,[7] then Nike CEO Phil Knight in a 1998 speech conceded that "the Nike product has become synonymous with slave wages, forced overtime, and arbitrary abuse."[8] This marked the turn around. Nike undertook a number of initiatives to fully understand supplier labor practices. They set up an internal monitoring system, created a corporate responsibility and compliance division with field staff conducting local audits, and established rigorous requirements to be accepted as a supplier. It joined various initiatives organized by NGOs and invited its toughest critics to review Nike's corporate responsibility report. Nike eventually published 90 percent of its supplier list for greater transparency. Today, Nike boosts a history of taking a stand on social and environmental issues[9] to the extent of being accused of commercializing social justice.[10] [11]

---

[1] https://hbr.org/1992/07/high-performance-marketing-an-interview-with-nikes-phil-knight.

[2] https://depts.washington.edu/ccce/polcommcampaigns/NikeChronology.htm.

[3] https://apnews.com/article/d3c0fa434245b6b92f83f05278f3cd2d.

[4] https://www.nytimes.com/1997/11/08/business/nike-shoe-plant-in-vietnam-is-called-unsafe-for-workers.html.

[5] Doorey, D. J. The Transparent Supply Chain: from Resistance to Implementation at Nike and Levi-Strauss. *J Bus Ethics* 103, 587–603 (2011). https://doi-org.ezproxy.library.bi.no/10.1007/s10551-011-0882-1.

[6] https://www.nytimes.com/1997/11/08/business/nike-shoe-plant-in-vietnam-is-called-unsafe-for-workers.html

[7] https://business.nmsu.edu/~dboje/nikestockstories.html.

[8] Cushman, J.: 1998, "Nike Pledges to End Child Labor and Increase Safety", New York Times (13 May 1998).

[9] https://purpose.nike.com/how-we-stand-up-for-equality.

[10] https://www.prweek.com/article/1492939/why-brands-will-follow-nike-social-justice.

[11] Hayhurst, L. M. C., & Szto, C. (2016). Corporatizating Activism Through Sport-Focused Social Justice? Investigating Nike's Corporate Responsibility Initiatives in Sport for Development and Peace. *Journal of Sport and Social Issues, 40*(6), 522–544. https://doi.org/10.1177/0193723516655579.

Arthur Andersen—from perceived as a responsible company to bankruptcy

At the start of 2001, Arthur Andersen & Co (AA) was one of the world's largest and influential accountancy firms with 85,000 employees generating $9 billion in revenue from over 30,000 clients.[12] The next year, AA declared bankruptcy and became the first accounting firm to have ever been convicted of a felony. The story of their downfall starts with the spectacular demise of one client, Enron, once ranked 7th on Fortune's 500 list of world's largest firms. AA provided Enron external auditing services, verifying the integrity of their financial statements to protect shareholders and potential investors.

In August 2001, Sherron Watkins, an Enron VP wrote an anonymous letter to the new CEO regarding concerns about the firm's accounting and also discussed it with a former colleague and audit partner at AA's Houston office, James Hecker. Although Enron was not his account, he took it to the partners. Enron was an important client, generating 27 percent of Houston office's revenue, 25 million in audit fees, and 27 million in consulting fees. On October 12th an AA lawyer contacted a senior partner at the firm to remind him that Andersen does not retain documents that are no longer needed resulting in a massive amount of Enron documents being shredded.[13] Shortly after, Enron announced a massive quarterly loss, the SEC initiated an investigation. By December, Enron filed for bankruptcy after it came to light, the company hyperinflated its revenues by 100 billion and hid debt using deceptive and fraudulent accounting tactics.

All attention turned to AA, their auditor.[14] The CEO denied having any previous knowledge of any of Enron's illegal behavior, rather argued the business model failed and information was withheld during audits.[15] First, the firm denied wrongdoing, arguing that the email to the Houston partners to shred the documents was just a reminder, urging compliance with a legal document-retention policy.[16] Then, AA denied knowledge at the executive level and pushed blame on a rogue partner.[17] Shortly after the indictment, the CEO resigned. AA was convicted of obstruction of justice and

(continued)

[12] https://www.forbes.com/2002/03/07/0307andersen.html?sh=508b50575001.

[13] The Fall of Enron, Paul M. Healy and Krishna G. Palepu, Journal of Economic Perspectives—Volume 17, Number 2—Spring 2003—Pages 3–26.

[14] Red Flags in Enron's Reporting of Revenues and Key Financial Measures. Bala G. Dharan & William R. Bufkinds, Governance and Intermediation Problems in Capital Markets: Evidence from the Fall of Enron (forthcoming 2004, Harvard Business School working paper 03-027.

[15] https://www.theguardian.com/business/2002/jan/21/corporatefraud.enron.

[16] https://www.economist.com/finance-and-economics/2005/06/02/not-guilty-after-all.

[17] https://www.wsj.com/articles/SB1011096414335724680.

(continued)

witness tampering for purging the Enron documents and surrendered its rights to practice before the SEC by August 2002. Even though the Supreme Court unanimously overturned the felony conviction 3 years later, AA's reputation was destroyed overnight, many of its clients ended their relationship with AA and the company was dissolved after 89 years of business.

VW Emissions Scandal—from being a top-rated responsible company to an under-performer

In March 2014, three researchers from the University of West Virginia presented a paper that would inadvertently ignite one of the largest scandals in automotive history. Since 1966, when the United States began setting emissions standards, new vehicles were always tested under controlled laboratory conditions on a stationary test rig in order to gauge CO_2. These researchers asked the question whether clean diesel engine cars have the same emissions under real-world driving conditions as in the lab.[18] *After test driving three different Volkswagen (VW) cars and a BMW, they found that no, the emissions were significantly larger. Sitting in the audience was the deputy head of CARB (California Air Resource* Board), who subsequently put together a team of experts to investigate the discrepancies and engaged the Environmental Protection Agency (EPA)

CARB and EPA sought clarification from VW regarding the discrepancies,[19] specifically that VW cars had nitrogen oxide emissions up to 40 times higher than permitted levels.[20] VW attributed them to technical issues and issued a limited recall to fix the problem.[21] In September 2015, the US EPA found that VW cars had a defeat device, illegal manipulation software that recognized when emissions were being tested, resulting in tests meeting standards. Only after the EPA threatened to withhold approval for its 2016 VW and Audi diesel cars to be sold on the US market, VW formally acknowledged that it rigged its cars and manipulated emissions tests.[22]

(continued)

[18] https://www.spiegel.de/international/business/the-three-students-who-discovered-dieselgate-a-1173686.html.

[19] https://www.nytimes.com/2015/10/24/business/international/directors-say-volkswagen-delayed-informing-them-of-trickery.html.

[20] https://www.bbc.com/news/business-34324772.

[21] https://www.npr.org/sections/thetwo-way/2015/09/23/442818919/volkswagen-ceo-resigns-saying-he-s-shocked-at-emissions-scandal.

[22] https://www.reuters.com/article/us-usa-volkswagen-deception-insight-idUSKCN0RO2IP20150924.

(continued)

The US CEO publicly admitted VW "totally screwed up".[23] However, senior management denied having any previous knowledge of the deception and blamed it on a few software engineers. The CEO immediately took responsibility and formally resigned. There are conflicting reports, when exactly management was aware going back as far as 2005, while regulators estimated executives must have known for at least over a year. In 2017, VW pleaded guilty to three criminal charges[24] and subsequently spent an estimated 34.69 billion USD in fines and settlements.[25]

The VW scandal snowballed to include Volvo, Daimler,[26] Renault, Jeep, Fiat, and many other major car manufacturers, which were also using defeat devices and manipulating emissions data.[27] However, VW was the first and it is just a matter of luck that the researchers from University West Virginia (UWV) had a limited budget to rent VWs and could not afford to use Mercedes in their study. In response to the political fallout, VW revised their company strategy and culture to transform itself to be a pioneer in sustainable mobility with the goal of becoming carbon neutral by 2050.[28]

Rana Plaza—the effect of public awareness of irresponsible companies

In late April 2014 in Dhaka, Bangladesh, workers noticed large, growing cracks in the concrete pillars that support the eight-story garment factory complex, Rana Plaza.[29] An engineer quickly assessed the building as unsafe, evacuating everyone.[30] However, the managers downplayed the risks. They had a deadline to meet with the 30 global brands that deducted 5 percent every week from every late order. Threatening to withhold monthly pay, all the garment workers went back to work the next day. Shortly after 9:00, the building collapsed killing over 1100 and injuring another 2400.

(*continued*)

[23] https://www.euronews.com/2015/09/22/volkswagen-admits-it-totally-screwed-up-as-emissions-rigging-scandal-spreads.

[24] https://www.justice.gov/opa/pr/volkswagen-ag-agrees-plead-guilty-and-pay-43-billion-criminal-and-civil-penalties-six.

[25] https://www.reuters.com/article/us-volkswagen-results-diesel-idUSKBN2141JB.

[26] https://www.justice.gov/opa/pr/us-reaches-15-billion-settlement-daimler-ag-over-emissions-cheating-mercedes-benz-diesel.

[27] https://www.motoringresearch.com/car-news/not-just-vw-30-dirty-diesels-accused-emissions-cheating/.

[28] https://www.dw.com/en/how-volkswagen-wants-to-drive-e-mobility-revolution/a-47586417.

[29] https://www.theguardian.com/world/2014/apr/19/rana-plaza-bangladesh-one-year-on.

[30] https://web.archive.org/web/20180425114547/https://www.nytimes.com/2013/05/03/world/asia/engineer-arrested-in-bangladeshi-building-collapse.html.

(continued)

From 2004, the garment industry, which is very labor intensive, exploded in Bangladesh, thanks to having the lowest wages in the world. By 2013, it was the second largest exporter of clothes and provided the country with 80 percent of its export earnings.[31] Hundreds of factories were built every year with little to no planning or oversight.[32] The Rana Plaza building was not designed to house factories with heavy machinery or the additional three floors that were added. Although Western brands had set up systems to monitor pay and working conditions in their supply chain, they did not think of conducting building inspections.

In the aftermath, some companies such as Primark quickly acknowledged they sourced from Rana Plaza and pledged to compensate its victims.[33] A joint fund was established with the goal of raising $30 million for the victims and families, while contributions were voluntary. Brands such as Benneton, Walmart, C&A, and Carrefour immediately denied having any connections. Many firms donated without confirming production, claimed they stopped ordering well before the disaster, or downplayed their relationship (C&A, Mango, and Walmart).[34] Only after Benetton labels were found in the rubble and documents showing work orders were publicized, five days after the disaster, the company acknowledged it had placed a one-time order.[35] It donated $500,000 USD to the respectable NGO, Bangladesh Rural Advancement Committee (BRAC) collecting money for the victims.

For two years, Benetton refused to take any responsibility. Only after a new CEO came onboard and activists launched a campaign on social media at select store locations, questioning their socially conscious branding with the slogan "Benetton: show your true colors", depicting a Bangladeshi woman rescued from the Rana Plaza rubble, the company decided to contribute an additional $1.1 million USD to the BRAC victim's compensation fund. The calculation was based on doubling a PricewaterhouseCoopers (PwC) estimate that Benetton accounted for about 2 percent of Rana Plaza's output for the prior year, sourcing 266,000 shirts.

Most firms including Benetton rapidly signed up to the Accord on Fire and Building Safety in Bangladesh (ACCORD), a joint initiative to verify the

(*continued*)

[31] https://jp.reuters.com/article/instant-article/idUSL4N0PL2ED20140710.

[32] https://www.theguardian.com/world/2014/apr/19/rana-plaza-bangladesh-one-year-on.

[33] https://www.aljazeera.com/opinions/2015/4/24/when-workers-die-no-company-can-walk-away.

[34] https://www.theguardian.com/world/ng-interactive/2014/mar/17/rana-plaza-factory-collapse-compensation-interactive-guide.

[35] https://www.nytimes.com/2013/05/01/world/asia/retailers-split-on-bangladesh-factory-collapse.html?_r=0.

(continued)

structural integrity of Bangladeshi garment factories.[36] Only one year later, ACCORD has shown progress with global brands beginning to pull out orders from around 30 percent of the garment factories housed in unsafe buildings impacting 1.5 million workers.[37]

5.6 Response Analysis of the Four Cases

The following is an analysis of the four cases relative to the six stages in the response framework (Fig. 5.2). This is the model and the analysis is a good tool for benchmarking one's own company performance as a basis for developing a sustainability strategy.

Stage 1: Ignore

This is a stage where companies ignore that they might have sustainability challenges, or they may be just completely unaware of them. Nike was a company aware of its own unsustainable behavior but chose to ignore the fact that its suppliers exploited their workers, despite years of negative press coverage. Sometimes companies operating in low cost countries include clauses in their contractual agreements with suppliers stipulating that they must abide by national laws and/or international principles established by the United Nations Guiding Principles on Business and Human Rights (UNGP) and United Nations Global Compact (UNGC) in their operations. This can be a standard clause in all the company's contracts. However, even if the supplier signed the contract, the majority of buyers do not have intentions nor resources to conduct proper due diligence and actually show up at the factory to check that the agreement is fulfilled. Some companies that actually conduct on-site inspections, it might turn out that the supplier has several facilities with different working conditions. Whereas the

[36] https://www.ft.com/content/f9d84f0e-e509-11e4-8b61-00144feab7de.

[37] https://www.reuters.com/article/us-bangladesh-budget/bangladesh-budget-offers-minor-incentives-for-garment-industry-safety-idUSKBN0EG1N020140605.

visited factory might fulfil the terms of the agreement with regards to working conditions, the supplier could actually fulfill the order from other locations, which do are not within the scope of the agreement. When Nike implemented a code of conduct, it did not create a rigorous process for actually monitoring suppliers' adherence.

In the Arthur Andersen and Volkswagen cases, employees at different levels must have been aware that their respective firms were "bending" the rules for quite some time. The schemes were too complex and involved too many people to place blame on only one person. It was evident that ignoring such transgressions had become part of the company culture. Employees who were aware of the facts were less likely to report them. Arguments that "This has been going on for a long time", "It is not my responsibility", "Everybody else does it the same way" are typical arguments for claiming ignorance. It is also uncomfortable to report on colleagues that they are not behaving in accordance with the law or bending the rules to accommodate this borderline behavior. Arthur Andersen auditors somehow did not catch that Enron inflated its revenues for years and hid debt. After Enron collapsed, Arthur Andersen claimed Enron held back information during audits and it failed due to its business model.

These kinds of rationalizations can be explained by neutralization theory (Sykes & Matza, 1957). People use one or more sets of argument to neutralize irresponsible behavior. Applying neutralization theory to the VW case would be along these lines:

- Denial of responsibility (It was not my fault; I only did what I was asked to. All our competitors are doing it too.)
- Denial of injury (It was not a big deal; emissions from these cars are very low anyways.)
- Denial of the victim (Every car pollutes; this does not make a difference.)
- Condemnation of the condemners (the managers are to blame; they knew about the defect devices and did not tell us to stop.)
- Appeal to higher loyalties justifies what is objectively irresponsible (if I told anybody about the defect device, I would lose my job. I have three children and cannot afford to be unemployed.)

In the Rana Plaza case, the tragedy did not challenge the reputation of just a single company, but numerous global companies sourcing from five different factories operating within the complex. Some of the companies involved were large well-known brands such as Benetton, Primark, and C&A. As noted in the case, Benetton initially denied any sourcing contracts at Rana Plaza. The irony of Benetton is that its core marketing focuses on developing a multicultural and socially conscious brand image. However, other firms such as Mango downplayed their role, noting they just ordered samples without a formal commercial relationship.

Stage 2: React

After being passive, companies are pushed to become active and respond to the deleterious event or incident. There are different reasons these four cases caught the public's attention, making it necessary for the companies to respond to accusations. Throughout the 1990s, numerous newspapers, magazines, TV programs, and media within Asia were covering the exploitive working conditions at Nike's supplier's factories.

At Arthur Andersen, a massive quarterly loss at Enron and subsequent SEC investigation precipitated a revelation of Enron's fraud, inducing a reaction from Arthur Andersen, their external auditors, who for years certified their books were in order.

In the Volkswagen case, after so many years of the cheating emissions testing, three researchers from UWV presented their surprising diesel emissions research at a conference attended by the head of the California Air Resources Board (CARB), who immediately started an investigation. And in the Rana Plaza case, the collapse of the building and high death toll triggered an international media storm.

It is when the incidents become public that the companies are bounded to react. The cases are all based on issues that have been going on for quite some time internally. If the cases had been resolved then, there would have been no public case to react to. So, there are two types of reaction; internal reactions to avoid public cases and ignorance over time, which finally result in public cases. This is yet another reason for following up possible cases internally, and, most important of all, avoid having unacceptable practices going on in the company.

Stage 3: Defend

There are generally two approaches companies use in defense; they either deny there is a problem or defend themselves from accusations, claiming for example that it is not the company's fault or that the company is not responsible.

In the Nike case, the firm strongly denied allegations for years. Later, as more convincing media reports surfaced and an external auditing report pointed to the same, the company was explicitly aware of the workers' exploitation. Nike continued handling the situation as a PR problem but addressed it more directly. In public statements, Nike maintained it was not the company's responsibility to investigate working conditions of its suppliers.

Arthur Andersen denied previous knowledge of Enron's fraudulent practices, claiming that its business model failed and that its executives withheld information from Arthur Andersen's partners. First it denied wrongdoing, noting it was a standard policy to dispose of unnecessary documents. Arthur Andersen would also later deny knowledge of the order from the HQ level to destroy the documentation, spinning it to be the work of a rouge partner.

Whereas Primark in the Rana Plaza case quickly acknowledged they sourced garments from Rana Plaza and pledged to compensate the victims, Benetton completely denied any business relationship hence culpability. Then as Benetton labels and documentation surfaced days later, this turned out that was not the case. They were bounded to react.

When confronted by the EPA and CARB with data showing discrepancies in emissions, VW attributed them to technicalities, indirectly denying there was anything further to investigate. It also issued a limited recall. When the EPA threatened to not allow VW's 2016 diesel cars to be sold on the US market without further clarification, VW was pressed to respond.

Stage 4: Accommodate

At this stage, firms concede by acknowledging their bad behavior and/or mistakes in order to move on from the scandal. By taking responsibility, expressing regret and concern, and providing a comprehensive list of corrective actions, they put themselves in a position to accommodate criticism. This open approach consequently takes away the interest of media. Acknowledgment and regret—even though the company might not fully agree that they did something wrong—is the typical approach. Also, it is a common practice to replace the CEO, whether or not the CEO is directly involved, demonstrating accountability in their leadership.

The culmination of negative press coverage and active human rights groups made the Nike CEO concerned with Nike's reputation and whether these accusations were finally impacting growth. He publicly acknowledged their brand became synonymous with exploitation of labor and embarked on turning around Nike image. They implemented a rigid monitoring system of their suppliers' working conditions with local Nike employees, created a corporate responsibility and compliance division issuing annual reports, engaged their hardest critics, and published their supplier list for transparency.

Two years after the Rana Plaza collapse, Benetton's new CEO stated, "We accept and agree that it's a shared responsibility for those who were there." Immediately after the accident, Benetton donated 500,000 to the largest international NGO, Bangladesh Rural Advancement Committee (BRAC), which collected money for victims. However, donating to a charity avoids the presumption of responsibly and liability. It is different than directly compensating the Rana Plaza victims. After consulting with PwC to establish a reasonable amount, Benetton finally paid $1.1m into The Rana Plaza Trust Fund to compensate the victims and their families. They excused the delay based on how the fund provided no guidance and contributions were voluntary. At this point, Benetton considered the Rana Plaza matter closed on its part. Going forward it would upgrade and consolidate its supply chain as well as collaborate with other brands on safety initiatives.

After the EPA's threat to ban VW diesel cars on the US market, the company admitted to regulators it manipulated emissions tests with defect devices. The CEO denied knowledge, but accepted the responsibility for the irregularities in emissions, formally submitting his resignation. Since VW pleaded guilty to three criminal offenses and paid over $34.69B in fines and settlements. VW and its subsidiaries, Audi and Porsche were also not allowed to sell any new or used diesel cars on the US market for the two years.

Whereas the Arthur Andersen case ended quite differently. The firm went bankrupt and the accommodation stage was not a relevant option. It lost most of its clients after the indictment. The CEO stated, "The fact is that improper shredding of documents took place on my watch … it is now in the best interest of the firm for me to step down from the CEO position." Arthur Andersen was found guilty, but continuously defended it did nothing wrong. Years later, Arthur Andersen was exonerated in a unanimous verdict by the highest court in the United States, the Supreme Court. The judges called the case by the government prosecutors, "weird". The jury was never instructed to find a link between the document destruction and any official investigation in which the documents were requested. However, it would later come to light that Arthur Andersen was the external auditor in a number of scandals involving fraudulent accounting, such as WorldCom, Waste Management, and Sunbeam Products. As a result, its collapse led to systematic change in the auditing industry. Auditors would be more willing to stand up to clients, comprehensive legislations (Sarbanes-Oxley Act) were enacted, and regulatory agencies created, and it actually made the industry more profitable, generated a lot more demand for accountants and lawyers.

In general, the first move when such deleterious incidents are uncovered is to go through the company processes to find out how this could have happened. The next step is to repair the system. When the company has reached a level where they perceive themselves as in control and having a complete overview of their responsibilities, they can either finish there or move to the next step—proactive.

Stage 5: Proactive

Tragedies and crisis are inflection points, which create opportunities as the common saying goes, "Never waste a good crisis". That is what Nike did. The company was one of the first, if not the first, company to be open about all their suppliers and transparently published them. Anyone can now consult Nike's websites and see where the products are produced. That can be categorized as advanced Accommodation. Nike also moved to the next stage with regards to products. It has promoted environmental issues through its product design. Today 75 percent of all Nike products contain some recycled material, and in the industry, no one uses more recycled polyester (Nike News, 2018). Nike also has a reuse-a-shoe program where shoes (including athletic shoes from other manufacturers) at the end of their life can be dropped off at a participating Nike retail store. The shoes then become part of a recycling process and are designed to accommodate for this circularity process. Nike's circular principles will be further addressed in the next chapter on circular economy.

Nike has also made controversial decisions to support social issues, when for example it signed Colin Kaepernick, a civil rights activist and former American football quarterback, who kneeled during the US national anthem to protest police brutality and racial inequality. It was a choice between David (Kaepernick) and Goliath (NFL) for Nike. After he played out his contract, not a single NFL team would sign him on as a player. Instead, Nike ran the campaign "Believe in something. Even if it means sacrificing everything. Just do it." It was good for business, increasing Nike's value by $6b. Although very risky, its success even led to accusations of commercializing social justice, the direct opposite of its image in the 1990s. It was not only social issues that became part of Nike's strategy. In 2019, Nike launched its "Move to Zero" strategy, fighting environmental and climate change.

Brands that outsourced from Rana Plaza complex, engaged in several initiatives to improve the situation, both through industry networking and more global initiatives in cooperation with governments and NGOs. Supply chain labor standards initiatives like the Ethical Trading Initiative (ETI) received increased attention, and issues like maximum working hours, minimum pay, employees' freedom of association, investigating of previous poor conditions, and so on were followed up. Country level multi-stakeholder initiatives, initiatives that include the workers into the process, workers helpline for reporting and assistance, robust monitoring, increased transparency, capacity building, brand buyer accountability and better sourcing and purchasing practices, aligning targets and incentives are examples of initiative resulting from the Rana Plaza collapse. These initiatives were not only associated with factories in the Rana Plaza area, but in the sweatshop in industry in general (see Chap. 4 on regulations associated with Human Rights and Corporations). Global brands and NGOs have also become more conscious and active in conducting building safety inspections in their audits, something they didn't consider doing before the tragedy. In Bangladesh, many firms joined the ACCORD initiative and have pulled out orders from garment factories from which operations are housing in unsafe buildings.

VW also moved into the proactive stage. It announced it would stop manufacturing gas and diesel engines by 2026 and focus on electric cars. VW is in the process of transforming itself to be a pioneer in sustainable mobility with the goal of becoming carbon neutral by 2050.

Evident from the tragedies and scandals presented in the cases above, unsustainable development can have major negative repercussions for companies. The immediate interventions of companies from a sustainability standpoint are therefore, not surprisingly, to reduce contagion and mitigate further risks for such incidents.

5.7 Business Models for Sustainability

The risk of negative effect of behaving irresponsible and the opportunity for better business when behaving responsible and sustainable have made companies to take a proactive approach to sustainability. Integrating sustainability into the company's identity is becoming increasingly common.

Companies do not have to go through the Five Stages of the model to respond to scandals and tragedies. Rather, by not ignoring potential challenges and opportunities, companies are maybe already at the "Accommodate" stage, having implemented at sustainability program that identified what to do. Changing the company's name and vision is also part of the accommodation process and can also be part of advancing to the proactive stage. Today, about 12 percent of companies in the S&P 500 list address the triple bottom line in their strategy documents, "caring for the people" and "safeguarding the planet" appeared respectively in 34 and almost 15 percent of the companies (Baral & Pokharel, 2017)

In Chap. 7 *Strategy to approach sustainability in companies*, the necessity of anchoring the work on sustainability in top management is put forward. New more sustainable visions and missions are crucial, and examples of how this is applied in companies are provided.

Today, most large companies are in stage four, improving social and environmental performance through reducing negative impact. In order to attain a sustainable future, companies have to move to stage five—proactive. The real opportunities in a sustainability setting are the business opportunities.

A business model is about Creating, Delivering, and Capturing Value (Kapland, 2012). To pursue a sustainable future, new and more sustainable elements must be included in the model—and the final product will be different and more sustainable. The three elements of the business model have to be extended to include social and environmental issues.

If the cost of gasoline reflected its external environmental and social cost, the price per liter would be multiplied, and the variables in the business model will have to include that. The company still has to create, deliver, and capture value—only that the outcome of the model, the product, and the value are changed. The companies which are succeeding in this process are the ones which manage to redesign the product to be more sustainable—and still preferred by consumers. Limiting production can contribute to increased profit and thus reducing the use of resource. Collaboration between different disciplines such as ecology, psychology, and sociology is necessary to change production and consumption and ensure the negative impact of products is minimized—and the SDGs are great tools to evaluate the impact.

During the COVID-19 pandemic, many companies had to change their business models. Companies with a business model delivering an *Active holiday experience in Africa*, had to change to providing an *Active holiday experience in Norway,* since people in Norway were not allowed to leave the country. But it is not only pandemics that have the capacity to change business models, it is also the introduction of taxes reflecting the product's external costs that lead to changes in business models. With an increase in fuel prices, long distance travelling has become more expensive and less people can afford too far. Then too it can be an alternative and good business model to focus on local holiday experiences. Some companies are agile and manage this shift in a business model well, whereas other companies do not cope well with new situations and fail to change their business models. To be prepared for environmental and social challenges, the business model of a company has to move to the "Proactive" phase.

New companies today often emerge directly from the "Proactive" stage of the model. Some examples of new companies' business models that have a purpose, which contributes to sustainable development, include Airbnb and TooGoodToGo. Airbnb facilitates sharing housing. TooGoodToGo sells left over food with the purpose of "Save the Food help the Planet".

A system change to a circular economy is a promising business model and a good example of the proactive stage of doing business. This will be the focus in the next chapter.

In the midst of chaos, there is also opportunity.

References

Baral, N., & Pokharel, M. P. (2017). How sustainability is reflected in the S&P 500 companies' strategic documents. *Organization & Environment, 30*(2), 122–141. https://doi.org/10.1177/1086026616645381. https://login.ezproxy.library.bi.no/login?qurl=https://search.ebscohost.com/login.aspx?direct=true&db=bth&AN=123161373&site=ehost-live&scope=site

Bhattacharya, C. B., Sen, S., & Korschun, D. (2008). Using corporate social responsibility to win the war for talent. *MIT Sloan Management Review, 49*(2), 37.

Brand Finance. (2015, September 25). VW risks its $31 billion brand and Germany's national reputation. https://brandfinance.com/press-releases/vw-risks-its-31-billion-brand-and-germanys-national-reputation

DiMaggio, P. J., & Powell, W. W. (1983). The iron cage revisited: Institutional isomorphism and collective rationality in organizational fields. *American Sociological Review, 48*, 147–160.

Ditlev-Simonsen, C. D. (2010). From corporate social responsibility awareness to action? *Social Responsibility Journal, 6*(3), 452–468. https://doi.org/10.1108/17471111011064807

Ditlev-Simonsen, C. D. (2014). Are non-financial (CSR) reports trustworthy? A study of the extent to which non-financial reports reflect the media' perception of the company's behaviour. *Issues in Social and Environmental Accounting, 8*(2), 116–133. https://doi.org/10.22164/isea.v8i2.85

Ditlev-Simonsen, C. D., & Midttun, A. (2011). What motivates managers to pursue corporate responsibility? A survey among key stakeholders. *Corporate Social Responsibility and Environmental Management, 18*(1), 25–38.

Fombrun, C. J. (2005). Building corporate reputation through CSR initiatives: Evolving standards. *Corporate Reputation Review, 8*(1), 7.

Freeman, R. E. (1984). *Strategic management: A stakeholder approach*. Pitman.

Friedman, M. (1970). A Friedman doctrine—The social responsibility of business is to increase its profits. *The New York Times*. https://www.nytimes.com/1970/09/13/archives/a-friedman-doctrine-the-social-responsibility-of-business-is-to.html

Hoffmann, A. J. (2018). The next phase of business sustainability. *Stanford Social Innovation Review, 16*(2), 34–39. https://ssir.org/articles/entry/the_next_phase_of_business_sustainability

Hursthouse, R. (1999). *On virtue ethics*. Oxford University Press.

Jensen, M. (2001). Value maximisation, stakeholder theory, and the corporate objective function. *European Financial Management: The Journal of the European Financial Management Association, 7*(3), 297–317. https://doi.org/10.1111/1468-036x.00158

Juetten, M. (2014). Pay attention to innovation and intangibles—They're more than 80% Of your business' value. *Forbes*. https://www.forbes.com/sites/maryjuetten/2014/10/02/pay-attention-to-innovation-and-intangibles-more-than-80-of-your-business-value/?sh=12c143b11a67

Kanter, R. M. (1999). From spare change to real change. The social sector as beta site for business innovation. *Harvard Business Review, 77*(3), 122–210.

Kapland, S. (2012). The business model innovation factory: How to stay relevant when the world is changing. In *Business models 101: Creating delivering, and capturing value*. Wiley. https://doi.org/10.1002/9781119205234

Nike News. (2018, May 15). Nike's latest sustainable innovations and environmental impact. https://news.nike.com/news/sustainable-innovation-air-bag-manufacture

Porter, M. E. (1998). Clusters and the new economics of competition. *Harvard Business Review, 76*(6), 77–90.

Sustainable Brands. (2019, July 3). Measuring and managing brand reputation: How CSR and other factors influence reputational value [Video]. *YouTube*. https://www.youtube.com/watch?v=JKzZlyJD1Z0

Sykes, G., & Matza, D. (1957). Techniques of neutralization: A theory of delinquency. *American Sociological Review, 22*(6), 664–670. https://doi.org/10.2307/2089195

Williamson, O. E. (1964). *The economics of discretionary behavior: Managerial objectives in a theory of the firm*. Prentice Hall.

Wilson, I. H. (1975). What one company is doing about today's demands on business. In G. A. Steiner (Ed.), *Changing business-society interrelationship*. Graduate School of Management, UCLA.

World Commission on Environment and Development. (1987). *Our common future*. https://sustainabledevelopment.un.org/content/documents/5987our-common-future.pdf

Zadek, S. (2004, December). The path to corporate responsibility. *Harvard Business Review*. https://hbr.org/2004/12/the-path-to-corporate-responsibility

6

Circular Economy: New Business Models

From the time humans made their first attempt to control the environment until industrialization accelerated, there has been a circular economy. Trees grew, shed their leaves in the autumn and decayed into organic matter, which would then fertilize the trees. Big fish ate small fish and when the big fish died, its remains underwent a biological process to become food for other small microorganisms, which were later eaten by small fish. Both these cycles continued. In the past, there was a balance of life in the ocean, but today, overfishing, so fishing at a rate at which the stock cannot replenish itself, has eroded that delicate balance. In 1990, 90 percent of fish stocks were at levels considered to be biologically sustainable and in 2017, this percentage dropped to 66 (Food and Agriculture Organization of the United States, 2020).

Wild animals are still part the natural ecosystem. One rarely sees a dead wild animal, unless it has been run over by a car. In most cases, when an animal dies, the carcass provides food and nutrients to other species. Nature takes care of it. In contrast, car wrecks are manmade, and cleaning them up is not taken care of by nature. Plastic is another example of how humans have a negative effect on nature. A plastic bag is used for an average of 12 minutes, only one percent of all bags are recycled,

C. D. Ditlev-Simonsen, *A Guide to Sustainable Corporate Responsibility*,
https://doi.org/10.1007/978-3-030-88203-7_6

and it takes 500 years for them to degrade in a landfill. In the meantime, 100,000 marine animals are killed annually by eating plastic bags (Center for Biological Diversity, n.d.).

Before humans started depleting the Earth's resources at an unsustainable rate, there was a circular economy. Today, the majority of the man-made economy is linear: Take, Make, and Dispose. Given the current situation in which human demand on nature is greater than its ability to regenerate, a difference referred to as an ecological "deficient" or "over-spending", it is imperative that we return to a circular economy.

As economic growth accelerates, consumption increases, and greater volumes of waste are accumulated. To provide perspective, waste generated daily in India amounts to 0.34 kg per person, whereas in the United States, it is more than seven times as much, at 2.6 kg per person. When looking at the composition of global solid waste, 44% comes from food and green waste, 17% from paper and cardboard, and 12% from plastic (The World Bank, n.d.). Of this, 33% is openly dumped, 25% is sent to landfills, and only 13% is recycled. In 2012, the average European used 16 tons of materials and only 40 percent of that amount was recycled or reused (Hannon, 2016). The fact that one third of the total global food production is either lost or wasted, while people are starving, shows that something is obviously wrong.

The problem of the linear economy is recognized across the world. It is a common understanding that recycling is the solution for what to do with waste. Much effort has been put in to increase recycling or in other words, avoid dumping waste into landfills. A circular economy, however, is a system in which there is no waste. Figure 6.1 illustrates the move from a linear to circular economy. In the middle of the model is the recycling economy where the products are partly remanufactured. The waste goes into other "lower level" products, before it is dumped. New products with elements of used plastic bottles are some examples of recycling, whereas reuse of plastic bottles is closer to a circular economy.

For a sustainable future, we need to transition from a linear economy to a circular economy. This involves changes in the whole production process: from design, logistical issues, shelf life of perishable food, customer behavior, government regulations, education, and the need for innovation.

In this chapter, I will address the key challenges of a society with a linear economy, the concept of circular economy, its potential, and

Fig. 6.1 From a linear to a circular economy

associated challenges. I will provide numerous examples to illustrate each case. The role of different stakeholders in the process of achieving a circular economy will be discussed. Lastly, the move from selling products to providing services will be addressed.

6.1 Why Do We Have a Liner Economy: Generating So Much Waste?

The answer to why today's economy is linear is found partly in the price of natural resources. These prices do not reflect its real costs. If external costs associated with for example correcting the environmental damage were included, the sales prices would have been much higher and the consumption resulting in much more efficient use of the resources—or replacement of the product. Take coal for example, the majority of electricity worldwide is based on this cheap commodity.

The life cycle process of coal includes extraction, transport, processing, and combustion. There are negative consequences linked to health and the environment, especially CO_2 emissions at each phase. It is estimated that including the cost of these negative consequences would increase the price of electricity generated from coal with 17.8 cents/kWh (the low estimate being 9¢/kWh and the high estimate 26.89¢/kWh) (Epstein et al., 2011). Including the external cost of electricity generated from coal would thus make the price of electricity made from wind and solar energy much more competitive and at least financially make extraction less economical across most of the world.

One way to approach the issue is to claim that as long as there are wastes and negative environmental consequences of production and use, the price of the resources the product is made of is too low.

6.2 Key Elements in Circular Economy

The circular economy begins with design. Products have to be designed to last longer, reuse, repair and, remanufacture. We also need a change in peoples' attitudes to reducing over consumption and willingness to use fewer products longer. We need regulators to include the negative environmental impact of resources in pricing. We also need regulations that motivate and support a circular economy. The concept of a circular economy is well illustrated in the circular economy system diagram, the Butterfly diagram. This diagram was developed by the Ellen MacArthur Foundation (Ellen MacArthur Foundation, n.d.). A simplified version of the diagram is presented in Fig. 6.2.

The middle of the butterfly diagram is the production process. The "wing" to the right is the technical cycle, products and materials such as metals, which are kept in the cycle for as long as possible. Products such as cars, tools, and construction should be maintained for as long as possible, then, when that is no longer possible to reuse, repair, or refurbish, it enters into the last phase, recycle.

The "wing" to the left concerns renewables, such as textiles, paper, food, and sewage. The goal here too is to keep the resources in the loop as long as possible. First, by extending the life of products, and thereafter

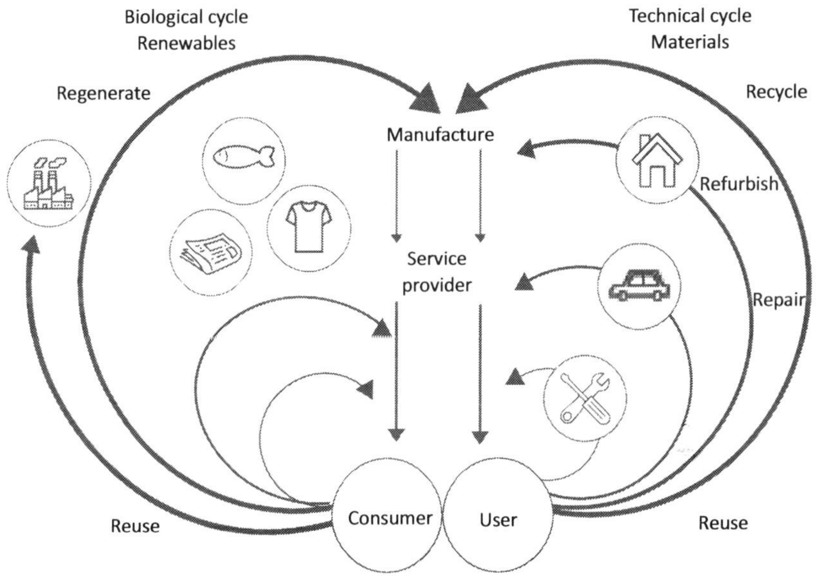

Fig. 6.2 A simplified version of the Ellen MacArthur foundation butterfly diagram

to gradually to make use of the products through different treatments. It could be to make new dishes of leftover food; waste food becoming animal food; providing a second-hand market for clothing; making insulation of used newspapers or crab sticks from fish cut offs; energy generation from sewage and composting food waste and using it as fertilizer. The best, however, is to reduce the consumption of the products—and finish what is on the plate.

In the circular economy, there is a hierarchy of measures to attain indifferent orders. A number of elements in the circular economy are named with terms starting with the letter "R". Some examples of these Rs in alphabetic order include re-assembly, recapture, reconditioning, recollect, recover, recreate, rectify, recycle, redesign, redistribute, reduce, re-envision, refit, refurbish, refuse, remarket, remanufacture, renovate, repair, replacement, reprocess, reproduce, repurpose, resale, resell, re-service, restoration, resynthesize, rethink, retrieve, retrofit, retrograde, return, reuse, reutilize, revenue, reverse, and revitalize, and all are relevant. Studies have mapped the popularity of the different Rs and debated how many should be included in the model (from 3Rs to 10Rs) (Reike et al., 2018). Instead for engaging in this discussion, I will address the circle economy as a whole.

6.3 Refuse and Reduce: Using Less

By far the most efficient approach to sustainable consumption is to reduce consumption—either by stopping to using certain products such as meat or reducing consumption of meat. In the industrialized world, we have so much we do not need and so much we do not even use. For example, Norwegians on average have 359 garments in their wardrobe and of these eight percent of these are never used (Dæhlen, 2016).

To make one pair of jeans requires 7500 liters of water. Considering that one in three people in the world do not have access to safe drinking water, this is definitely very unfair (World Health Organization, 2019). The same amount of water that goes into making one pair of jeans is approximately what an average person drinks over a period of seven years (United Nations News, 2019). Further, CO_2 emissions from the textile industry are almost equivalent to that of the automobile industry (Doboczky, 2019).

Taking into account that people in the developed world generally have considerably more clothes in their wardrobes than they actually need, so even a small change in consumer buying behavior can lead to a large positive change. The carbon footprint and energy use associated with clothing mainly comes from the production process and transport. Keeping the garments longer and purchasing less can have a considerable impact. If each garment is used twice as many times, before it is thrown away, almost half on the negative impact of resource and production is mitigated (Sandin et al., 2019). Companies like Nudie Jeans and Patagonia facilitate repairs and have made sustainability part of their business model.

Still, there is a need for a major shift toward sustainability among all manufacturers—as well as customers. From 1995 to 2010, textile waste grew from 29,000 tons to 52,000 tons in Norway (Mayer, 2017). The growth of online shopping has also not been necessarily good for the environment.

Other positive initiatives from individuals, other than having less clothes and using them longer, are to change food consumption. Becoming a vegetarian has for example a significant impact on greenhouse gas emissions. Replacing red meat and dairy with vegetables just one day a week can reduce an individual's carbon footprint to what is the equivalent of a 1000 mile car trip (McCartney, 2009). This is almost the same distance as from Paris to Africa, from California to Canada, and from Bangladesh to Thailand. Such initiatives as Meat-Free-Mondays that encourage people to reduce their meat consumption have a positive effect on both the environment and peoples' health.

Most people in the industrialized world can reduce their consumption. Despite knowing about the rising levels of waste, pollution, and environmental degradation, people still continue to increase their consumption. Increased awareness is just not enough. However, what does change consumer behavior is price. Governments play a key role here with regulations. Increasing the price or passing some sort of deposit legislation would lead to less consumption. Adding a 5 pence charge on plastic bags in the UK resulted in an 85% reduction in the use of plastic bags (Smithers, 2016).

6.4 Reuse: Extending the Life of Products

Refundable deposit fees on products are an efficient tool to influence consumer behavior. Since 1902, Norway has collected deposits on certain types of bottles. When this deposit was increased from two to three NOK (approx. \$0.24 to 0.36 USD) in 2018, 88% of plastic bottles and 84% of aluminum soft drink cans were returned for a deposit refund (Infinitum). Since safe drinking water is ubiquitous in Norway, the use of bottled water is less compared to other countries where it is not safe to drink from the tap. Now imagine the potential impact of a deposit system implemented in countries where safe drinking water is only available in bottles!

Car deposits programs are another good example of initiatives that promote higher recycling rates. In Norway, scrapping a car earns the owner a NOK 3000 (\$360 USD in 2016) refund. When for a limited time this refund was doubled, the number of scrapped cars increased from what is typically 120,000 to 220,000 cars (Njarga, 2016). This scheme provides a motivation to properly depose of old cars, but, as it is typical for many environmental initiatives, there can be negative consequences as well. If the return fee is too high, owners are incentivized to replace their old car sooner than its useful life. However, if the car is replaced with an electrical car, it would be better for the environment to get the gas guzzler off the roads. On the other hand, if the old car is rarely used, it would be better to keep the old car and not replace it. A good environmental accounting system or Life Cycle Analysis (LCA) is necessary to capture the optimal environmental solution.

The best solution for a circular economy is however to prolong the useful life of products by providing such things as repair options. However, as of now, it is often too complex and expensive to repair or refurbish products. To illustrate the complex challenges of prolonging life of products, I will use mobile phones as an example.

Today, there are more than five billion mobile devices worldwide, and almost three billion are smartphones. People upgrade to a new phone about every 11 months. Two reasons to purchase new phones are that the old one cannot be repaired and/or a new model is released. A study conducted by Greenpeace found that more than three out of ten people bought a new phone in order to have a more up to date version (Boztas, 2016). Often, there are only very minor differences between the old and the new phones, but manufacturers need to launch new products in order to ensure turnover and profit.

Companies such as Apple claim to be concerned with reducing their negative environmental footprint, when it announced that all products will be "made entirely with clean energy by 2030" (Apple, 2021). Still, those reductions apply only to the production process, but in fact, the most negative impact on society is the accumulated electronic waste, when the phone is replaced (The Irish News, 2018). It is only through reducing the number of new models with minor changes and providing affordable repair services that manufacturers can reduce the aggregate negative societal impact. Customers are also critical regarding the continuous release of new models and not having access to repair services (Boztas, 2016).

In a typical mobile phone, there are 62 different types of metals. More than 25% of these are classified as rare-earth metals, found and refined in rural China (McMaster, 2017). Still, less than 10% of smartphones are recycled. One ton of iPhones would deliver 300 times more gold than a ton of gold ore and 6.5 times more silver than a ton of silver ore (Nogrady, 2016).

Retrieving these and other metals like copper, lead, zinc, and coltan would reduce the need for mining and refining. Most smartphones today are impossible to repair and valuable metals are not removed or reused. That throwing away used phones is an indication that the resources it is made of are priced too low.

Fairphone is a mobile phone manufacturer established in 2013 with the purpose and goal of delivering sustainable smartphones, taking both social and environmental issues into account throughout the entire life cycle process—circular economy. This includes reducing the negative social impact of mining by using conflict-free minerals. In design, they focus on delivering longevity and repairability. In the manufacturing process, providing safe working conditions and fair wages are in focus. Regarding the life cycle, Fairphones are for use, reuse, and safe recycling (Fairphone, 2016).

The company was launched by concerned citizens, who became aware that mobile phones generally contained conflict minerals from the Democratic Republic of the Congo. It began initially as a campaign against the use of conflict minerals, before taking a more constructive approach by establishing a company manufacturing sustainable smartphones. With a Fairphone, the owner can replace the glass screen if it is broken and replace the battery by simply removing the plastic back (Gibbs, 2020). By 2016, 100,000 Fairphones have been sold—which is a microscopic share of the total mobile phone market, still proof that more sustainable product solutions can be realistic.

Responding to market trends and consumer demand, mobile phone manufacturers have increased their focus on environmental and social issues. In 2018, Apple introduced Daisy, a robot that disassembles iPhones to recover valuable materials. Daisy can pull apart 1.2 million iPhones annually (Martin & Sherr, 2019). However, taking into account Apple sold more than 35 million iPhone 11s in the first half of 2020 (Gadgets Now, 2020), the robot may be a great start and generate a good image, but so far it makes a neglectable impact. To make a real impact, the circular economy approach needs to start at the design stage, developing phones that can be repaired and which are simple to take apart—not requiring it to be shipped to a fulltime robot to do the job.

Many companies make efforts to be part of a circular economy, but the main limitation is the lack of a reuse culture among customers. Renting cars when travelling and renting formal attire for events such as weddings are however something people in general are comfortable doing, because it tends to be practical and cost effective.

Such rental services have existed for decades, but what is new is that not only rental companies or services, but well-known brands are experimenting with such business models. At Filippa K is a “sustainable fashion brand”. At its stores, it is possible for customers to rent cloths for four days, paying only 20 percent of retail price. Upon returning the garments, the customer gets the remaining 80 percent of the value back (Sivertsen & Zakariassen, 2016).

Bergans, a Norwegian outdoor clothing and gear company, also offers rental services. Such renting schemes benefit customers in more ways than just saving money. Tents, for example, are not used very frequently, yet the quality of tents is continuously improving. Renting a Bergans tent for a trip, instead of using a purchased tent, will probably provide a tent of better quality on an annual basis. The company also offers repair services. It even has a service car driving around Norway collecting and repairing clothes. Though repairs by Bergan are less expensive than having the same job done at a tailor, it is still costly—even though the service is subsidized by the company. As of now, it is not a profitable business. A change in attitude and behavior among customers is a key in the pursuit of making circular economy good for business.

6.5 Challenges and Opportunities in a Circular Economy: The Impact of Law and Regulations

Alcohol and cigarettes are products that society is aware have a negative impact on public health. To deter consumption, many countries regulate sales and levy taxes on such products. In Norway, more than half of the price of a package of cigarettes goes to the government in the form of fees designed to capture the societal costs linked to smoking. So, in that sense, this is an example of full cost pricing. It is also interesting to consider that smoking leads to more sick-leaves, hospitalizations, and shorter life expectancies, so from an economic, societal point of view, smokers are actually net contributors to national accounts because they will draw shorter pensions, thus saving money for society. Some claim that smokers are funding the health of non-smokers (Edseth, 2009).

There are still several regulations, and new are launched, which actually decrease incentives to extend the use of a product. If an electrical car in Norway is less than five years and needs repairs, often for simple issues like broken light or a dent in the hood, owners prefer to scrap it and get a new car as that is part of the guarantee period. Laws like that do not motivate getting repairs done and keeping the car.

Another example of existing regulations actually working against sustainability is the sugar tax in Norway. When soda bottles and boxes are close to their expiration date or the box has a dent, it is less expensive for the producers to throw away the soda instead of donating it. As the law works now, producers only recoup the sugar fee if the soda is thrown away and not if it is donated. One of Norway's largest soda producers pours out around 25,000 liters of soda daily (Grimstad et al., 2019).

There are several positive examples of positive effects of governmental initiatives. France was the first country to make it illegal for large supermarkets to throw away food. Up until 2016, foods that pass their best-before date were thrown away, but now it is donated to charities. Even prior to this new law, people would search waste containers of supermarkets, so-called "dumpster diving" and salvage these thrown away food items. Sometimes this became so messy that the supermarkets locked off the waste containers.

Although the law was advocated by a grassroot campaign, large supermarket chains welcomed the change (Chrisafis, 2016). Besides benefiting charitable food banks, business opportunities have also emerged. The Too Good to Go company is a mobile application, connecting surplus food from stores and restaurants to the general public. Taking into account that one third of all food produced in the world is thrown away, there is great potential for improvement (Mattilsynet, 2019). As what is available from stores today usually are part of international regulations, it is important that international regulations are first movers toward a circular economy. The European Union has taken such a role in the circular economy setting.

In 2015 the European Commission launched the first Circular Economy Action Plan. This was a very positive initiative, even though the path forward will take time. Key actions in the plan are:

- Make sustainable products the norm in the EU.
- Empower consumers and public buyers.
- Focus on the sectors that use most resources and where the potential for circularity is high such as: electronics and ICT; batteries and vehicles; packaging; plastics; textiles; construction and buildings; food; water and nutrients.
- Ensure less waste.
- Make circularity work for people, regions and cities.
- Lead global efforts on circular economy. (European Commission, 2020)

The EU made a concrete initiative in 2020 related to battery regulations and standards. All batteries in the EU markets are to be part of a circular economy throughout their lifecycle, from manufacturing to recoverage of valuable raw materials. From 45 percent of portable batteries being collected and recycled, the goal is to raise this figure to 65 percent in 2025, and 70 percent in 2030.

Today, less than 40 percent of electronic waste in the EU is recycled. This is due to the fact that many of these electronic products such as hairdryers, shaving machines, dishwashers, and so on cannot be repaired, often because spare parts are no longer available. To change this, the *Right to Repair* bill was proposed in 2021. This is a law requiring companies to fix electronic goods for up to 10 years (Euronews, 2021). Still, others argue that this is not the source of the problem, rather the cost of repairing the goods is prohibitive and it is less expensive to purchase a new product.

Governments can have a great impact in setting the right laws and regulations. However, another key contribution from governments is to change its own consumption. The public/governmental sector is the largest consumer in most countries. If their purchasing policies required reuse of products, that would have a great effect—both on consumption and as a role model. Governments also have the responsibility to ensure that students are becoming familiar with the circular concept through education.

6.6 From Product to Service

So far, the main environmental focus has been to reduce waste from products. Whereas the focus on the *purpose* of the product, that is why we need the products, has received less attention. A move from the "end of pipe" to product purpose has a great potential in a circular economy. A popular anecdote to illustrate the move from cleaning up the waste to avoiding another generation of waste is the following. You come home and find water all over the kitchen floor. Do you start to clean up the water, or do you try to stop the tap from where the water is pouring out?

Instead of thinking about the product, companies are beginning to focus on services the products offer. What is the function of the product the company is selling—and is it necessary to attend to the need?

A good example of the difference between product and service is in the transport sector, sale of car versus sale of mobility as a service. This also illustrates the business opportunities in the circular economy. The purpose of the car is transport. However, an average European car is parked 92% of the time (Ellen MacArthur Foundation et al., 2015). So, instead of focusing on how to dispose of the car when it is obsolete, the focus should be on making its use more efficient during its life cycle. By finding ways to make use of the car during the time it would otherwise been parked has great potential. This way the need for cars could be significantly reduced.

Car sharers emit between 240 and 390 fewer kilograms of CO_2 per person than car owners per year. 13 to 18 percent of CO_2 emissions are attributed to car ownership (Nijland & van Meerkerk, 2017). Traditional car rental companies such as Avis and Hertz see this car sharing model as a new business opportunity, making it more convenient to car share through memberships, easy bookings, and more access points, all facilitated by digital solutions.

When it comes to larger modes of transport, such as buses, ferries, and planes, we are already comfortable with buying services as opposed to ownership. With these products, owners want them to last for a long time to reduce the cost per year. Furthermore, their customers are not very sensitive to whether or not the bus or ferry is the latest edition or not. So public transportation maintains products longer and behaves more circular than private ownership.

For companies however, it is often best for business that customers continuously replace their products. Therefore, many companies regularly launch new product models. The last version of products such as cellphones might only have minor differences from prior models. Still, marketing the new version and people wanting to have the last edition is a challenge for the concept of extending the use of products. Some products are even produced for planned obsolescence, that is, they are not made to last.

The case of lightbulb consumption is a good example of the positive environmental effect of moving from the product concept to the service concept. Today, there is one lightbulb that has lasted for 115 years. So, when that bulb was made, the producers might have had the knowledge to make bulbs that could last for a long time. However, this was not a good business for producers like Osram, GE, and so on. Through the "Phoebus cartel" in the 1920s, these companies agreed to reduce the lifetime of their products to 1000 hours.

EU regulations mandated a shift from incandescent bulbs in 2009 and phasing out halogen lightbulbs by 2016. People are required to use LED bulbs, which could last for 10,000–50,000 hours. Even though LED bulbs are much less expensive over the course of their lifetime, the price was significantly higher than traditional bulbs. That made customers prefer traditional lightbulbs until these were no longer sold in stores. This is a good example of the necessity for active use of laws to make changes, which dampen negative impacts on the environment.

If companies such as Osram and GE were offering lighting as a service when they started production over 100 years ago, lightbulbs would probably be engineered to last for much longer than they do now. Today, there are companies experimenting with this business model in this industry, such as Philips, offering tailor-made lighting services at a fraction of the energy cost (Philips, n.d.).

Another example of a service-based business model as opposed to selling physical products is copy machines. In offices today copy machines are often rented or leased from the producer. Xerox has provided this service since 1980 without naming it circular economy—it was its business model. If something goes wrong with the copy machine, maintenance personnel from Xerox come to fix it (EREK, n.d.). Since it is leased, Xerox wants it to last as long as possible. If the customer had purchased the photocopier, it would then be better business for Xerox to manufacture with planned obsolescence, so that the customer would purchase a new photocopy machine.

Carpet companies also provide services like floor coverage. Art companies rent out pictures. Corporations such as IKEA are testing the concept of leasing furniture. For students renting an apartment far from home, it is more convenient to rent furniture and cutlery/appliances for one year, instead of purchasing and later reselling them when they move. Construction stores are increasing the variety of tools and machinery to rent. With the ease of connecting with people on internet, privately sharing tools and goods like outfits are becoming increasingly easy and convenient. A change in attitudes will make a great contribution to extend the life of products and reduce the need for manufacturing. Still the same initiatives which are good for society might not be as good for companies because it leads to reduced turnover and sales. There is a conflict between the environment and profit part in the Triple Bottom Line model.

The major challenge for companies is that they want to be sustainable, but sometimes this is not in line with profitability. Repairing a phone is less profitable than selling a new one. Selling disposable products, requiring customers to make new purchases is good for business. Take the Nespresso company for example. The company's business concept involves disposable coffee capsules. The company works toward sustainability by collecting the coffee capsules—often by providing free return postage—which is good. However, the best would be to sell coffee without disposable capsules. At the same time that would be the end of the business concept of Nespresso and thus the company.

Summing up, the key barriers for business and their circular economy are:

1. Products are not designed with circularity in mind. They are too complex and contain too many elements to be part of a circular economy.
2. Lack of access to used products. In order to reuse or repair of products there is a need for a minimum level of volume and access. If you only get refund for your bottles one place in the city, the likeliness of it being thrown away is much higher that if you can deliver your bottle for reuse at any food store.
3. Not available to refurbish or recycle used product in a cost-effective way. Too expensive to dismantle and lack of access to spare parts.

4. Customers discount the value of refurbished or remanufactured products. Quality of refurbished and manufactured products are perceived as lower quality than new products (Atasu et al., 2018).

Three approaches to overcome these abovementioned challenges to circular product economy are:

1. Implement modular product architecture
2. Lease instead of selling (at least some products)
3. Expand the refurbishing operations (Atasu et al., 2018)

The following are inspirational examples of initiatives which are circular and profitable presented by the European Circular Economy Stakeholder Platform and Ellen Mac Arthur Foundation case studies.

Fil&Fab has developed a technique to transform disused end-of-life fishing nets into plastic sheets, which are then used to create a series of new plastic products (France).

- Bio2Materials is a company which makes a 100% biodegradable "leather" from apples, based in Poland, the largest producer of apples in the EU and third in the world.
- I:CO is an international circular solutions provider for the collection, certified sorting, reuse, and recycling of clothing and shoes. They aim to support innovative new recycling technologies which help close the loop of production cycles.
- Better World Fashion produces new quality products from waste materials. Their primary material, leather, is from discarded post-consumer products collected by NGOs (European Commission the European Economic and Social Committee, n.d.).

A proliferation of business models for the circular economy

Five New Business Models for Circular Growth

1. Circular Supply-chain
2. Recovery and Recycling
3. Product Life-extension

(continued)

(continued)

4. Sharing Platform
5. Product as a Service

Waste to wealth, The Circular Economy Advantages

The Circular Business Model—Three Strategies for Circularity

1. Retain product ownership (RPO)
2. Product life extension (PLE)
3. Design for recycling (DFR)

HBR The Circular Economy Business Model

Circular Economy Strategies

- Business models describe the organizational and financial structures where an organization converts resources and capabilities into economic value.
- Innovation is required to deliver business models that create value from cycling products, parts, and materials.
- Strategies from three elements—circular value creation, circular value proposition and circular value network—can be combined to form a circular business model.

Circular Economy—Sustainable Material Management, IIIEE Lund University

References

Apple. (2021). *Environment: We're carbon neutral. And by 2030, every product you love will be too. How it's designed.* https://www.apple.com/environment/

Atasu, A., Agrawal, V., Rinaldi, M., Herb, R., & Ulkü, S. (2018, July 3). Rethinking sustainability in light of the EU's new circular economy policy. *Harvard Business Review*. https://hbr.org/2018/07/rethinking-sustainability-in-light-of-the-eus-new-circular-economy-policy

Boztas, S. (2016). Phone companies release too many new models, say consumers. *The Guardian*. https://www.theguardian.com/sustainable-business/2016/aug/15/phone-companies-release-too-many-new-models-consumer-survey-greenpeace

Center for Biological Diversity. (n.d.). *10 Facts about single-use plastic bags: The problem with plastic bags*. https://www.biologicaldiversity.org/programs/population_and_sustainability/sustainability/plastic_bag_facts.html

Chrisafis, A. (2016). French law forbids food waste by supermarkets. *The Guardian.* https://www.theguardian.com/world/2016/feb/04/french-law-forbids-food-waste-by-supermarkets

Dæhlen, M. (2016). Vet du hvor mange klesplagg du har? *forskning.no*. https://forskning.no/miljo-historie-naeringsliv/vet-du-hvor-mange-klesplagg-du-har/406500

Doboczky, S. (2019). Ending the era of dirty textiles. *World Economic Forum.* https://www.weforum.org/agenda/2019/09/ending-the-era-of-dirty-textiles/

Edseth, R. F. (2009). *En kritisk vurdering av tobakksavgiften* [University of Oslo]. https://www.duo.uio.no/bitstream/handle/10852/17570/RemyxEdsethxtobakksavgift.pdf?sequence=1&isAllowed=y

Ellen MacArthur Foundation. (n.d.). *Infographic: Circular economy system diagram.* https://www.ellenmacarthurfoundation.org/circular-economy/concept/infographic

Ellen MacArthur Foundation, SUN, & McKinsey Center for Business and Environment. (2015). *Growth within: A circular economy vision for a competitive Europe.* https://www.ellenmacarthurfoundation.org/assets/downloads/publications/EllenMacArthurFoundation_Growth-Within_July15.pdf

Epstein, P. R., Buonocore, J. J., Eckerle, K., Hendryx, M., Stout Iii, B. M., Heinberg, R., Clapp, R. W., May, B., Reinhart, N. L., & Ahern, M. M. (2011). Full cost accounting for the life cycle of coal. *Annals of the New York Academy of Sciences, 1219*(1), 73. https://doi.org/10.1111/j.1749-6632.2010.05890.x

EREK. (n.d.). Leasing extends end-of-life product cycles at Xerox. https://www.resourceefficient.eu/es/node/142

Euronews. (2021, March 1). EU law requires companies to fix electronic goods for up to 10 years. https://www.euronews.com/2021/03/01/eu-law-requires-companies-to-fix-electronic-goods-for-up-to-10-years

European Commission. (2020). *First circular economy action plan*https://ec.europa.eu/environment/topics/circular-economy/first-circular-economy-action-plan_en

European Commission the European Economic and Social Committee. (n.d.). *European circular economy stakeholder platform: Good practices.* https://circulareconomy.europa.eu/platform/good-practices

Fairphone. (2016, July). Fairphone fact sheet. https://www.fairphone.com/wp-content/uploads/2016/08/Fairphone-factsheet_EN.pdf

Food and Agriculture Organization of the United States. (2020). *The state of world fisheries and aquaculture 2020.* http://www.fao.org/state-of-fisheries-aquaculture/en/

Gadgets Now. (2020, November 20). 10 highest-selling smartphones in the world. https://www.gadgetsnow.com/slideshows/10-highest-selling-smartphones-in-the-world/apple-iphone-11/photolist/77882296.cms

Gibbs, S. (2020). Fairphone 3+ review: Ethical smartphone gets camera upgrades. *The Guardian*. https://www.theguardian.com/technology/2020/aug/31/fairphone-3-review-ethical-smartphone-gets-camera-upgrades
Grimstad, M. E., Jacobsen, G. E., & Bastiansen, J. E. (2019). Heller ut 25.000 liter drikke—hver dag. *NRK*. https://www.nrk.no/dokumentar/heller-ut-25.000-liter-drikke-_-hver-dag-1.14789395
Hannon, E. e. a. (2016). *The circular economy: Moving from theory to practice*. McKinsey Center for Business and Environment Special edition, Issue.
Martin, J., & Sherr, I. (2019). How Apple's Daisy iPhone recycling robot works. *CNET*. https://www.cnet.com/news/how-apples-daisy-iphone-recycling-robot-works/
Mattilsynet. (2019, November 7). Slik tar du vare på maten: Matsvinn. *Matportalen*. https://www.matportalen.no/matsmitte_og_hygiene/matsvinn-1
Mayer, M. L. (2017). Slik blir garderoben din mer miljøvennlig. *Putsj*. https://putsj.no/artikkel/slik-blir-garderoben-mer-miljovennlig
McCartney, P. (2009, December 8). Meat free Monday—the facts. https://www.paulmccartney.com/news-blogs/news/meat-free-monday-the-facts
McMaster, A. (2017). 3 ways your iPhone could be bad for the environment & workers. *Global Citizen*. https://www.globalcitizen.org/fr/content/iphone-x-apple-environment-pollution-smartphones-k/
Nijland, H., & van Meerkerk, J. (2017). Mobility and environmental impacts of car sharing in the Netherlands. *Environmental Innovation and Societal Transitions, 23*, 84–91. https://doi.org/10.1016/j.eist.2017.02.001
Njarga, B. B. (2016). Derfor bør ikke vrakpanten økes. *Dagbladet*. https://www.dagbladet.no/tema/derfor-bor-ikke-vrakpanten-okes/61663256
Nogrady, B. (2016). Your old phone is full of untapped precious metals. *BBC*. https://www.bbc.com/future/article/20161017-your-old-phone-is-full-of-precious-metals
Philips. (n.d.). *Lighting services has moved to signify*. https://www.lighting.philips.com/main/services
Reike, D., Vermeulen, W. J. V., & Witjes, S. (2018). The circular economy: New or Refurbished as CE 3.0?—Exploring Controversies in the Conceptualization of the Circular Economy through a Focus on History and Resource Value Retention Options. *Resources. Conservation and Recycling, 135*, 246–264. https://doi.org/10.1016/j.resconrec.2017.08.027
Sandin, G., Roos, S. R., Spak, B., Zamani, B., & Peters, G. (2019). Environmental assessment of Swedish clothing consumption. *Mistra Future Fashion Report* (2019:05). http://mistrafuturefashion.com/wp-content/uploads/2019/08/G.Sandin-Environmental-assessment-of-Swedish-clothing-consumption.MistraFutureFashionReport-2019.05.pdf

Sivertsen, E. V., & Zakariassen, G. (2016). Svensk kleskjede lar deg lease gardero-ben. *NRK*. https://www.nrk.no/kultur/filippa-k-lar-deg-lease-klaer-1.12835784

Smithers, R. (2016). England's plastic bag usage drops 85% since 5p charge introduced. *The Guardian*. https://www.theguardian.com/environment/2016/jul/30/england-plastic-bag-usage-drops-85-per-cent-since-5p-charged-introduced

The Irish News. (2018, March 02). How our smartphones are hurting the environment. https://www.irishnews.com/magazine/science/2018/03/02/news/how-our-smartphones-are-hurting-the-environment-1268849/

The World Bank. (n.d.). Trends in solid waste management. *WHAT A WASTE 2.0: A Global Snapshot of Solid Waste Management to 2050*. https://datatopics.worldbank.org/what-a-waste/trends_in_solid_waste_management.html

United Nations News. (2019, March 25). UN launches drive to highlight environmental cost of staying fashionable. https://news.un.org/en/story/2019/03/1035161

World Health Organization. (2019, June 18). 1 in 3 people globally do not have access to safe drinking water—UNICEF, WHO. https://www.who.int/news/item/18-06-2019-1-in-3-people-globally-do-not-have-access-to-safe-drinking-water-unicef-who

7

Strategy to Approach Sustainability in Companies: A Step by Step Model

Quick Check—Is your company a sustainable company?

1. Is the product sustainable?
2. Is the production system sustainable?
3. Is the global value chain sustainable?
4. Is the business a good citizen and transparent on its activities?

If you want to evaluate if the company and employer is a sustainable company, I recommend the quick check below. This "tool" is inspired by Jeffrey Sachs, professor at Columbia University and key actor in the development of the UN Sustainable Development Goals (SDGs). In the rest of this chapter, I will present a strategy for how to actually realize the potential of being sustainable and profitable company.

How the approach to sustainable corporate responsibility starts is often dependent on individuals. Who this person is, its interest and engagement, whereabouts in the company, department, power to impact, responsibility, and so on, all have a great impact on how the company as

C. D. Ditlev-Simonsen, *A Guide to Sustainable Corporate Responsibility*,
https://doi.org/10.1007/978-3-030-88203-7_7

a whole actually approach sustainability (Ditlev-Simonsen, 2010). If the person is head of marketing department, the approach to sustainability might be from a marketing perspective. Internal involvement and commitment might receive less attention. If it is somebody from the information and communication department picking up the issue, it might include more information in general—both internally and externally. If external investors ask for a sustainability report, the approach to sustainability might be shaped for investors, or department of accounting. The approach will then probably be more on reporting backwards, that is, things that have already happened, not visions and forward looking strategies. In Chap. 5, I reviewed what often is the corporate sustainability approach—in this section, the focus will be on what the strategy ought to be.

The following six steps, presented in Fig. 7.1, will guide companies on how to approach social responsibility and sustainability (Ditlev-Simonsen, 2013).

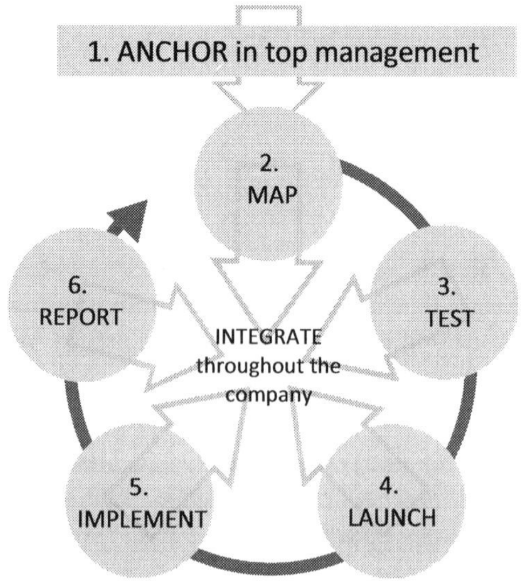

Fig. 7.1 Sustainability strategy model

7.1 Step 1: ANCHOR in Top Management and INTEGRATE Throughout the Company

In order to approach sustainability strategically, the initiative needs to come from or at least be *anchored* in top management—or even better—requested or endorsed by board of directors. Still, it is more common that an individual in the company takes the initiative. That is fine, but this person should get the message through to top management, not start a "local" project. As addressed earlier, it is important that the work on sustainability is integrated across the company. So, it is important also that the sustainability focus is not left at "the top" but involves all employees—or at least give them the opportunity to be involved.

Sustainability should not be an "add on" for the company but needs to be *integrated* throughout the company. It is not necessary with new channels for sustainability, but rather these activities should be integrated into already existing operations—business development, marketing, customer communication, reporting employee bonus, and so on. Formulating a vision, purpose, or mission statement, explicitly expressing the company's commitment to sustainability is important. This can be done after Step *3 Test and set goals* is completed. Examples of such corporate sustainability claims are presented in the Step 3 section. Corporate sustainability plans with concrete goals as well as visions and missions rarely go through without thorough work in top management and often requiring board approval. This strengthens the anchoring of sustainability in top management and commitment throughout the company.

7.2 Step 2: MAP

When the focus on sustainability is anchored in top management, getting an overview on the current status and draft plan for future work is necessary. Companies are complex organizations, and in order to get an overview of the company, it is useful to put together a task force to follow up the call from top management. As much as possible, the task force should represent all the divisions within a company—including representatives from HR, accounting, information department, and so on. It is important that the group is not too big in order to ensure good dialogue; it should be less than ten people. Still, I urge to allow other employees to contribute as well. Using a digital survey to announce the work and ask for input and comments is a simple and effective approach to collect relevant information and ensure buy-in.

The next involves mapping the company's social and environmental impact. If the company is in the oil and gas industry, relevant issues to address are for example CO_2 emissions and HMS issues. If it is a small company in the textile industry, for instance, running a clothing store importing from Bangladesh or Cambodia, emissions associated with dyeing of textiles and working conditions among employees among the suppliers are more relevant. My experience with companies is that the first thing they are looking for is where the company is doing something good. They focus on that and not in the area where there are real problematic challenges facing the company.

> "Did You Lose the Keys Here?" "No, But the Light Is Much Better Here"
> (Are your sustainability challenges in this area? No, but we have so much more nice things to tell from our activities in this area.)

Using the UN SDGs as a checklist is a good approach to mapping the current situation, opportunities, and challenges. Some of the 17 goals will be more relevant than others. Identify the goals that are the most relevant and depending on the size of the company, more of the goals can be selected. For small companies, it is perfectly fine to focus on one goal and how the company can contribute to that, whereas for larger companies, it can be useful to work with several goals. Some multinational companies choose to address all 17 goals—and sometimes it seems like they want to "cover their backs" not to leave anything out.

A good approach to use in mapping the relative importance of different elements of the company's impact is through a materiality assessment.

Materiality Assessment

Materiality assessment is a practical framework to discuss with colleagues and other stakeholders on what to prioritize and what matters for whom. Depicting the different items visually furthermore gives a good overview and basis for a sustainability program. It serves as a good decision tool. It is common to use materiality assessments in large companies, but it is also useful for small-to-medium enterprises (SMEs).

The materiality assessment concept consists of a matrix with two axes. The x-axis addresses business impact/relevance, while societal and stakeholder impact/relevance is on the y-axis. In Fig. 7.2, the materiality model is presented. Depending on the impact on society and business, issues are placed at different areas on the matrix.

The unit of measurement on each of the two axes is Low and High. Issues in the Low-Low area are rarely put into the matrix. In this case, we are talking about issues which have a low impact on society and are low on relevance for business. An example could be a bakery located in

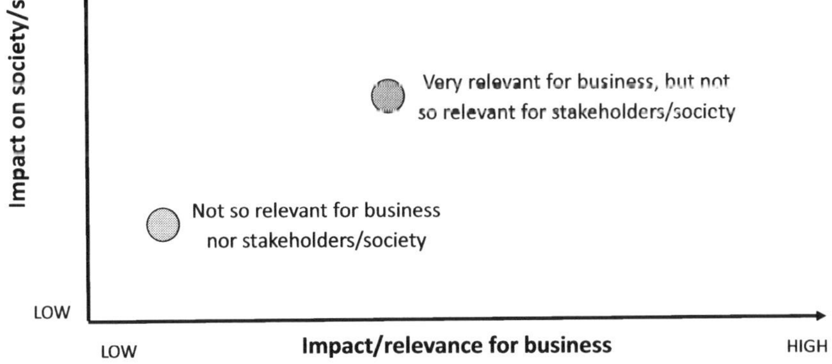

Fig. 7.2 Generic model for materiality assessment

Norway making its own products. For this company, working conditions are strictly regulated by the Norwegian government. Customers are also not likely to be very concerned about employees' working conditions when they make purchases at the bakery. So low impact and low relevance should be placed in the Low-Low area. In the High-High area for the same bakery, the number of ingredients produced with low levels of pesticides would be an issue. Avoiding palm oil for example would be relevant and placed in the High-High area.

Unilever, a multinational consumer goods company, places climate change as a High-High issue, signaling that the company recognizes that climate change is very relevant for society and its stakeholders. It also signalizes that the company actually can contribute to the reduction of greenhouse gas (GHG) emissions. Unilever has set a target to move to zero emissions in its operations by 2030, by among others decarbonizing raw materials, shifting to renewable energy, and eliminating deforestation in its supply chain (Unilever, 2020). The company perceives talent and development as very important (High), but with a low impact on society and stakeholders in general (Low).

Some companies post the relevant SDGs in their materiality matrix. Canon, a company providing network solutions for business, perceives its impact on Life in Water, SDG# 14 as Low-Low. That makes sense as the company is not in the marine industry and its stakeholders are not specifically concerned about the marine impact of Canon's products and services. SDG# 9 however, Industry, Innovation and Infrastructure, is perceived as High-High for Canon. Working to reduce the cost of making chips and helping to automate factories to improve productivity are in the scope of Canon's core business operations. This SDG goal is therefore important and relevant for Canon as well as their stakeholders such as customers (Canon Global, 2021).

In a company, not all employees or other stakeholders immediately agree on where the different issues should be places relative to importance. That is why materiality assessments are an important tool in evaluations on what really matters. This again will contribute to different stakeholders eventually having a common agreement on what happens—and if they do not, they know where and how they disagree.

Current Situation and Goal Drafting

After the key areas of environmental and social impact are identified and mapped, the company has to take account of what they are already doing in these areas—that is, the current status. Often companies realize that they are actually doing a lot in the pursuit of sustainability—they just do not call it sustainability or corporate responsibility.

Several companies which have come to me for advice are worried that all their competitors work on sustainable corporate responsibility but they themselves are not. After the mapping exercise, they get somewhat reassured when they become aware of the current situation on environmental and social issues within the company. Still, they also realize that they need to organize this work and put it into a system. Benchmarking or assessing the current situation in different areas of relevant sustainability issues in the company is addressed in Chap. 5.

Using a simple example, a transport company, whose main impact is through gasoline usage (CO_2 emissions), "Ignore" would be to not be aware of or address the issue at all. "React" would be to identify the issue, but not do anything. "Defend" would be to argue for no need to do anything (everybody else uses gasoline cars, it is too expensive to replace the transport cars, etc.). "Accommodate" would be to replace the gasoline cars with electric cars. And finally, "Proact" would be to reflect on ways to coordinate transport, share cars, pickup-sites, and so on.

The next step then is to set concrete goals associated to the areas where the company has major social and environmental impact. For example, training of employees in sustainability; number of hours within specific time, reduction of CO_2 in tons within a certain set time, and so on.

Then the company's key social and environmental impact is assessed and a plan with concrete goals is put forward. Reduce CO_2 emissions by 10% by 2023, stop using plastic packaging by 2024, Meatless Mondays from 2022, and so on. It is important also to have some more far-reaching goals, maybe not reachable within time, but to stretch innovation. For a small clothing store, it could be that 20 percent of their sales should be used clothes within a year. For an oil company, it can be to be an oil-free energy company within 10 years.

The next step is to consult with stakeholders to collect feedback on the plan.

7.3 Step 3: TEST

Stakeholders are crucial for companies, and their relevance is obvious. Still, companies often overlook the key stakeholders in the process of developing their sustainability plan. More emphasis is often on marketing the sustainability plan to stakeholders after the program is ready. However, if stakeholders are involved in the developing the program, or at least asked, the likeliness that they will buy-in is much greater.

It is the customers who know what they expect and prefer from the company, it is employees in the production process, who know how to make the production process more sustainable and it is the suppliers, who know the challenges and the solutions in the supply chain. Research shows that employees want to be more involved in the sustainability process than they actually are (Ditlev-Simonsen, 2012). Engaging employees and soliciting their feedback by for example asking which of the SDGs they think are relevant for their job can be quite useful for the company as well as getting employees onboard. A simple online survey to employees is all that is needed to collect the necessary information.

The success of the sustainability program is much more likely if the program is tested on stakeholders prior to launch. Stakeholder management is the topic of Chap. 8, but the following are some examples of relevant stakeholders in different sectors and areas of business.

For a large company in the oil and gas industry, consulting environmental organizations, customers, suppliers, and employees in general could be some relevant stakeholders. A consultancy company could also be a relevant stakeholder.

For the small clothing store, asking the customers on their views as well as to check the relevance and possibility of their goals with their agent is a good approach. Maybe what the store asks from their agent, information on the working conditions in the producers' factories, is not possible to obtain. Still, raising the issues pushes the agent to follow up the request which itself has an impact. This should be included in the store's sustainability plan.

Present the plan with concrete goals for different and relevant stakeholders. Reflect on their comments and, most likely, you are inspired to make revisions. The final plan has to be approved by the top management—and preferably the board of directors too. Developing a revised company vision, mission, and purpose statement associated with sustainability can be an efficient approach to signaling new corporate priorities and values. The following are some examples of such statements in large corporations—the process is equally relevant in SMEs:

Bosch is committed to sustainability and constantly evolving in this respect. The corresponding strategic foundations are anchored in our "New Dimensions—Sustainability 2025" target vision.

Tesla mission—"To accelerate the world's transition to sustainable energy".

Coca-Cola—"Our vision is to craft the brands and choice of drinks that people love, to refresh them in body & spirit. And done in ways that create a more sustainable business and better shared future that makes a difference in people's lives, communities and our planet."

Beyond Meat—"We believe there is a better way to feed our future and that the positive choices we all make, no matter how small, can have a great impact on our personal health and the health of our planet. By shifting from animal to plant-based meat, we can positively impact four growing global issues: human health, climate change, constraints on natural resources, and animal welfare."

TATA "To be the most reliable global network for customers and suppliers, that delivers value through products and services. To be a responsible value creator for all our stakeholders."

Philip Morris Int.'s new vision being "A Smoke Free Future."

VW Group "We are a globally leading provider of sustainable mobility."

Northvolt—"Our mission is to build the greenest battery in the world with a minimal carbon footprint and the highest ambitions for recycling to enable the European transition to renewable energy."

The next step then is to launch the sustainability plan and new vision.

7.4 Step 4: LAUNCH

Many companies are very happy after developing a good sustainability strategy with concrete plans and goals. However, often it ends up there—a good plan and that is it.

The launching process, making the plan and the responsibilities known among key stakeholders such as employees, suppliers, customers, officials, and so on, is as important as the plan.

There are many channels of communication—everything from including aspects of the plan on company indoor information screens, on products, to include as parts of bids and offers.

Educating and contributing knowledge to external stakeholders is relevant. Educating employees on how to increase sustainability focus and planning is also important. Employees need to know the reasoning behind changes associated with the pursuit of sustainability. In the clothing store example, making the store employees aware of the current situation and goals will make them proud of their workplace. It is a good pitch for sales and the employees will be good ambassadors for the store.

Many companies are eager to inform employees and other stakeholders on their sustainability engagement. My experience is however that if these activities are not impacting the receivers of the information, the receivers will not pick up on it. The information has to be based on communication and dialogue, especially with the employees.

7.5 Step 5: IMPLEMENT

The implementation process actually ensures that set goals are being realized and it is the foundation for actually making change happen. Sometimes, sustainability goals are not explicitly part of the job description of employees or part of the usual day-to-day operations. Therefore, follow-ups though dialogue and meetings are useful. The most efficient approach is to include the company's sustainability plan as part of other progress evaluations and follow-ups, like for example in sales and budgets.

A good and efficient tool and checklist for implementation is Kotter's 8-Step Process for Leading Change (Kotter, 2012):

1. *Create a sense of urgency*—let employees, customers, and other stakeholders know that your sustainability program is important and need attention—link it to concrete issues.
2. *Build a guiding coalition*—pinpoint the stakeholders involved in the process of developing the sustainability plan—they are part of the team.
3. *Form a strategic vision and initiatives*—the focus on sustainability should be clearly expressed in the company vision and the initiatives are part of the sustainability strategy.
4. *Enlist a volunteer army*—involve employees as "ambassadors" and credit stakeholders involved in the sustainability plan.
5. *Enable action by removing barriers*—include elements from the sustainability plan in the procurement criteria.
6. *Generate short-term wins*—announce when goals in the sustainability plan are achieved, and even when you come half-way
7. *Sustain acceleration*—use the achievements as drivers and motivators for that it is possible
8. *Institute change*—the awareness and success of sustainability plan can have long lasting impact across the corporation—as well as customers and suppliers. Make it part of company policy.

It is to be expected that not all goals in the sustainability plan will be met, and even to discover that some of the set goals were not optimal after all. All this is part of a learning process and important to track. An open environment for employees to be able to report on challenges and voice new ideas or replacement of goals is crucial. Channels such as an e-mail address dedicated to such dialogue can be useful. Employees as well as other external stakeholders can use this venue to contribute with feedback. In large companies, set-up for reporting is a relatively simple process. For the small clothing store, having an email or Instagram site for feedback and suggestion can be a simple and good channel. This continuous dialogue with stakeholders is often forgotten—both in large and small companies.

The most efficient way to ensure implementation of the sustainability plan is, however, to include elements of it in the company's performance bonus system. When employees can document their work, reach the goals, and receive a bonus, that is a game-changer.

It is argued that there is a distinct difference to succeed leading a sustainability process relative to leading other corporate changes. Focus on authentic leadership theory has received increased attention. Authentic leadership is about leaders being aware of their moral attitudes and integrate these in their day-to-day work. Pursuing a sustainability venue requires that leaders are good role models. When the company, endorsed by company leaders, urges employees to avoid traveling by plane and the managers travel by private planes generates a dissonance. A leader that applies sustainability in his or her day-to-day behavior is a powerful way to make employees implement sustainable changes in their work (Ditlev-Simonsen, 2009).

7.6 Step 6: REPORT

The final step in this model is the reporting phase. Reporting on the sustainability plan together with the annual report is a good approach. This illustrates that sustainability is an integrated part of the company's performance. When companies started reporting on first environmental and later social and sustainability issues, the reports were often very separate from the annual report, likely because sustainability was not integrated in the company—but something separate.

Now more and more companies are integrating their non-financial reports in their annual report. The term non-financial report is in many ways a wrong reference to corporate performance on social and environmental issues, because it can definitely have a financial impact. Some companies apply the term "extra-financial reporting" which is a much better description.

Reporting on social and environmental issues with figures and numbers, like change of CO_2 emissions in tons, percent of recycled material in products in tons, and so on show that the company is treating these issues as part of day-to-day operations. Companies should also report on goals, which were not achieved, and why it is so. As mentioned above, maybe the goals set were wrong or impossible. This should be part of a learning process. In line with transparency, challenges and problems should also be reported. Such openness truly shows that the company actually integrates sustainability into operations.

In the small clothing store, the goal to increase sales of reused clothing could have been set to 20 percent. It turns out that the increase of sales was only ten percent. Why was that so? One approach to find out is to ask the customers. This illustrates how measuring and addressing the results can help improve the company's performance.

When the first round of the *Step-by-Step* sustainability strategy is concluded, the process continues on from Step 1, updated with experience from the first round. Furthermore, some of the goals set in the first round could be long-term goals, which have to be followed up on again. For example, as mentioned previously several companies have set goals to be carbon neutral by 2030. The degree to which the company is on track has to be benchmarked and reported annually. Reporting is in itself often backward looking. Sustainability reports should also be forward looking, sharing goals to be reached in within different timeframes. Many of the sustainability goals need time to be reached. Becoming carbon neutral for what is today an oil and gas company will probably need decades.

References

Canon Global. (2021). *CSR activities: Materiality and SDGs*. https://global.canon/en/csr/sdgs/index.html

Ditlev-Simonsen, C. D. (2009). Fordrer det noe spesielt å lede en samfunnsansvarlig bedrift. *Magma, 2*, 22–33.

Ditlev-Simonsen, C. D. (2010). From corporate social responsibility awareness to action? *Social Responsibility Journal, 6*(3), 452–468. https://doi.org/10.1108/17471111011064807

Ditlev-Simonsen, C. D. (2012). The relationship between Norwegian and Swedish employees' perception of corporate social responsibility and affective commitment. *Business & Society, 54*(2), 229–253. https://doi.org/10.1177/0007650312439534

Ditlev-Simonsen, C. D. (2013). Ny proposisjon om samfunnsansvarsrapportering. *Magma, 2*, 12–14. https://www.magma.no/ny-proposisjon-om-samfunnsansvarsrapportering

Kotter, J. P. (2012). *Leading change*. Harvard Business School Press.
Unilever. (2020, December 14). *Unilever to seek shareholder approval for climate transition action plan*.https://www.unilever.com/news/press-releases/2020/unilever-to-seek-shareholder-approval-for-transition-action-plan.html

8

Stakeholder Management

In the field of corporate responsibility and sustainability, stakeholder management is maybe more relevant than many other issues companies have to take into account. There is no absolute agreement on what is a sustainable company and what is not—and many stakeholders have different opinions of what companies should do. Even peripheral stakeholders can have great impact on companies. This is an important consideration that companies need to be aware and take into account. In this chapter, I will explore the roles of different kinds of stakeholders such as owners (including investors), employees, governments, suppliers, customers, NGOs, and media. I will address the function of these stakeholders explicitly as well potential areas for positive collaboration. The power and impact of NGOs on corporations will receive special attention as they often act as representatives for environmental and social interests—and bring such issues to the attention of others.

Initially owners and investors were the key stakeholders in companies. The focus then was on procuring resources at low cost, producing at low cost, and achieving sales with quick profit. This worked in a time when employees had little power and owners had full control. There was no minimum wage, employees were often not allowed to organize, and there

C. D. Ditlev-Simonsen, *A Guide to Sustainable Corporate Responsibility*,
https://doi.org/10.1007/978-3-030-88203-7_8

were limited regulations with regards to working hours and typically poor working conditions. Resources were often free or easy to appropriate while exploring new territories (e.g., the Gold Rush in the late 1800s). Many companies dumped their waste in rivers and oceans without penalty.

Gradually, employee-rights, regulations of working conditions, taxes on emissions, and so on changed the way of doing business. Now, with a complex and connected society, managing a variety of stakeholders' interests is an issue for corporations, especially with regards to sustainable development and responsibility.

For today's companies, responsibility must go beyond the boundaries of the firm and extend to their choice of business partners. This is also a crucial part of system change in a circular economy setting. Environmental and social issues throughout the supply chain also have to become part of a company's responsibility. The challenge of keeping track of and ensuring good working conditions is crucial.

Edward Freeman's stakeholder model from 1984, as presented in Chap. 2 (Fig. 2.5), is the "classic" stakeholder concept model. The model seems rather straightforward with the company in the middle circled by a variety of different stakeholders. In reality, the model is much more complex.

Today, there are many more and new stakeholders. In our digital society, new stakeholders such as Facebook, Twitter, and LinkedIn can have strong impact on corporations. Civil society can encompass different stakeholders, for instance, NGOs, with different goals and purposes. Furthermore, firms can have more of the same type of stakeholders in the model. For example, most companies do not have just one supplier but several. Finally, there is a direct connection between the different stakeholders, for instance customers are impacted by critical NGOs. So, the linkages are not only between the firm and the individual stakeholders in Freeman's model.

One thing is that there are many more stakeholders (Customer 1, Customer 2, Customer 3, etc.) in "the real world" and each of the stakeholders can have a different impact in terms of both size and scope. Finally, different stakeholders do not only relate to the company on an individual basis—but can also have a dialogue between one another. A more realistic stakeholder model, which more accurately represents the complexity of a few selected stakeholders, is presented in Fig. 8.1.

Given the large range of stakeholders, not all can be included and taken into account. The challenge for the company is to listen to the "right" stakeholders in the right way and make the right decision depending on the topic. This is especially relevant when it comes to corporate responsibility for sustainability. Balancing different interests in the best way is eventually what forms the basis for a company's success or failure.

A company in a short-term horizon can narrow down the number of, and focus on, stakeholders. For instance, the customers of street vendors in tourist areas can be less concerned about product quality and trust among customers. If something goes wrong with the product the tourist has brought home, there are not many options for return and refund. The same is true when purchasing goods from low cost countries through eBay or other online platforms.

However, if a product is purchased from a brand name store close to where the customers live, the likeliness of confronting customer reactions is much higher. Furthermore, if journalists detect that the product is manufactured under poor working conditions in low cost countries or if

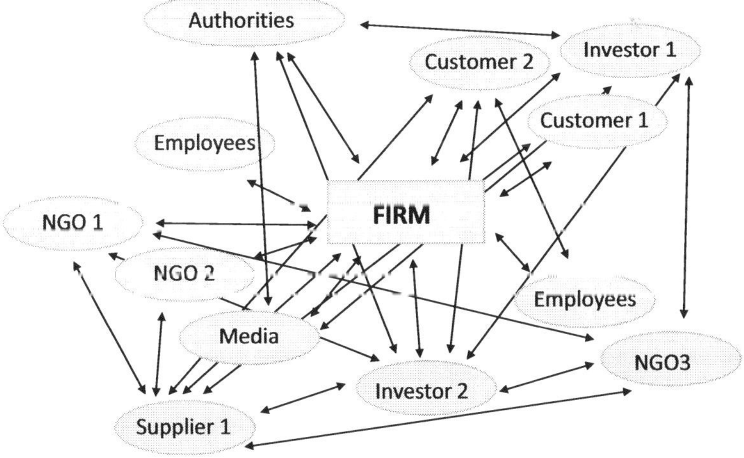

Fig. 8.1 Stakeholder model revised—in illustrating several versions of same stakeholder and dialogue between stakeholders

authorities find that the products do not fulfil regulations, both can pose major challenges to the product brand. NGOs are often actors or stakeholders, which identify negative social and environmental elements associated with the production line of a product. That can be a risk and a threat for companies. At the same time, customers, media, and NGOs can be stakeholders, which can make positive contributions toward companies. They can rate similar products from different companies and recommend which are the best from an environmental and social perspective. This often guides customers in their purchasing process.

So, different actors agree that taking stakeholders into account is important, but how to do this in practice is less clear. In the rest of this chapter, I will take a closer look at the role and relevance of some more relevant stakeholders.

8.1 Owners, Shareholders, and Managers

How the company perceives it responsibility for society and sustainability depends upon the owners and the managers. In private companies, where the manager is often the owner, as is the case in many small-to-medium enterprises (SMEs), it is very much up to the manager how the company operates from a sustainability point of view. This also relates to the values of the owner. Some managers find sustainability to be relevant for the company and work on making products more sustainable, whereas other managers and owners do not care. In the same sector, companies can address sustainability issues very differently.

In companies with several owners, shareholders, it is less up to a hired manager, who is not an owner, to think about sustainability if the board of directors do not care. For some shareholders, the priority is short-term profit. Some have a limited investment perspective and speculate on a certain increase in shareholder price within a set timeframe. In this case, long-term payoffs for behaving sustainably might not be prioritized.

On the other hand, the company might have shareholders which require the company to behave in a certain way in order to invest. Environmental, Social, and Governance (ESG) requirements issues are increasingly relevant to shareholders. Relative to such shareholders, the company has to fulfil different sustainability requirements. A good example of how shareholders can change company focus happened in May 2021. The shareholders voted to replace two of the company's twelve board members with new climate concerned candidates. When the majority of the board of directors is dedicated to make the company more sustainable, the change can actually be realized. The shareholder perspective of sustainability issues will be closely addressed in the next chapter.

Companies registered on a stock exchange often have to report quarterly on results. The shorter the timeline for showing positive results, the more challenging it is to invest in better and more long-term sustainable technologies. This short time horizon is a major challenge and obstacle for companies to take measures to become more sustainable. When Paul Polman, CEO in Unilever 2009, decided not to issue quarterly earnings reports, there was an outcry. Later research has shown that increased frequency in reporting is associated with a decline in investments in US companies (Kraft et al., 2018). It is also evident that companies managed by equity companies with a longer investment horizon are also more keen on integrating sustainability for long-term profitability.

The Business Roundtable (BRT) is association formed in 1972 consisting of nearly 200 CEOs of leading American companies, together employing more than 15 million people. In line with most companies, the organization had defined the corporation's principal purpose as maximizing shareholder return. When BRT overturned its original purpose in 2019, it received a lot of attention. Their new purpose statement was "companies should serve not only their shareholders, but also deliver value to their customers, invest in employees, deal fairly with suppliers and support the communities in which they operate" (Business Roundtable, n.d.). This statement has been welcomed by many stakeholders, while others have been critical and claim it is only window dressing. At the same time, ensuring sustainable business is in many cases a prerequisite for good and profitable business. Focus on short-term profit does not render profit in the long term.

The importance of the company sustainability work being anchored in the management team is addressed in Chap. 7. In addition, when it comes to sustainability, it is not enough that manager(s) claim that sustainability is important, they also have to behave sustainable themselves. They have to be good role models. If the CEO of public transportation urges people to commute on public transportation, the same CEO cannot commute with a gas guzzler herself. Sustainability needs to be integrated as part of the corporate culture (Ditlev-Simonsen, 2009).

8.2 Employees

Employees are key stakeholders for corporations. Their competence, knowledge, and experience are crucial assets. Without employees most companies would not survive—or not even exist. How companies treat their employees impacts among other, employees' motivation, trust, willingness to contribute, well-being, and commitment. Having committed employees is positive for retaining and avoiding expenses for recruiting new employees. "55% of respondents said that strong sustainability programs improve morale, and 38% said they increase loyalty" (Whelan & Douglas, 2021).

How companies deal with society outside the company also impacts employees' attitude and performance. Sustainability issues such as to which extent the company is involved in pollution, levels of climate gas emissions, environmental and social issues in the supply chain, bribery, and so on all relate to employees. So, a company's level of social responsibility and sustainability is both relevant and important with regards to employees' perception of the employer and performance. In fact, research shows a perception of corporate social responsibility among employees is a significant predictor of affective commitment (Ditlev-Simonsen, 2012). Affective commitment again is associated with reduced absenteeism, better performance, and lower turnover.

More than 90 percent of the workforce claims to be willing to reduce wages for greater meaning at work (Achor et al., 2018). A large portion of the millennials claim that positive societal impact was more important than wages, and "societal impact and ethics are the most common reasons for millennials change their relationship with businesses" (Deloitte, 2019).

A challenge for companies is the fact that not all employees have the same perception of what a sustainable company, or employer, is.

Companies have many different "types"/cultures and levels of employees, differences in ages, genders, cultures, and so on, that all impact perceptions of sustainability. Depending on employees' position, part-time, full time, interns, production operators, managers, directors, and so on, the view of sustainability and what is important can vary. Employees need to adhere to company values, but it might be even more important that they support their employer and how it operates.

When it comes to production and design, companies produce what sells. If employees in the production line do not like the design or color of a product, it is irrelevant as long as customers choose to buy the product—and as long as the product does not have significant negative societal or environmental impacts. When it comes to sustainability however, it involves more than values and beliefs. Having employees "on board" is therefore not as simple as producing products that sell. Therefore, it is important to involve employees in the process of developing a common sustainable attitude in the company.

Too often the decision on what is the scope of the sustainability strategy is made solely on the top. There are many examples of initiatives taken by top management for sustainability and responsibility engagement that part of the company workforce disagrees with. Most of the time this disagreement is not discussed openly, but it still exists and can impact employee work performance. Other times, employees' disagreement with employers have resulted in negative consequences for employers outside the company as well. Microsoft's support of the "Gay Rights Bill" was against some employees' beliefs. For them the fact that in the Bible it is stated that people of the same gender should not be partners was enough to make this a media case resulting in Microsoft withdrawing their support for the Bill (Kershaw, 2005).

Discussing the employee perspective of sustainability, the challenges of too much top-management-driven engagement are reoccurring. It is quite obvious that employee engagement is important; however, it is surprising how little attention is paid to it. One of the reasons for this may be that mangers implicitly assume that employees share their view and personal beliefs of what is important when it comes to sustainability and responsibility issues. That is one key reason for involving employees in the sustainability process (Ditlev-Simonsen, 2012).

There are many examples of companies engaging in voluntary community work, involving employees and even giving them time off to contribute. This can be a positive experience for employees, both through feeling good for doing good, teaming up with co-workers, and good for society. However, this is not directly associated with doing business. Maybe the greatest potential of involving employees in the company work on sustainability is the potential for new and more sustainable production and products. Just as the "post-it" note was developed by a 3M employee, employees in most companies will have ideas related to sustainability—but they need to be asked and involved (Prather & Turrell, 2002).

8.3 Governments: The Public Sector

The concept of the "tragedy of the commons" was first introduced in 1969 by the evolutionary biologist Garrett Harding. However, what it describes has been around since the beginning of time. The problem begins with the assumption that people act in their own self-interest and individuals take more common resources than they need without thinking of the long-term consequences. People in general are short-sighted and neglect societal interests in the pursuit of personal gains. The outcome can be devastating for everyone—including the next generation. This is not sustainable and therefore, we need regulations of common goods. A commonly cited example illustrating the "tragedy of the commons" is fishing in the ocean. If there were no regulations, people would catch as many fish as they could as fast as they could, eventually depleting stocks to extinction. To prevent overexploitation, fishing regulations have been put in place to preserve a balance ensuring availability of fish over the long-term. Still the regulations of common goods go too slow. The same applies to regulations related to climate issues and biodiversity in general. Governments thus need to regulate the use of common goods to ensure a fair distribution and well-being in countries, that is, sustainable development.

Historically, industrialization developed, faster than the regulatory regime, companies had to take on societal responsibility in order to get started and operate. Today, industries establishing businesses in developing countries or rural and unpopulated areas often need to take on responsibilities which are usually provided by public services in developed countries: housing, school, medical services, and so on for employees.

A good example of the development history of corporate responsibility is Norsk Hydro, a Norwegian company in the fertilizer sector established in 1907 in a small city in the middle of Norway, Rjukan. Today Hydro is Norway's largest employer. Prior to this startup, there were only a few farmers living in Rjukan, and the energy generating potential of large waterfalls was not realized. After three years of operations, there were 2200 people living in Rjukan, and in 1920 over 8000 people were living there. People moving to Rjukan to work could not afford housing, so this had to be provided by Norsk Hydro. This situation is often the same when companies are starting up in poor countries.

At that time in Norway, and similar to the situation in many poor countries today, a good public welfare framework is missing. For many of the employees coming to such sites, in the Norsk Hydro example in 1907 as well as in low cost countries today, the company owner has to take care of the workers. Norsk Hydro followed up on this responsibility and provided living conditions which were much better than where the employees came from, with indoor access to sanitation as well as health services. Not all companies starting up in low cost countries provide the same services to their employees today.

The following is another example of taking care of employers by Norsk Hydro. Rjukan is a narrow valley with steep mountains on the sides resulting in almost no sunlight during the winter. That is one reason why people did not want to live in Rjukan. However, the high mountain provided the waterfalls generating the energy for production, and having workers living there was a prerequisite for doing business there. In order to provide sun to the employees the founder of Norsk Hydro provided a cable car lifting the employees almost 900 meters up to experience the sun, also during the winter. This is a good example illustrating how corporations have taken responsibility—beyond wages—for employees. For Norsk Hydro providing such societal services was good for long-term profit as well. If the employees did not see the sun for several months or lived under poor conditions, they were more likely to get ill and not able to do their work, or unhappy which also impact negatively their work performance. Today, governments in developed countries have taken over most social service initiatives and financed these through taxes.

In developing countries with weak governments, the situation for companies is often similar to those in developing countries a century ago. Some companies use this as an opportunity for low cost production under poor conditions, whereas others take more responsibility for their employees. In this international setting, many companies also seek to reduce or avoid tax. Companies like Starbucks, which are working hard to portray themselves as sustainable companies, are criticized for avoiding tax in the UK (Bergin, 2012). The company claims that what it does is legal. Here reflecting on how far companies should go to use the system to increase profit from an ethical perspective is relevant to reflect on.

Still, companies and governments have realized that a closer dialogue is necessary in the pursuit of sustainable development and that public-private partnerships have contributed to positive experiences and sustainable outcomes (Spraul & Thaler, 2019). Moving from companies opposing regulations from government, there is now a trend that in their pursuit of sustainability, companies are urging governments to pass stricter regulations. When companies try to go beyond what is required by government, for example by installing technologies which lead to less pollution, this can initially be costly. Competitors, which are not installing the same type of technology, can provide products at lower prices. In such instances, companies with better environmental performance urge government to set stricter requirements. This will be good for both business and the environment. Too often, the government regulations are behind what is technically possible with regard to environmental issues and prices of resources do not often cover the negative effects. It is argued that governments have the responsibility of representing "nature" as nature has no "voice". Subsiding the fossil fuels industry is an example of how governmental actions are negative for the environment and society as a whole (Coady et al., 2015; Shindell, 2015).

It is not only companies which are opposed to governmental regulations. When governments take initiatives to reduce the use of cars, with for example toll roads, major opposition from the groups and individuals is common. Introducing and increasing fees reduces the chances of political parties to be reelected—even when we are talking environmental taxation.

Digital shopping has made it easy to buy low price products from low cost countries, like China. Digital platforms like eBay make it simple for individuals to purchase such production online. It is almost impossible to ensure that the produces are manufactured under good working conditions or determine their environmental impact. The low price implies a great challenge and unfair competition for manufacturers producing under good working conditions and environmentally friendly processes in a high-cost country. It is much easier to verify products from these companies with regards to working conditions and environmental issues in the supply chain. Still, when companies demand higher tolls and taxes on products imported from low cost countries by individuals, there is much opposition—and so regulators are slow to take measures to avoid such unsustainable behavior among individuals.

Free market and social democracy have led to many public services, such as the telephone network, managing roads, hospitals, and so on, which are run by private companies. In many cases, this has led to more social and environmentally friendly operations—but not always. Government's role in controlling such operations is becoming even more important at the same time as it is challenging.

An important contribution from governments and public institutions is to make and increase sustainability as part of their purchasing policy. In the OECD countries, one third of the total public spending is purchase of goods and services. Moves like the EU Green Public Procurement can contribute to a shift to more sustainable production. Furthermore, new EU requirements in the line of producers of certain electrical goods need to make their products repairable for at least 10 years. Still, it is often the price of not repair that outweighs the price of purchasing new products—not repair.

Still, the most important contribution to sustainability from governments is implementing public policy that makes business and individuals act in a more sustainable manner. Higher environmental taxes on primary raw materials and on waste, making it mandatory to use secondary raw materials in products, increase Extended Producer Responsibility, raise knowledge on sustainable production and consumption among people and companies are some examples of initiatives that would contribute to sustainability.

Since there is a growing consensus that a carbon tax, so price on emitting carbon, might be the most effective tool in reducing emissions, governments have the power to decarbonize an economy. This implies they have a great responsibility. Increasing the price of CO_2 emissions leads to increased energy efficiency. Today, carbon offsets are priced for less that $5 USD per metric ton CO_2, which does not provide the sufficient incentive for businesses or people to change enough. By taxing emissions and setting it sufficiently high, this induces change away from business as usual and investment into sustainable alternatives. However, by raising the cost of GHG emissions, it will also raise costs for businesses that will be later passed on to the consumer. For governments, this is a difficult policy initiative to promote. In developed countries, higher living expenses could mean the political party is voted out of office in the next election. In developing countries, a carbon tax is difficult because many are already living in poverty and can barely afford the basic necessities, never mind a carbon tax that would push even more people into poverty. So, will politicians act in self-interest to maintain power and do nothing or will they take the chance of being voted out for an unpopular carbon tax which is in the greater good for society and its future generations? The question remains.

8.4 Suppliers

As international trade has grown, import of goods and services has increased. Worldwide imports of goods and services were less than 14 percent in 1970 and have more than doubled today (The World Bank, n.d.). Improved transport efficiency and reduced cost have contributed to an increased global trade. The Nike case in Chap. 5 illustrates the challenges of moving manufacturing to low cost countries. Since then, we have learned a lot—and most large companies are working actively to avoid poor working conditions and child labor. Still, as the Rana Plaza case illustrates, production in low cost countries is too often proven to be under par. Figure 8.2 depicts the complexity of the supply chain concept, illustrated with a fraction of the number of suppliers which is usually the case for companies.

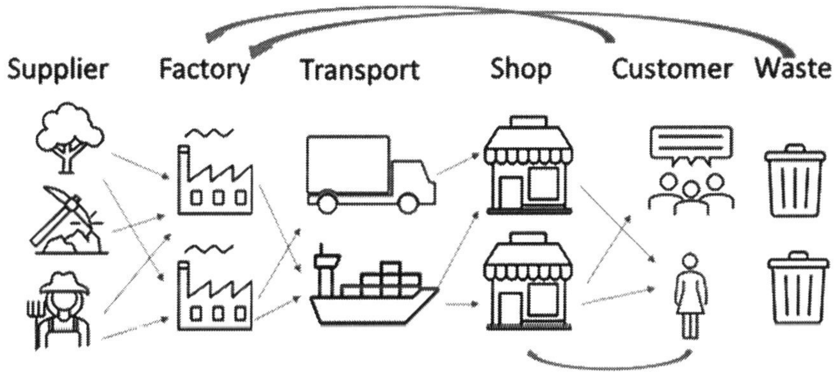

Fig. 8.2 Traditional supply chain—added circular reuse and return systems

Typical challenges in the supply chain are forced and slave labor, human trade, child labor, discrimination, lack of employees' rights, working conditions, right to get organized, wage and working hours. Environmental issues such as uncontrolled emissions and pollution are also a challenge. Large companies often have contracts with hundreds of suppliers which are hard to follow up. SMEs too can have several suppliers and for them travelling around to ensure acceptable working conditions and environmental performance are not affordable. Even with a signed supplier contract where good environmental and social issues are guaranteed, there is almost no way to control that the agreement is actually implemented. There are furthermore several incidents where large corporations have visited their suppliers' facilities and ensured good working conditions. Later it turns out that the facility, the company had visited was only a "show off" site, whereas the majority of products were manufactured at other sites not fulfilling the requirements. Actually, 65 percent of companies have limited knowledge of their supply below the factory tier of the supply chain (Blyth, 2020).

The Norwegian telecommunications company Telenor, which is partly own by the Norwegian government, has been very focused on taking a social responsibility. For 12 years, Telenor was rated among the top companies in the telecom sector on the Dow Jones Sustainability list. Yet, several times, unacceptable working conditions have been uncovered among suppliers in Bangladesh, even though the company had worked hard to avoid such incidents.

Often companies withdraw when unacceptable conditions are uncovered among suppliers. However, that might not be the best solution. Intuitively one would expect that children would not want to work and employees in general would not want to work overtime and on weekends. However, for seasonal workers, the main goal is to work as much as possible to earn as much as possible before they travel back to their families. They prefer to work and make money instead of having leisure time far away from their families. This is not only a challenge for seasonal workers in poor countries, carpenters from Poland and nurses from Sweden face the same challenge in Norway. They often want to work overtime but as that adds up to more hours than is allowed per week in Norway, this is not possible.

In the supply chain, social issues, like working conditions, receive most attention. Equally important in the supply chain are environmental challenges. Supply chains are responsible for about 90 percent of companies' environmental impact (Blyth, 2020). Just as it is hard to verify the social issues in the supply chain, it is equally hard to follow the environmental impact in the supply chain. Even though new human rights laws required companies to follow the supply chain and ensure quality with regards to social and environmental issues, acting upon this is a challenge. Goods such as cotton are traded on mercantile exchanges. In such incidents it is impossible to track the bushel of cotton back to the exact cottonfield it was produced.

Workers in low cost countries need knowledge with regard to their rights. Also talking with employees on the production floor, not only the management, gives one a better understanding of the working conditions present at the factory. Finally, companies can also work on providing long-term contracts with the suppliers—and time to plan. A challenge for suppliers is often that buyers want to test out new seasonal products, and, as soon as they learn what customers prefer, they want immediate delivery. That leaves the supplier and its employees in a challenging situation. In order to fulfil the order, unpaid overtime is often required. Just-in-time production, that products are not produced before a buyer contract is signed, is often presented as a good solution from an environmental perspective. It implies less overproduction. On the other side, for seasonal products it often demands large production in short time—and overtime for employees.

Suppliers and especially distribution is crucial with respect to environmental issues. In a linear economy, as addressed in Chap. 6, the process is Take—Make—Waste (Take—Make—Use—Dispose). This is a one-way direction in which products end up as waste. In a circular economy, suppliers can, through Extended Producer Responsibility (EPR), be required to take back or collect products for reuse, repair, refurbish, remake, and so on. This will have a great impact on organizing the supply chain and changing the distribution system.

8.5 Customers

Companies need customers to survive. Customers in general claim to be increasingly concerned about the social and environmental quality of the products they purchase. More than half of the Norwegians say it is important to know where the goods they buy are produced and even more say they want to steer clear of companies that can be linked to human rights violations or unsustainable environmental management. Forty percent claim to have opted out of a product due to suspicion that the product contributes to child labor. But, when it comes to what the customers actually purchase, it is often not the most responsible product—but rather the product with the lowest price (Devinney et al., 2006; Ditlev-Simonsen, 2015).

According to a study investigating purchasing patterns in Norwegian clothing stores, customers hardly ever ask about environmental and social issues related to the products they purchase. Those who did ask were mainly interested in knowing whether parts of the product contained leather or skins—because they were vegetarians. At the same time, some of the employees thought that customers who were interested in environmental and working conditions would check the company's website in advance. Other studies found that some customers do not even want to know about ethical issues at the production stage because if that product does not meet ethical standards; it can result in unpleasant issues for the customer.

Companies have a great responsibility to produce products that are environmentally friendly. However, we as consumers also have a responsibility to choose sustainable products—and not buy too many of these but rather keep and use the products for a longer period. Authorities have a responsibility to make it profitable for companies to behave in a sustainable way—and that we as customers make the right choices.

It is not only the gap between attitude and behavior when it comes to purchasing patterns, but also the volume of shopping that is a problem when it comes to sustainability. Consumption among Norwegians has continuously grown. As addressed in the chapter on the circular economy, Norwegians have on average about 359 garments in their wardrobe. Many of these garments are rarely used and some of them have never been used. To show responsibility, many companies in the clothing industry respond with offers for renting garments as well as offers to repair garments. Nevertheless, so far, the majority of consumers are less interested in taking advantage of these offers, but this is gradually changing in a positive way. For a few companies, such offers have paid off, but for most, it is not profitable and more for posturing. With a change in attitude, this will be a good business in time. Online initiatives to purchase and sell used products, and simple ways to ensure secure payment and transportation have increased reuse of textiles, and are also contributing to developing a more circular culture.

Still, educating people on how to behave more sustainably is important. At finn.no ("find.no"), Norway's largest online trading site for used products, the purchaser can see how much CO_2 was "saved" through purchasing the product used, not new. So far, few people know that how often we clean our clothing and whether or not we use cold or warm water have the second largest CO_2 and water use impact of a pair of jeans, after the fiber production, according to Levi's. So in addition to purchasing more sustainable, it is a lot we can do for the environment in our consumer care of what we have purchased.

8.6 Non-Governmental Organizations

A non-governmental organization (NGO) is a "voluntary group of individuals or organizations, usually not affiliated with any government … formed to provide services or to advocate a public policy" (Karns, n.d.). There are currently thousands of international NGOs. Most are relatively small, but a few are quite large and powerful. These can set sustainability agendas, shape policy, and impact and convince individuals across the world—especially in a world where social media has great power. NGOs are usually nonprofit organizations and many of them work on environmental and social issues. NGOs can be divided into several groups, but in a sustainable setting, these two groups are the most relevant: charitable and service NGOs and participatory and empowering NGOs.

The first, charitable and service NGOs are organizations such as the Red Cross, CARE International, *Médecins Sans Frontières (MSF)*, *BRAC*, and *Oxfam*. Their key activities initially involved collecting money to help others or save the environment. Some of these organizations are invaluable in their work during natural catastrophes and others also help people, plants/biodiversity, and animals in need.

During the last decades, it has become more common for such organizations to collaborate with corporations. A typical type of "collaboration" is one that companies, and employees donate money or products to the organization. But more constructive collaboration is also emerging. The Norwegian Red Cross for instance has several cooperative partners. These range from law firms working pro bono to a consulting company contributing with homework help and developing good IT solutions, construction companies building housing, telecom companies donating free use of mobile broadband as well as financial donations and volunteer work by employees. There has been a shift from pure donation of money to collaboration based on products and competence.

Another type of NGO, that goes beyond helping people in need, is a participatory and empowering NGO. These too can have the purpose of helping others; however, the approach is often different than that of charitable NGOs. Organizations like Amnesty international, Greenpeace and Bellona, World Wide Fund for Nature (WWF), and People for ethical treatment of Animals (PETA) are working more on lobbying, demonstrations, protest, and boycott to draw attention to different issues. Unfair treatment of individuals, unacceptable working conditions, environmental damage caused by corporations are typical issues these participatory and empowering NGOs engage in.

During the last few decades, these organizations have moved from merely criticizing corporations to collaborating with them on solutions. Sometimes it is a challenge to be both a partner and an opponent. Amnesty International for example invites companies to be project partners, supporters, and also to donate money. At the same time, the partner companies might unexpectedly be involved in unacceptable situations associated with social and environmental issues. This will be a challenge for both the NGO and the company. In situations like these, some NGOs choose to cancel the contract, whereas others collaborate with the company to improve the situation.

NGOs have great power to move opinions among individuals as well as governments especially through social media. The following are example illustrates this power.

Lego is a privately own Danish company producing plastic construction toys called Lego. The company was launched around 1950 and the brand as well as the product are well-known across the world. Since around 1960, Lego collaborated with Shell through Shell-branded toys and sold them at Shell gas stations. In 2012, Greenpeace launched the "Save the Arctic" campaign with the goal to stop oil drilling and as Shell was planning to drill in that area, Lego became a target for Greenpeace.

In 2014, Greenpeace launched a campaign against Lego. The argument was that Shell was damaging the future of the children by drilling and producing oil and that Lego supported this by collaborating with Shell. Lego had for a long time been recognized as a respected and responsible company working on energy efficiency and from their use of renewable energy, as well as alternatives to plastic to manufacture the toys. Even though Shell had partnerships and collaborations with several other companies and institutions, Greenpeace chose to focus the attack on Lego which was involved in producing toys for children—the next generation who will experience the negative consequences of global warming.

Greenpeace set up a campaign calling Lego to drop its collaboration with Shell. The NGO produced the two-minute film "Everything is not awesome". In the film, Greenpeace used Lego blocks to depict a Shell team drilling in the Arctic. Gradually, in the film, oil was covering the land and killing people and animals including polar bears. In the background, there is a sad song. This film is still available on YouTube and seen by almost nine million people. This way of portraying Lego and the resulting public awareness was very negative for the Lego brand. As a result, Lego eventually ended its partnership with Shell.

Most collaborations with NGOs and corporations have a positive effect. Whereas donations of money or products were the most common approach previously, partnership and collaboration are becoming more common. This type of collaboration can have a very positive effect for companies, the organizations, and society. This, however, requires a well-planned and organized cooperation.

How to Develop a Constructive Win-Win(-win) Partnership with a NGO?

Collaboration between companies and NGOs must be anchored in a good strategy—along the lines of business in general. Previously, the relationship between companies and NGOs was characterized by philanthropy and donations. It was usually based on private initiatives with little focus on measuring impact and results. Oftentimes, NGOs were selected based on managerial preferences.

A partnership ought to start from the point where the company reviews it business and identifies NGOs that are relevant to the company's area of business. For a company involved in production in low cost countries,

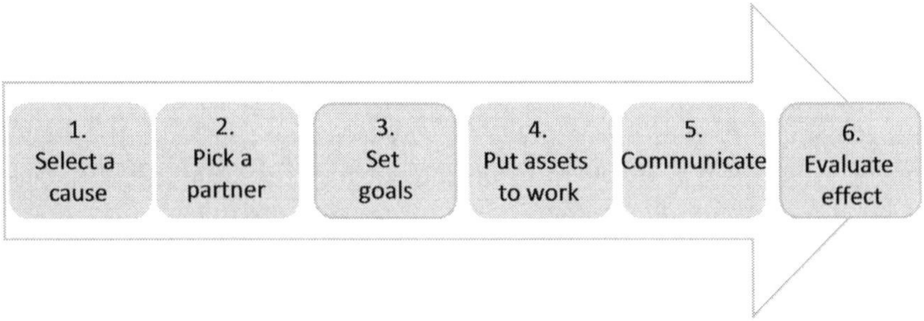

Fig. 8.3 The revised model of NGO interaction (Ditlev-Simonsen, 2017)

supporting schools for children in the same area could be relevant collaboration with local NGOs. For service companies in big cities, job-training and internship programs for youth struggling with drugs can be an alternative example. Today, some companies actually invite NGOs to submit suggestions on how to collaborate and they choose the ones with the best and most constructive ideas.

After the partner is selected, the company and the NGO have to agree on the goals and metrics of the partnership are and how to reach them. For example, how many children are to attend school as a result of the project, how to evaluate what they learned, how many of the youth struggling with drugs managed to get a job, and so on. As the projects start, the partners have to communicate and share. Finally, the result of the collaboration needs to be evaluated. Did the project reach the goals? Evaluating the results is a valuable process with useful knowledge for further partnership. The collaboration model is presented in Fig. 8.3.

How Corporations Collaborate with Different Stakeholders: Some Examples

For large companies, it is common today to report on which stakeholders the company focuses on and how it engages with them. On the horizontal line, the company reveals how it communicates with these stakeholders. H&M identifies the following ten stakeholders: customer, colleagues, communities, business partners, supply chain, industry peers, policy-makers, NGOs, academia and science, and investors. The engagement is based on both formal and informal communication. Surveys in different formats are used to collect information. In this way, the company can get a broader understanding of stakeholders' concern. Issues like supply chain working conditions, environmental impact, peaceful conflict resolutions, product labeling and sustainability disclosures, microfibers and microplastics, and circular innovations are issues H&M are working on with different stakeholders.

Huawei identifies customers and consumers, employees, suppliers, governments, NGOs, media and communities as key stakeholders. Huawei claims that working with stakeholders is an integral part of the company's sustainability work. In the matrix, presenting their stakeholder engagement, key concerns, communication channels, and Huawei strategy is presented. Also, here surveys, dialogue, training, participation at events, disclosure, and transparency are key issues through different platforms.

For Coca-Cola partnering for success is their approach to stakeholder engagement. Key stakeholder engagements presented are related to bottling partners, suppliers, consumers, and customers. Some examples of engagement include partnerships are directed to finding innovative ways to reduce packaging and waste and recycling education for communities.

Philip Morris International had grouped their 31 identified stakeholders into ten groups: adult consumers, employees, regulators, public health community, supply chain, retailers and wholesalers, business community, civil society, financial community and media. Means of engagement range from dialogue, surveys, training, formal gatherings, regular or ad hoc visits, hotline to call centers.

Listing stakeholders and forms of communication is common practice, but some companies take it a step further, to provide concrete results of their interaction. IKEA for example, pinpoints the important input they get through dialogue with stakeholders and how crucial the input from NGOs is for the company to make the right decisions. The World Wide Fund for Nature (WWF) is for example perceived as a key stakeholder and partner. The result of this collaboration includes among others a reduction of pesticide usage from almost 40 percent of their suppliers, reduction of water use by 37 percent, and an increase of gross margins of 24 percent (IKEA, 2021). The WWF can also be a critical organization. So, by establishing a positive working relationship early on helps IKEA avoid criticism from the WWF in the future.

8.7 Other Stakeholder: Journalists, Social Media, Researchers, and More

Finally, media is also a key stakeholder for companies. Often companies issue press releases on their positive sustainable behavior, but media is more interested in being critical and publishing negative coverage. There are many instances in which investigative journalists have uncovered breaches of laws and regulations.

The International Consortium of Investigative Journalists for example has uncovered several cases which have led to major changes in ways of doing business. Two examples include Walmart using widespread bribery to dominate the market in Mexico (Meyersohn, 2019; The Pulitzer Prizes, 2013) and the Paradise Papers in which the bank DNB facilitated tax evasion which led to the recovery of $ 1.3 billion (McGoey, 2021).

Also, filmmakers produce documentaries uncovering and exposing unacceptable conditions. Heather White's *Complicit* is a good example. The film shares the story of a Chinese migrant worker's effort to eliminate life-threatening benzene from workplaces producing smartphones practices. More mainstream documentaries such as *Super Size Me* explore how unhealthy McDonald's food can be and also uncover the negative impact of corporations (Spurlock, 2004). Still, not all journalists and filmmakers do thorough research and the cases presented are not always portrayed in a balanced way. Cases involving negative issues can be blown out of proportion and often these cases become quite popular with readers. In this regard, researchers and academic institutions have a great responsibility in providing objective analysis. Many cases have also been uncovered through research which has led to positive changes.

Corporate initiatives to fight COVID-19

The following examples of how companies responded to face COVID-19 challenges illustrate that companies are taking creative and constructive societal responsibility.

When COVID-19 was declared a pandemic in March of 2020, initially companies' main focus was on their own employees—how to ensure they did not get ill, and then to ensure financial security. Then the focus shifted, more than half of the world's population was under some form of lockdown, which impacted virtually every part of the economy and way of life. Companies have also donated large sums to help develop medicines and care for people in different ways. Many companies have also come up with creative positive initiatives illustrating social responsibility. Below are some examples:

Several companies, like **Coca Cola, Hermes, and a Gin Producer,** pivot factories to produce hand sanitizer.

Ventilux—emergency lighting specialist quickly launched temperature scanner, which can capture data in busy places such as shopping malls, hospitals, venues, and so on even wearing hats and masks.

Ford Motor Company—partnered with the United Auto Workers, GE Healthcare, and 3M lent manufacturing and engineering expertise to help build respirators and ventilators, assemble face shields, and use its 3D printing capacity to produce parts used in other personal protective equipment.

Coca Cola, McDonald's, Audi, and **VW** temporarily changed their logos to promote social distancing.

Scania—heavy truck maker, partnered with Karolinska University Hospital and is converting trailers into mobile testing stations and directed some 20 highly skilled purchasing and logistics experts to locate, acquire, and deliver personal protective equipment to health care workers.

Cozy—a restaurant in Vilnius, Lithuania placed of mannequins on seats, helping to ensure customer distancing while making the restaurant seem busy. The mannequins were dressed by local designers to advertise their clothing lines.

DAKA—Tyrol, Austria based waste-disposal company, repurposed snow cannons for disinfecting large areas like train stations or production halls.

Uber—expanded the services on offer and is now delivering products such as medication.

Doctolib—French tech company that develops appointment-scheduling software, offered free-of-charge service to French and German doctors, leading to 2.5 million online appointments.

Nike—when stores closed, staff engaged with Chinese consumers digitally by offering at-home workouts.

EasyJet and Virgin Atlantic—staff members were offered jobs in temporary NHS Nightingale hospitals.

McDonalds—in Germany created an employee-leasing agreement with Aldi grocery stores to help with surging demand, while the restaurant was closed.

References

Achor, S., Reece, A., Kellerman, G. R., & Robichaux, A. (2018). 9 out of 10 people are willing to earn less money to do more-meaningful work. *Harvard Business Review Digital Articles,* 1–7. https://hbr.org/2018/11/9-out-of-10-people-are-willing-to-earn-less-money-to-do-more-meaningful-work

Bergin, T. (2012, October 15). Special Report: How Starbucks avoids UK taxes. *Reuters.* https://www.reuters.com/article/us-britain-starbucks-tax-idUKBRE89E0EX20121015

Blyth, N. (2020). Sustainable development goals and the business community. *DailyFT.* http://www.ft.lk/opinion/Sustainable-development-goals-and-the-business-community/14-695549

Business Roundtable. (n.d.). *One year later: Purpose of a corporation.* https://purpose.businessroundtable.org/

Coady, D., Parry, I. W. H., Sears, L., & Shang, B. (2015). *How large are global energy subsidies?* IMF Working Paper, 15 (105). https://www.imf.org/external/pubs/ft/wp/2015/wp15105.pdf

Deloitte. (2019). The Deloitte global millennial survey 2019. https://www2.deloitte.com/content/dam/Deloitte/global/Documents/About-Deloitte/deloitte-2019-millennial-survey.pdf

Devinney, T. M., Auger, P., Eckhardt, G., & Birtchnell, T. (2006, Fall). The other CSR: Consumer social responsibility. *Stanford Social Innovation Review.* https://doi.org/10.2139/ssrn.901863

Ditlev-Simonsen, C. D. (2009). Fordrer det noe spesielt å lede en samfunnsansvarlig bedrift. *Magma, 2,* 22–33.

Ditlev-Simonsen, C. D. (2012). The relationship between Norwegian and Swedish employees' perception of corporate social responsibility and affective commitment. *Business & Society, 54*(2), 229–253. https://doi.org/10.1177/0007650312439534

Ditlev-Simonsen, C. D. (2015). The gap between attitude and behavior in environmental protection—the case of Norway. In P. E. Stoknes & K. A. Eliassen (Eds.), *Science based activism.* Fagbokforlaget.

Ditlev-Simonsen, C. D. (2017). Beyond sponsorship—exploring the impact of cooperation between corporations and NGOs. *International Journal of Corporate Social Responsibility, 2*(6). https://doi.org/10.1186/s40991-017-0017-9

IKEA. (2021). *IKEA culture and values.* https://about.ikea.com/en/about-us/ikea-culture-and-values

Karns, M. P. (n.d.). Nongovernmental organization. *Encyclopædia Britannica.* https://www.britannica.com/topic/nongovernmental-organization
Kershaw, S. (2005). Microsoft comes under fire for reversal on gay rights bill. *The New York Times.* https://www.nytimes.com/2005/04/22/us/microsoft-comes-under-fire-for-reversal-on-gay-rights-bill.html
Kraft, A. G., Vashishtha, R., & Venkatachalam, M. (2018). Frequent financial reporting and managerial Myopia. *The Accounting Review, 93*(2), 249–275. https://doi.org/10.2308/accr-51838
McGoey, S. (2021). Panama papers revenue recovery reaches $1.36 billion as investigations continue. *ICIJ International Consortium of Investigative Journalists.* https://www.icij.org/investigations/panama-papers/panama-papers-revenue-recovery-reaches-1-36-billion-as-investigations-continue/
Meyersohn, N. (2019). Walmart settles with US government over international bribery. *CNN.* https://edition.cnn.com/2019/06/20/business/walmart-bribery-mexico-brazil-fcpa-sec
Prather, C. W., & Turrell, M. C. (2002). Managers at work: Involve everyone in the innovation process. *Research-Technology Management, 45*(5), 13–16.
Shindell, D. T. (2015). The social cost of atmospheric release. *Climatic Change, 130*(2), 313–326.
Spraul, K., & Thaler, J. (2019). Partnering for good? An analysis of how to achieve sustainability-related outcomes in public–private partnerships. *Business Research, 13*, 1–27.
Spurlock, M. (2004). *Super Size Me* [Film]. https://www.imdb.com/title/tt0390521/
The Pulitzer Prizes. (2013). The 2013 Pulitzer prize winner in investigative reporting: David Barstow and Alejandra Xanic von Bertrab of The New York Times. https://www.pulitzer.org/winners/david-barstow-and-alejandra-xanic-von-bertrab
The World Bank. (n.d.). Imports of goods and services (% of GDP): 1960–2019. https://data.worldbank.org/indicator/NE.IMP.GNFS.ZS
Trove Research. (2021). Ten-fold increase in carbon offset cost predicted, UCL web June 4th, 2021 https://www.ucl.ac.uk/news/2021/jun/ten-fold-increase-carbon-offset-cost-predicted
Whelan, T., & Douglas, E. (2021). How to talk to your CFO about sustainability. *Harvard Business Review, 99*(1), 86–93.

9

Sustainability and Finance: Environment, Social, and Governance (ESG)

In the last few years, the focus on Environment, Social, and Governance (ESG) investment and socially responsible investment (SRI) has "exploded". How and to which extent investment criteria are taking into account are relevant for sustainable development.

Even though terms like ESG, SRI, and ethical investment seem new, some of the first examples of socially responsible investment can be traced back to the 1760s, when Quakers, a Christian community, decided not to invest money in companies which made products using slave labor. Later, companies involved in issues associated with unacceptable civil- and women' rights and political issues have been excluded from investments by concerned citizens. This type of exclusion has been sporadic, and many based on individual beliefs. Over the past 20 years, ESG has attracted more attention as a way to reduce risk and detect new business opportunities. Also, the fact that the world's largest sovereign wealth fund, Norway's Government Pension Fund Global, introduced Ethical guidelines further increased the awareness and interest in ESG, SRI, and ethical investment. Recognizing the critical role and responsibility of investors in the pursuit of sustainable development, the UN initiative Principles for Responsible Investment (PRI) was launched in 2006. The PRI is an international network of more than 1700 signatory investors

C. D. Ditlev-Simonsen, *A Guide to Sustainable Corporate Responsibility*,
https://doi.org/10.1007/978-3-030-88203-7_9

representing clients that control more than half of the world's wealth. The first of the six PRI principles illustrates the commitment required of its signatories to be part of this network: "We will incorporate ESG issues into investment analysis and decision-making processes".

Investors commitment to the ESG is reflected in the growth of investor sustainability strategies. In 2012, only one of nine dollars under professional management in the United States had some form of sustainable investment strategy. This number increased to one out of every six dollars in 2014, and in 2018, one out of four dollars under professional management had some sort of responsible investment strategy. In 2020 one in three dollars (33 percent) of the total US assets under professional management use sustainable investing strategies (US SIF: The Forum for Sustainable and Responsible Investment, 2020).

In 2021, the Net-Zero Banking Alliance was established representing over 40 percent of global banking assets. These financial institutions are now committed to aligning their lending and investment portfolios with net-zero emissions by 2050. Given the need for financing that is required to realize the SDGs, such initiatives from the investment sector are crucial. In this chapter, I will address what ESG, SRI, and ethical investments are about, as well as different investment strategies taking these into account. Further dilemmas that arise will be introduced, such as: What is a sustainable sector or product and how this varies depending on peoples' values. The switch from addressing sustainability issues as a risk reduction activity to a business opportunity will also be discussed. Finally, the Norwegian Pension Fund will be used as an example with regards to product-based and conduct-based exclusion.

9.1 Environmental, Social, and Governance (ESG)

Traditional financial analysis has always taken into account a variety of factors, like revenues, liabilities, cash, inventory machinery competitors, and so on. ESG are additional factors that can be included in the evaluation. The goal of including these additional factors can be to reduce risk and or improve financial results.

Typical issues related to the "E" Environmental are energy consumption, pollution, climate change, waste generated, water scarcity, biodiversity, and deforestation

Typical issues related to the "S" Social are child- and forced labor, human rights, community engagement, stakeholder relations, health and safety, employee engagement, customer satisfaction, gender and diversity policies.

Regarding the "G" Governance, the quality of the board and management as well as executive and board compensations, transparency and disclosure, audit, lobbying, political contribution are some examples of content.

Data generated to evaluate the level of corporate performance on the E, S, and G is collected from annual reports, company website, NGO website, stock exchange, Corporate Social Responsibility (CSR)/sustainability reports, new sources/media as well as surveys and interviews.

There are several ESG data providers, Morningstar, Bloomberg, Sustainalytics, and Morgen Stanley Capital International (MSCI). These data providers collect and evaluate the data. Up to 450 ESG data points can be collected. A data point can be for example a type of energy used, level of emissions, waste types generated, volume, production sites, and so on. As data points can be measured in different ways, results will also differ.

A typical approach to calculate an overall ESG score begins by collecting datapoints on corporate sector and operations, and then these are divided into different categories of ESG scores, which are weighted according to own evaluations. Finally, the ESG overall score is provided. This can be presented in the form of letters from AAA for companies and funds with the best ESG performance/score to CCC with companies with the relatively worst ESG performance. The following are some examples of ESG data providers. These companies have traditionally provided company information on financial performance and have since expanded their operations to also cover ESG data.

MSCI (Morgen Stanley Capital International) has more than 150 ESG analysists studying companies' performance. Media coverage, NGO reports, research, and the companies' own sustainability and CSR reporting are sources of data collection (Dieschbourg & Nussbaum, 2017).

Bloomberg's database covers more than 11,000 companies and their ESG data is based on MSCI data as well as other data collecting services (Bloomberg Professional Services, n.d.)

Morningstar has more than 400 global employees colleting and processing company data (Schmelzer, 2020). In addition to data from publicly available information, interviews are also conducted to collect information.

Whereas companies like MSCI, Bloomberg, and Morningstar have a long history of providing data for company analysis and have expanded to also provide ESG data, **RobecoSAM** was founded in 1995 with the purpose of assisting in the process of sustainable investment. To collect ESG data, RobecoSAM mainly uses a questionnaire. Collecting data and answering around 100 questions, which is later evaluated by RobecoSAM, required lots of work for a company. The Dow Jones Sustainability Index (DJSI) RobecoSAM annually publishes a list of best-in-class sustainability benchmarks with the top 10 percent of companies in each sector based on data from RobecoSAM.

The value of the different scores of different companies is only as good as the data on which it is based. If the data put in the analysis is not trustworthy, the outcome or the rating is not trustworthy either. There have been several examples of companies that have been on the top the DJSI list and suddenly were removed when it turned out that the data used to analyze the company was incorrect. Volkswagen for example had a great score on all the above ratings, however, when it turned out that the company had been tampering emission technology to convey better performance, making the point that that ESG scores are not necessarily right. Same with the palm oil giant Golden Agri-Resources, which was also removed from the DJSI after a bribery and corruption scandal in 2018.

Rating providers use different quantitative metrics and weight the results differently. This has led to a variety of results. One company is scored high by one rating company and low by another. It turns out that the correlation between ESG ratings from the six leading ESG providers was 0.61 (Mayor, 2019). This makes it hard for investors to evaluate a company's ESG profile. That combined with the fact that more and more funds have started to name themselves "Green funds" have made investors skeptical. The reputation of such green funds has begun to fringe, and the term "greenwashing" employed when referring to such funds. Greenwashing is about conveying a false impression that the company is taking the right environmental measures when in fact the company is deceiving the investors and customers. When claiming to provide "green products," the claim has to be supported with facts and figures. This lack of clarity of what is green and what is not is partly the motivation for the development of the EU Taxonomy, a regulation intended to help stakeholders evaluate more objectively to which extent a company is environmentally sustainable or not and to make it easier for companies to report.

9.2 The EU Taxonomy

Given the increasing interest in ESG and "Green funds", it is no wonder that in the last few years we have seen a significant growth in the share of green funds—many renamed as green without any actual changes in companies which consist the funds. It is evident there are many ways to categorize what a sustainable company is, and it is a challenge to understand how the ratings are calculated. Partly as result of this, the EU Taxonomy was launched in 2019.

The EU Taxonomy is part of the plan to finance sustainable growth. Financing sustainable growth is a key element in the European Green Deal. The EU Green Deal, launched in 2019, is a strategy and plan to make EU the first climate-neutral continent by 2050. More investment in climate neutral, energy- and resource-efficient, and circular projects is needed. It is estimated that an additional annual investment of 175 to 290 billion EUR will be needed to reach the climate-neutral goal (European Commission, n.d.-c). The EU Taxonomy provides a common framework for assessing whether or not investments are sustainable and supporting the Green Deal. Such a common framework will help investors to objectively compare corporate performance in the field of sustainability, saving time and money for both companies and investors.

The EU Taxonomy is part of the Sustainable Finance Action Plan (SFAP), a major policy objective by the EU to promote sustainable investment. There are six environmental objectives of the Taxonomy and in order to qualify as "green" the investment needs to contribute to at least one of these objectives and do no significant harm on any of the other:

1. Climate change mitigation
2. Climate change adaptation
3. The sustainable use and protection of water and marine resources
4. The transition to a circular economy
5. Pollution prevention and control
6. The protection and restoration of biodiversity and ecosystems (European Commission, n.d.-a)

The Taxonomy is focused on the industries which are the main contributors to climate gas emissions and/or high-emitting sectors: agriculture and forestry, manufacturing, energy, water, transport, information and communications technology (ICT), and buildings.

The Taxonomy is not rating companies as such but provides investors a list of relevant criteria to evaluate companies. This makes it easier to compare companies in terms of sustainability. The Taxonomy is dynamic and will adapt to new knowledge from for example science and experience.

The following is a practical example of how the Taxonomy can contribute to raising capital. A company in the oil and gas industry wants to raise capital to diversify into alternative and renewable energy, like wind power. Since this contributes to climate change mitigation and even a potential reduction in oil production, this fulfils the criteria for issuing an EU Green Bond.

There are several short and practical how-to-do guides for the EU Taxonomy, for example the FAQ-What is the EU Taxonomy and how will it work in practice? (European Commission, n.d.-b). The Taxonomy Technical Report (EU Technical Expert Group on Sustainable Finance, 2019) which consists of several hundred pages can be used as a reference, where each company can assess whether or not their products and services are compatible with and in line with the goals of the Paris Agreement.

9.3 To Which Extent Does Focus on Sustainability and Applying the "Right" ESG Impact Profit?

Traditionally, focus on ESG has either been based on personal value or risk reduction. Supply chains today are vulnerable to natural disasters, climate change, water scarcity, and poor labor conditions and thus represent a risk. A majority of suppliers claim that climate change represents risk which could have a significant negative impact on their operations and earnings.

Hundreds of studies have been conducted to see if it pays off financially to include ESG either to reduce risk or increase turnover and profit. Not surprisingly, this analysis depends on the ESG criteria. What is found, however, is that companies that focus on relevant sustainability issues outperform firms with poor ratings (Khan et al., 2016). And the other way around. That is, if a company involved in the oil and gas industry focuses its sustainability engagement on donating money to poor children in Africa, this is good for society, but not for profit. If the same company focuses its sustainability work on reducing CO_2 emissions, that is on materiality issues, the company is more likely to outperform companies involved in non-materiality issues. According to a review of over 2000 empirical studies, including review studies, 90 percent of the studies found a nonnegative ESG-CFP (Corporate Financial Performance) and a large majority of these studies report positive findings (Friede et al., 2015).

There are many examples of negative impact on share price after incidents of corporate irresponsible behavior. Volkswagen tampering with the emission technology led to a significant drop in the shareholder price as was the case with BP after the Deep Horizon disaster. The price of shares in the coal industry furthermore dropped after that Paris agreement was announced.

9.4 SRI Strategies

As is evident from Fig. 9.1, there are different avenues to act on socially responsible investment (SRI) in funds. The most common approach to SRI/ESG funds is, as illustrated in Fig. 9.2, to exclude certain sectors. In the next section, I will address different criteria for exclusion and which ones are most commonly applied. But first, a short review of the different approaches.

The Best-in class approach, or positive screening, is to choose the companies which are the best on ESG performance relative to other industries in the same sector.

Norm-base screening is about selecting companies that perform in accordance with key sustainability standards, such as the UN Global Compact, OECD Guidelines, ILO (International Labor Organization), or the UN sustainable development goals (SDGs).

ESG Integrating in the company investment analysis is conducted either to reduce risk or increase results—or a combination of both. Companies are evaluated based on different ESG factors, and the

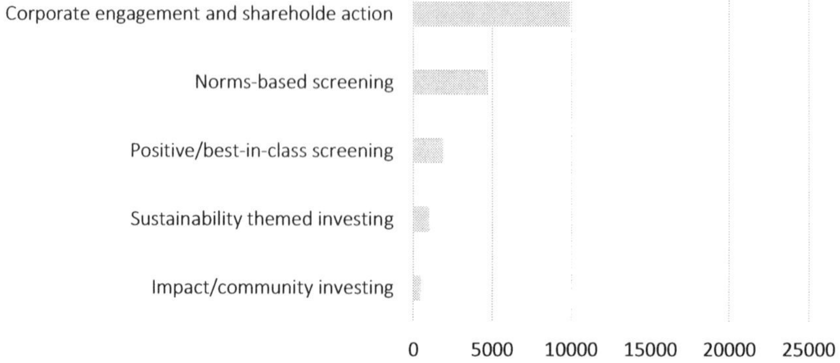

Fig. 9.1 Responsible investment strategies Eurosif

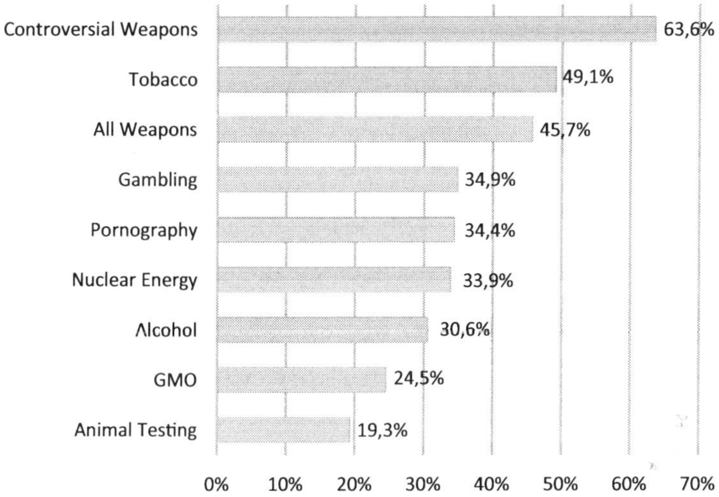

Fig. 9.2 Top exclusion criteria Eurosif

outcome is, as discussed above, dependent upon which ESG elements are selected and how they are weighted. Some of the ESG elements have more impact on returns than others. For example, gender equality in top management might have less of an impact on returns than the degree of CO_2 emissions relative to other companies in the same sector.

Engagement and voting are the second most common approaches to responsible investment. This is a long-term process in which investors try to move the company toward a more sustainable way of doing business by using its shareholder voting rights. However, in order to capture these rights, one has to be a shareholder. By excluding certain sectors and companies, the investor loses the voting rights in these companies. By keeping the shares, the investors potentially have a much stronger impact on the company. Sometimes NGOs which are opposed to certain sectors, go in and purchase shares in these companies in order to vote in shareholder meetings. In many cases, investors can have a much stronger impact on sustainable development by pushing "bad" companies in the right direction as opposed to excluding the same companies from their portfolios.

The most common strategy for responsible investment is however the exclusion strategy. The challenge, however, is that there are very many different understandings of what sectors or companies are responsible, and should be excluded, and which are not.

Figure 9.2 gives an overview of which sectors are the most common to exclude. And, as evident from the bottom of the figure, Controversial Weapons, that is, nuclear, chemical, and biological weapons and cluster bombs, are the most common industries to exclude.

The second most common industry to exclude is tobacco followed by All Weapons, or weapons in general, Gambling, Pornography, Nuclear Energy, Alcohol, and GMO (genetically modified organisms), and products which are developed using Animal testing. These are the collected rating of exclusion criteria. However, there are individual and cultural differences for opinions on what to exclude.

In a study at BI Norwegian Business School, we asked master's students what would be their main exclusion criteria if they were to choose for their own personal pension portfolios. For them controversial weapons, the most common exclusion criterion in Europe, was on the top of the list. However, the order of the priority list was quite different from what is the trend in Europe in general. For the students in Norway, animal testing is positioned at second place, whereas tobacco is in the second place across Europe. The students were least likely to exclude alcohol from their investment universe. Tobacco, which is a very typical exclusion criterion, was also not so important to exclude. Comparing the list of exclusion criteria in Europe in general to the list drafted by students in Norway illustrates the variation in values and preferences. This is closely related to culture.

9.5 Investors' Dilemma: What Is a Sustainable and Responsible Company?

One thing is a personal belief of whether or not investing in alcohol or tobacco is responsible. Another issue is how to invest to solve more general societal challenges in sustainability. Society's main challenges are CO_2 emissions and global warming. Industry is working to find alternatives to coal and other fossil fuels as energy sources. Wind power is such an alternative. However, even though people in general are positive with regards to wind power, nobody wants to have “it in their backyard”.

There are many examples of how Norway’s public opposition to onshore wind has threatened the growth wind power generation. The opposition has become so hostile that demonstrators set fire to excavators. The Norwegian Minister of Energy has furthermore been harassed on social media and accused of being a traitor, who should be in jail for supporting building wind power installations in Norway (Taraldsen et al., 2020).

Another industry in which people disagree whether it is sustainable or not is nuclear energy. The nuclear energy generation does not emit any negative climate gases. However, the main challenge in this sector is the accumulation of dangerous waste byproducts and the risk of meltdown. And again, people disagree on the solution. As we see from Fig. 9.2, nuclear energy is one of the most common sectors to exclude from responsible funds. At the same time, Bill Gates, the founder of Microsoft, who is known to be very concerned about environmental issues, and especially global warming, supports nuclear energy as part of the energy solution (Gardner, 2020).

9.6 The Norwegian Pension Fund

Norway’s oil fund, or the Government Pension Fund Global, is based on income from the oil discovered in the North Sea in 1969. This is one of the world’s largest fund with a market value of about 10 trillion NOK (1.3 trillion USD in 2021)—or about two million NOK per each Norwegian citizen. The fund’s portfolio includes about 9000 companies in 74 countries and it considers “environmental and social issues, and publish clear expectations of the companies we invest in” (Norges Bank Investment Management, 2019). In 2004, the fund’s Council on Ethics was established and over the years different criteria for investment have been implemented. The fund has been a frontrunner for taking ethics and sustainability into account and therefore it is a good example to use in illustrating how ESG criteria are applied in practice. As of March 2021, 144 companies are excluded from the fund.

The fund has two major exclusion criteria: product-based and conduct-based.

Product-based exclusion is when companies producing certain types of products are excluded. Conduct-based exclusion is based on a company's behavior, that is, the product can be acceptable, but the conditions under which they are being manufactured are not. Environmental damage and poor working conditions are typical examples of conduct-based exclusions.

Criteria for product-based observation and exclusion of companies (Norges Bank Investment Management, 2016)

(1) The Fund shall not be invested in companies which themselves or through entities they control:

   (a) produce weapons that violate fundamental humanitarian principles through their normal use
   (b) produce tobacco
   (c) sell weapons or military material to states that are subject to investment restrictions on government bonds as described in the management mandate for the Fund, section 3-1(2)(c).

(2) Observation or exclusion may be decided for mining companies and power producers which themselves or through entities they control derive 30 percent or more of their income from thermal coal or base 30 percent or more of their operations on thermal coal.
(3) In assessments pursuant to subsection (2) above, in addition to the company's current share of income or activity from thermal coal, importance shall also be attached to forward-looking assessments, including any plans the company may have that will change the share of its business based on thermal coal and the share of its business based on renewable energy sources.
(4) Recommendations and decisions on exclusion of companies based on subsections (2) and (3) above shall not include a company's green bonds where such are recognized through inclusion in specific indices for green bonds or are verified by a recognized third party.

There are several sectors which are excluded, but I will only focus on a few of them as examples. The first is weapons that violate fundamental human rights, in line with controversial weapons. This exclusion pertains mostly to nuclear weapons, but also to companies manufacturing chemical and biological weapons and cluster bombs.

Lockheed Martin Corp was for example excluded in 2013 due to its production of key components for nuclear weapons. The company claimed that it was producing “defense weapons”. Another example is in the tobacco industry. Philip Morris International Inc. was excluded from the fund in 2010 for its production of tobacco. The third example involves companies which derive more than 30 percent of its income from thermal coal. So, if 25 percent of the company’s income is based on coal, it is ok, but if more than 30 percent of its income, the company is excluded. Korea Electric Power Corp is an example of exclusion based on production of coal or coal based in energy. The company was excluded from the fund in 2017.

The following are the criteria for conduct-based observation and exclusion of companies.

Companies may be put under observation or be excluded if there is an unacceptable risk that the company contributes to or is responsible for:

(a) serious or systematic human rights violations, such as murder, torture, deprivation of liberty, forced labor and the worst forms of child labor
(b) serious violations of the rights of individuals in situations of war or conflict
(c) severe environmental damage
(d) acts or omissions that on an aggregate company level lead to unacceptable greenhouse gas emissions
(e) gross corruption
(f) other particularly serious violations of fundamental ethical norms.

Examples of companies excluded based on the above criteria include African Israel Investment Ltd (2014), which was excluded due to serious violations of individuals’ rights in situations of war or conflicts associated with the company's involvement in building settlements in the West Bank. The Luthai Textile exclusion is based on poor conduct, among other serious violations of human rights, poor working conditions, harassment, restricted access to toilet facilities. This large Chinese company is actually breaking international laws. The company has customers concerned about quality and responsibility in their supply chain, and it can therefore be very negative for Luthai's business and brand to be excluded from the pension fund.

Companies which have been excluded based on non-acceptable conduct can be reintroduced into the fund again if they improve their behavior. And many companies which have been excluded based on conduct, work hard to improve to be included in the fund again. It is not good for the reputation of the company to be excluded from the Norwegian pension fund—even though not all companies agree on the reason for why they are being excluded.

On the fund's website, there is an overview of companies that are excluded or under observation with explanations. It can seem like a paradox when the Norwegian pension fund excludes tobacco, yet cigarettes are sold in food stores across the country. Furthermore, Airbus is a typical commercial aircraft excluded from the fund due to production of nuclear weapons. Yet both Norwegians in general, as well as government officials travel around in aircrafts produced by Airbus.

As mentioned, whether or not a responsible investment strategy renders more or less return depends upon the criteria applied. For many years excluding tobacco led to reduced returns for fund. In one study, we asked a group of 500 people in Norway, a representative sample of the population; "In your own pension fund management, would you choose ethical investment if it means that your pension would be reduced?" 40 percent answered yes and 32 percent answered no. This implies that Norwegians are not all that ethical if it implies reduced earnings. In another group of 500 people, we asked what they thought about Norwegians in general: "In their own pension fund management, do you think most people would choose ethical investment if it means that their own pension will be reduced?" 20 percent answered yes and 56 percent answered no. So, the conclusion is: Norwegians in general prioritize to "earn" more pension, relative to taking ethics and responsibility into account if it decreases earnings. And we also think we are more ethical and responsible than other people around us (Ditlev-Simonsen & Wenstøp, 2016)

9.7 The Effect of Sustainable Investment Focus in a Long-term Perspective

From being something mainly of interest to environmentalists and church funds, sustainable finance has become an issue engaging investors and fund managers across the world. This surge in institutional demand and interest for green funds motivates companies to pay attention. If a company is required to report on how it deals with environmental and social issues in order to get access to finance, sustainability issues suddenly become much more relevant and of interest. Investor demand is an important driver for companies to work on sustainability in a more strategic manner.

Having witnessed how poor environmental performance has a negative impact on share price, referring to the Volkswagen case (Chap. 5), the BP Deep Horizon spill which led to a share price loss of 54 percent (Pistilli, 2021), and the decline in coal companies' valuations as renewable energy companies share value increased after the launch of the Paris agreement (Kar-Gupta et al., 2015). But taking sustainability into account is no longer only driven by risk reduction. A lower cost of capital and increased return on investment through sustainable products such as alternative energy, are other effects of a sustainable business model. These are a few of the many examples illustrating that companies have to focus on sustainable business, and also that it can be profitable if done in the right way.

The Value Driven Model presented in Fig. 9.3, is a practical tool developed by the PRI and UNGC that sums up key areas of growth, productivity, and management in which applying sustainability can increase returns on capital.

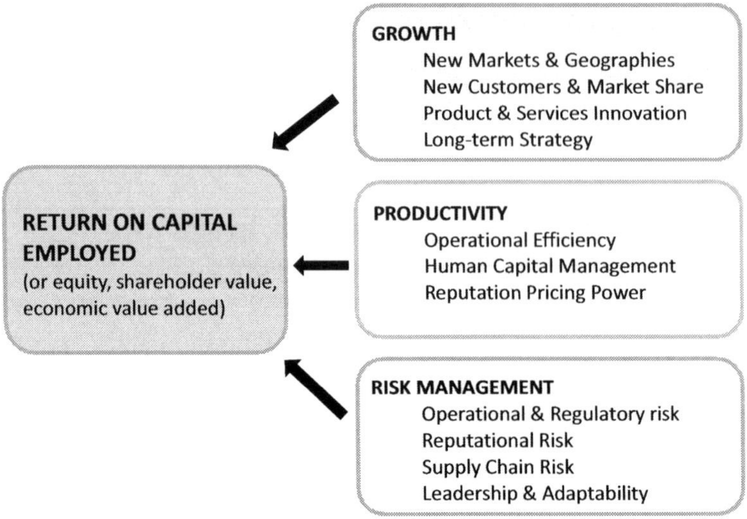

Fig. 9.3 The UN Global Compact and Principles for Responsible Investment (PRI) value driver model

References

Bloomberg Professional Services. (n.d.). Sustainable finance. *Bloomberg Professional Services*. https://www.bloomberg.com/professional/solution/sustainable-finance/?gclid=Cj0KCQjwhr2FBhDbARIsACjwLo2mRzuHPuTxpfY9WBNFF9YL6_p7G-qDvwAUNCipzqv8Hb-HtTiBKWwaAriZEALw_wcB#scores/?utm_medium=Adwords&utm_campaign=ESG&utm_source=pdsrch&utm_content=esgscores&tactic=342352

Dieschbourg, M. T., & Nussbaum, A. P. (2017). No places to hide thanks to Morningstar, Bloomberg, MSCI and Multiple global data providers. *Investments & Wealth Monitor*. https://investmentsandwealth.org/getattachment/fdf4d0e3-adc0-487a-bbe0-624cdefb3b2f/IWM17NovDec-

Ditlev-Simonsen, C. D., & Wenstøp, F. (2016). Attitudes towards ethical pension management among Norwegians. *Beta (Oslo, Norway), 30*(2), 100–118. https://doi.org/10.18261/issn.1504-3134-2016-02-01

EU Technical Expert Group on Sustainable Finance. (2019). *Taxonomy technical report*. https://ec.europa.eu/info/sites/default/files/business_economy_euro/banking_and_finance/documents/190618-sustainable-finance-teg-report-taxonomy_en.pdf

European Commission. (n.d.-a). *EU taxonomy for sustainable activities*. https://ec.europa.eu/info/business-economy-euro/banking-and-finance/sustainable-finance/eu-taxonomy-sustainable-activities_en

European Commission. (n.d.-b). *FAQ: What is the EU taxonomy and how will it work in practice?* https://ec.europa.eu/info/sites/default/files/business_economy_euro/banking_and_finance/documents/sustainable-finance-taxonomy-faq_en.pdf

European Commission. (n.d.-c). *Financing sustainable growth—factsheet*. https://ec.europa.eu/info/sites/default/files/business_economy_euro/banking_and_finance/documents/200108-financing-sustainable-growth-factsheet_en.pdf

Eurosif. (2018). *European SRI study 2018*.

Friede, G., Busch, T., & Bassen, A. (2015). ESG and financial performance: Aggregated evidence from more than 2000 empirical studies. *Journal of Sustainable Finance & Investment, 5*(4), 210–233. https://doi.org/10.1080/20430795.2015.1118917

Gardner, T. (2020). Bill Gates' nuclear venture plans reactor to complement solar, wind power boom. *Reuters*. https://www.reuters.com/article/us-usa-nuclearpower-terrapower/bill-gates-nuclear-venture-plans-reactor-to-complement-solar-wind-power-boom-idINKBN25N2U8?edition-redirect=in

Khan, M., Serafeim, G., & Yoon, A. (2016). Corporate sustainability: First evidence on materiality. *The Accounting Review, 91*(6), 1697–1724. https://doi.org/10.2308/accr-51383

Mayor, T. (2019). Why ESG ratings vary so widely (and what you can do about it). *MIT Thinking Forward Newsletter*. https://mitsloan.mit.edu/ideas-made-to-matter/why-esg-ratings-vary-so-widely-and-what-you-can-do-about-it

Norges Bank Investment Management. (2016). *Guidelines for observation and exclusion from the fund*. https://www.nbim.no/en/organisation/governance-model/guidelines-for-observation-and-exclusion-from-the-fund/

Norges Bank Investment Management. (2019, February 27). *About the fund*. https://www.nbim.no/en/the-fund/about-the-fund/

Pistilli, M. (2021, January 13). What was the BP stock price before the deepwater Horizon spill? *Investing News*. https://investingnews.com/daily/resource-investing/energy-investing/oil-and-gas-investing/bp-oil-stock-price-before-spill/

Schmelzer, R. (2020, October 1). Automating data collection for AI at Morningstar. *Forbes*.

Taraldsen, L. E., Poulsson, L., & Starn, J. (2020). Wind farm backlash grows in oil-rich Norway ahead of election. *Bloomberg*. https://www.bloomberg.com/news/articles/2020-12-09/wind-farm-backlash-grows-in-oil-rich-norway-ahead-of-election

US SIF: The Forum for Sustainable and Responsible Investment. (2020, November 16). The US SIF foundation's biennial "trends report" finds that sustainable investing assets reach $17.1 trillion. https://www.ussif.org/blog_home.asp?Display=155

10

Anti-corruption

Corruption is "the abuse of entrusted power for private gain" (Transparency International, n.d.)

Corruption is a global challenge. Typical forms of corruption are associated with bribery, facilitation payments, gifts, hospitality and expenses, political contributions, charitable contributions, sponsorships, voluntary community contributions, trading in influence, and conflict of interest and impartiality. According to a survey conducted by PWC among 5000 respondents across 99 territories about their experiences over the past 24 months, almost half of those surveyed had experienced one or more frauds such as customer fraud, cybercrime, and asset misappropriation. Almost half of these were internal frauds. It is estimated that the total cost of these kinds of crimes amount to US$ 42 billion (PwC, 2020). It is estimated that 2.7 percent of the global GDP is laundered annually, and corporations seeking tax-free jurisdictions cost governments close to $ 600 billion annually (Financial Accontability Transparency & Integrity, 2021).

The tenth principle of the UN Global Compact (see the next section) states that "Business should work against corruption in all its forms, including extortion and bribery". One of the reasons behind this is that

C. D. Ditlev-Simonsen, *A Guide to Sustainable Corporate Responsibility*,
https://doi.org/10.1007/978-3-030-88203-7_10

corruption is a major obstacle to economic and social development and that implies a negative impact on sustainable development especially affecting poor countries.

SDG Goal #16—Peace, Justice, and Strong Institutions includes "commitments to corruption, increase transparency, tackle illicit financial flows and improve access to information". This goal is thus critical to the entire 2030 Agenda, because corruption undermines progress on all other SDGs.

So how to reduce and avoid such corruption and crime? In this chapter, I will address the corruption challenges, how they are addressed by corporations and key international laws as well as challenges associated with norms and behavior. Anti-corruption is a huge topic and challenge. However, when addressing sustainability, it cannot be left out, but one should rather draw a framework for key issues.

10.1 Key Elements in a Plan for Anti-corruption

One of ten principles in The UN Global Compact, Principle 10, is about Anti-Corruption. The UNGC includes six ways to promote transparency and accountability in companies:

1. Commit: Make anti-corruption part of your company culture and operations. Show your employees, customers, and suppliers that your company has a zero-tolerance policy on bribery and corruption.
2. Assess: Know your risks and prepare for them. Recognize opportunities to improve your business by improving compliance.
3. Define: Define what success means for your company. Develop goals, strategies, and policies and get buy-in from colleagues by clearly showing the importance of these policies.
4. Implement: Make anti-corruption programs and policies integral throughout your company, including your value chain.
5. Measure: What gets measured gets done. Monitor and measure the impact of your anti-corruption policies to identify what's working and what still needs work.

6. Communicate: Consistently communicate your progress to stakeholdersS, always striving for continuous improvement.

10.2 Anti-corruption Regulations and Corporate Policies—and Effect

Stronger laws and institutions as well as greater transparency, international cooperation, and strong punitive sanctions when breaking laws are all crucial issues to reduce corruption. The UN Convention against Corruption (UNCAC) which entered into force in 2005 is the only legally binding universal anti-corruption instrument. The Convention is signed by 140 countries and covers five main areas: preventive measures, criminalization and law enforcement, international cooperation, asset recovery and technical assistance and information exchange. Bribery, trading in influence, abuse of functions, and various acts of corruption in the private sector are also covered (United Nations Office on Drugs and Crime, 2003).

There are many excellent guides that provide a good framework for anti-corruption as well. The UN Office on Drugs and Crime (UNODC) serves as the Secretariat for UNCAC and has provided a practical guide for business to avoid corruption. This practical guide pinpoints the importance of including among others support and commitment from top management, establishing a clear, visible and accessible program, apply the program, communicate and train stakeholders and incentivize compliance, follow up, report, and revise the anti corruption program (United Nations Office on Drugs and Crime, 2013).

There are also a multitude of national laws and regulations to combat corruption, and the number of these is increasing. A good example of how international laws lead to national changes reducing corruption comes from Norway. Until 1995 expenses associated with bribery of foreign officials could be deducted as an expense, entitling tax reductions for the company in Norway, but in 1999 this became illegal. The implementation of the OECD anti-bribery convention was a driver for an explicit section on corruption in Norwegian Criminal Law (Civita, 2013). Today, being involved in corruption can lead to fines as well as jail time up to 10 years (Straffeloven [The Penal Code], 2005§ 387–388).

10.3 Key Anti-corruption Challenges

Most large companies today have established a code of conduct or ethical guidelines addressing anti-corruption issues. The two key motivators for companies to adopt anti-corruption measures are to protect the company's reputation and avoid prosecution (OECD, 2020). These come in different forms, including length, focus, and depth. Some have programs to train employees, suppliers, and customers; with regard to other code of conduct manuals, only few employees are aware that they exist, and they are rarely used in practice. Companies involved in the major corruption scandals in the world usually had a well-established internal code of conduct addressing anti-corruption. The two companies involved in scandals, Siemens and Enron both had well-established anti-corruption guidelines and programs (Lemus, 2014; Transparency International, 2019). It is a paradox that major corruption scandals, including environmental and social scandals, are main drivers for a large number of companies to take measures in order to avoid this happen to them. It is a paradox that major social scandals along the lines of corruption actually improve the field in a longer term perspective.

Typical challenges are associated with gifts and other personal offers, fake companies, fake competitions, kick-back, agents claiming fees beyond the value of their actual work, and so on. Corruption is often more prevalant with international business and operations in countries with weak regulations. Corruption is especially a challenge in poor countries, and corruption in fragile and conflict-affected states (FCAS), corruption is not an exception but a rule (Charbatke-Church & Chigas, 2019). New Zealand and Denmark are ranked as the least corrupt countries in the world, Somalia and Sudan as the most corrupt (179). Tanzania is ranked 94th and Norway is in the 7th place (Transparency International, 2020). However, corruption is still a big challenge in countries like Norway with strong anti-corruption regulations and a regulatory framework to follow up.

It is crucial to have an international framework, national laws, and corporate code of conduct established to combat corruption. However, research shows that is not enough to avoid corruption. Maybe the biggest challenge related to anti-corruption is social norms.

10.4 Social Norms and Anti-corruption

Maybe too much focus has been on developing a good set of anti-corruption measures and training people to follow these rules without ever consulting the people this is actually related to. In order to avoid scandals and criticism, companies often require that suppliers in low cost countries abide and train employees in anti-corruption. However, this does not work in the long run if the social norms are not in line with the anti-corruption program (Charbatke-Church & Chigas, 2019).

In many fragile and conflict-affected states (FCAS), corruption and bribery is part of everyday life—both in private lives and business. Corruption is a norm (Chap. 2 on Duty ethics). In these countries, police officers are poorly paid and often accept bribes by drivers, civil servants can expect bribes providing favors to individuals and bribery in many cases is a necessity in order to win government contracts. Corruption is based on mutual expectations and peer pressure in informal groups like family, clans, friends, professionals, religions, and more. Serving and protecting these groups becomes more important than national laws and regulations. If individuals try to withdraw from this norm, it can result in negative consequences like disrespect, exclusion, and punishment.

To address corruption laws which make corruption more complicated may initially seem like a good approach. However, such laws are hard to define and even more challenging to implement and follow up especially in FCAS. Transparency through digitalization and reducing corruption opportunities has had a positive effect. For example, the paperless port clearing system in Ghana (online service), increased efficiency (reduced clearance time) and reduced the petty corruption opportunities (Wass, 2019).

Even though work on regulations, implementation, and follow-up is important, change in culture and behavior norms might be equally, if not more, important. More focus needs to be on understanding the social norms and what motivates corruption, the drivers. This is a long and complicated process. However, the awareness of the importance of addressing the divers is one important step. Instead of focusing on stopping corruption, the focus needs to shift to avoiding corruption because it is better for individuals and groups (Wass, 2019).

10.5 From the Grand Scandals to Petty Corruption

The major effects of corruption is not associated with the well-known scandals, but the daily petty corruption, money/cash paid to civil servants like police and government employees to get advantages, access, and avoid penalties and fines. Most people face dilemmas in their day-to-day work. Dan Ariely, a well-recognized expert in behavioral science, tested 30,000 people with regard to corruption but found only 12 "big cheaters" who stole a total of $150, while the 18,000 "little cheaters" stole a total of $36,000 (Ariely, 2012). Having good regulations and corporate programs for anti-corruption is important; however, understanding the human psyche, culture, and social norms is a prerequisite or even more important.

Case illustrating the challenge of avoiding corruption in countries with weak regulations

You are an agent for a fishing company. A delivery of fresh fish from your company is arriving at the port on a Friday and you are there to pick up and distribute to customers. However, the local person in charge of the customs process claims that she does not have time to approve the delivery before Monday. You know that on Monday the fish will no longer be fresh and cannot be sold. The customs officer chats about poor wages and no overtime payment, conveying that if you contribute 100 dollars, the person will check out the shipment today. What would you do? Pay the 50 dollars (which is like one-hour work for you) which is illegal or pay the 50 dollars to avoid spoiling the delivery worth 10,000 dollars? Such cases show the dilemma. What people decide in such situations vary.

References

Ariely, D. (2012). *The honest truth about dishonesty: How we lie to everyone*. HarperCollins Publishers.

Charbatke-Church, C. S., & Chigas, D. (2019). *Understanding social norms: A reference guide for policy and practice*. https://sites.tufts.edu/ihs/social-norms-reference-guide/

Civita. (2013). Korrupsjon og norsk næringsliv. *Civita-notat* (4). https://www.civita.no/assets/2013/03/Civita-notat_4_2013.pdf

Financial Accountability Transparency & Integrity. (2021, February 25). *UN Panel: End financial abuses to save people and planet*https://www.factipanel.org/press-release/un-panel-end-financial-abuses-to-save-people-and-planet

Lemus, E. (2014). The financial collapse of the Enron Corporation and its impact in the United States capital market. *Global Journal of Management and Business Research: Accounting and Auditing, 14*(4) https://globaljournals.org/GJMBR_Volume14/3-The-Financial-Collapse-of-the-Enron.pdf

OECD. (2020). *Corporate anti-corruption compliance drivers, mechanisms, and ideas for change*. https://www.oecd.org/corruption/anti-bribery/corporate-anti-corruption-compliance.htm

PwC. (2020). *PwC's global economic crime and fraud survey 2020*. https://www.pwc.com/fraudsurvey

Straffeloven [The Penal Code]. (2005). *Lov om straff* (LOV-2005-05-20-28). Lovdata. https://lovdata.no/dokument/NL/lov/2005-05-20-28/KAPITTEL_2-15#%C2%A7387

Transparency International. (2019, July 5). *Siemens: Corruption made in Germany*. https://www.transparency.org/en/news/25-corruption-scandals#Siemens

Transparency International. (2020). *Corruption perceptions index*. https://www.transparency.org/en/cpi/2020/index/nzl#

Transparency International. (n.d.). *What is corruption?*https://www.transparency.org/en/what-is-corruption

United Nations Office on Drugs and Crime. (2003). *United Nations convention against corruption*. https://www.unodc.org/unodc/en/corruption/uncac.html

United Nations Office on Drugs and Crime. (2013). *An anti-corruption ethics and compliance programme for business: A practical guide*. https://www.unodc.org/documents/corruption/Publications/2013/13-84498_Ebook.pdf

Wass, S. (2019). Paperless port system prompts import revenue growth in Ghana. *Global Trade Review*. https://www.gtreview.com/news/africa/paperless-port-system-prompts-import-revenue-growth-in-ghana/

11

Sustainability in Developing Countries: Case Sub-Saharan Africa

The first goal in the UN SDGs is No Poverty. Today 10 percent of the world's population lives on less than $1.90 USD per day. In contrast, industrialized countries' consumption is far beyond what is considered sustainable. This is not fair—we all have the same rights to our planets' resources and equal standards of living. To realize sustainability, consumption in developed countries needs to be reduced and living standards in developing countries must improve.

Since "sustainability in developing countries" is quite a broad topic area, this chapter will narrow down the focus to key issues pertaining Africa and business development. Africa consists of 56 sovereign states, which vastly differ in terms of size, populations, cultures, governments, stages of development, economic development, resources, political stability, and so on. Regarding sustainability as it relates to the first SDG, the focus of this chapter will be on how to improve the lives of people in Sub Saharan Africa, where the majority of the world's extreme poverty is concentrated. Since the poorest countries are becoming poorer, more focus is needed on the "Bottom Billion" (Collier, 2007).

Many dynamics have to change in Africa in order to accelerate sustainable development. African states confront political instability, conflict

C. D. Ditlev-Simonsen, *A Guide to Sustainable Corporate Responsibility*,
https://doi.org/10.1007/978-3-030-88203-7_11

and war, poor education, corruption, unemployment, poor access to finance, and a lack of transparency among many other problems. However, the biggest challenge for African countries today is high debt with states maintaining levels at about 70 percent of GDP. This figure has more than doubled in the last two decades (African Development Bank, 2021) and the COVID-19 situation will most likely only exacerbate this situation further. The focus of this chapter will be on sustainable business development and it will indirectly touch upon many of these challenges. If business is to be developed in a sustainable manner, it has the potential to make a positive impact in many aspects of these peoples' lives.

Business development is a prerequisite for better living standards, which makes sustainability evermore crucial. The majority of Africa's population is young with a median age less than 20 years old, compared to Europe with median age more than 40 years. With the fastest growing population in the world at 2.7 percent a year, Sub-Saharan Africa's population will double by 2050 to 2.5 billion people, one quarter of the global population. This signalizes that there will be a large surge in demand for work and resources in Africa in the coming years. (The Economist, 2020) Sustainable development can create the basis for future opportunities, while inaction or business as usual could only snowball current challenges. Ngozi Okonjo-Iweala, Director-General of World Trade Organization and the former Minister of Finance and Foreign Affairs of Nigeria, suggests if you want to help Africa, do business here (Okonjo-Iweala, 2007).

Thousands of books are written on how to solve the Africa's challenges, but finding agreement on what the right solution is proves elusive. What is striking is that the economies of African nations today have to a large extent been shaped by development aid. In the last 60 years, more than $1 trillion USD of foreign aid has been transferred to Africa, yet real per capita income today is lower than it was in the 1970s (Moyo, 2009). More than a fourth of Sub-Saharan countries are poorer than they were in the 1960s (Acemoglu, 2014).

Whereas development aid has received a lot of attention over the past several decades, business as a tool for a long-term sustained development has not. To avoid generalizations, I will use various, real world examples to illustrate the current situation in Sub-Saharan Africa. The chapter will focus specifically on sustainable business development and it will identify areas prime for development.

In 2020, Tanzania's economy was ranked as the ninth largest in Africa in terms of GDP. The country has a population of 56 million people. Agriculture is the cornerstone of the economy, employing 68 percent of Tanzania's workforce. Gold, coffee, cashew nuts, tobacco, and cotton are key export goods and 40 percent of the food is imported. The majority of agricultural production is categorized as small-scale subsistence farming. Less than half of the population has access to clean water[1] and only 35 percent have access to electricity. Undernutrition is still highly prevalent in Tanzania, yet morev than eight percent of the population is obese.[2] Adult literacy rates have been gradually increasing until now, 78 percent of the population can read and write in Swahili, English, or Arabic; 82 percent has mobile phone telephone subscription and 25 percent uses the internet. More than 95 percent of Tanzanians use charcoal for cooking. The ecological footprint of Tanzanians is 0.73 (2017) (Global Footprint Network, n.d.). Tanzania's footprint is quite sustainable in direct contrast to Norwegians, whose ecological footprint is 3.61 planet Earths. Tanzania has one of Africa's fastest growing economies increasing an average of seven percent in the last decade, compared to the global average of four percent. Relative to many other African countries, Tanzania has a stable political situation.

11.1 A Look Backward: Why Is the Situation as It Is?

There are many different opinions and theories on why countries in Europe, North America, and for example China and South Korea, have succeeded in industrialization and subsequently have increased living standards, whereas many countries in Africa have not. Some common explanations include: Africa's history of colonialism and resource extraction; lack of sound macroeconomic policies; low agricultural

[1] Those facilities designed to hygienically separate excreta from human contact.

[2] https://dashboards.sdgindex.org/profiles/TZA/indicators.

productivity; large deficits and debt; low savings and investment; poor education; and too little focus on export promotion (Goldin, 2019).

Poverty has been the primary driver for large influxes of development aid in Africa. Recipient countries have followed different allocation models, but it is often earmarked to fight famine and disease and to support economic development. To understand Africa's current business environment and its economic development, it is useful to have some background knowledge on Africa's history with international development aid.

11.2 Lessons Learned from Over 50 Years of Aid

Often developed countries assume they know best what people in other countries need and want. However, what is based on good intentions might not necessarily lead to good outcomes or expected results. Making assumptions without actually conducting the proper due diligence can lead to devastating results.

Only half of the World Bank and International Monetary Fund (IMF) funded projects have succeeded. The Chad-Cameroon oil pipeline to the Atlantic Ocean, Lesotho Highlands water project, Roll Back Malaria, and many more are examples of projects that are deemed as failures (NBC News, 2007). There are different reasons for each failure, but lack of local knowledge tends to be the common denominator (Short et al., 2020). It is a paradox that so many of these international development projects have actually made several African countries partly dependent on aid.

One would assume that after so many failed projects resulting in more harm than good would discourage similar initiatives in the future. After a failed tree planting project in the 1980s, the Turkana project in Kenya, only a few years later in 1995, Norwegian and Finnish aid organizations, private investment, and Green Resources AS started another tree planting project in Sub-Saharan Africa including among others Mozambique, Tanzania, and Uganda (Lyons & Westoby, 2013). Until today, it is one of the largest Norwegian private investments in Africa. The business model of the project involved planting trees to generate carbon credits to sell on the global market. Although it seemed to have good intentions and to be environmentally friendly, the largest plantation forestry operation on the African continent led to the forced relocation of local people, food insecurity, and the introduction of a new species that threatened the local plants. In 2020, financially, the project was deemed to have been a "massacre for the 'billionaire adventure' in Africa" (Bjergaard, 2020). Lack of knowledge and due diligence, assumed expertise, and not involving local people were deemed to the underlying reasons behind each of these failures.

Not all business projects that give rise to unintended, negative consequences are linked to state aid or large corporations. Some originate from individuals, who with good intentions want to contribute and help. People in developed countries have for a long time collected and donated used clothes via charities. These clothes however are not distributed for free; rather they create a multibillion dollar industry in which charities sell the used clothes in bulk to traders in developing countries, who retail them to locals. Donating used clothing could be perceived as a contribution to circular economy, and it might seem positive, but in the long-term, it works to the detriment of local businesses in the developing world. According to Oxfam, 70 percent of donated clothing goes to Africa (Kubania, 2015). Used clothing imports are estimated to be responsible for almost 40 percent of the annual decline in domestic production of clothing in Sub-Saharan Africa (Wilson & Hopewell, 2018).

If used clothes were not exported and instead used longer or resold by the original owner in the developed world. This would not only be more sustainable, but also indirectly support local businesses in Africa. Local production using local resources such as cotton would contribute toward gains in self-sufficiency. This is the reason why many states in Africa are banning imports of second-hand clothes (Reality Check Team, 2018). Another example of a well-intentioned initiative, that failed to achieve its desired results, was the case of a large company that spent millions to donate new computers to local schools. The organizers were not aware that there was no power grid in the areas, so no access to electricity in the region (Wharton University of Pennsylvania, 2007). These two examples illustrate the importance of consulting local knowledge and how partnerships and cooperation can help make projects work.

Even though many development aid-based projects in Africa have failed, there are many aid-projects, which have succeeded, especially in the health sector. The Melinda & Bill Gates foundation have created projects considered to be some of the most successful in Africa. The foundation has improved health, education, and quality of life for millions of people. Their goal is to have zero preventable deaths associated with malaria, TB, HIV, and malnutrition. Until 2016, the foundation had provided $9 billion USD in funding for projects on the continent. The budget for 2016–2021 was set to contribute another $5 billion (Philanthropy News Digest, 2016). It is estimated that the foundation has helped to save over 122 million lives through its work (Boseley, 2017).

Although the foundation's engagement in Africa is not directly related to business, it is estimated that every $1 USD on childhood immunization provides a $44 USD return in economic benefits (Boseley, 2017).

The focus has typically been on people outside Africa that help Africa. However, there are many noteworthy African philanthropists, who might also have a better understanding of what works and what does not work for Africa. Mo Ibrahim, a Sudanese billionaire, claims that Africa does not need help and it does not need aid. According to him, governance is the problem. Therefore, he financially supports political leaders, who have proven to provide among other things "sustainable economic opportunity" and "rule of law" (Jolis, 2012). Aliko Dangote of Nigeria and Mohammed Dewij of Tanzania are two more examples of wealthy Africans working on developing Africa, creating opportunities, and empowering the people (Nsehe, 2019). In addition, there are many Africans who have made a positive impact outside of the realm of philanthropy. In 1997, Dr Wangari Maathai started the grass-root movement to counter deforestation. Later in 2004, she received the Nobel Peace Prize for the impact of her work on the Green Belt movement and its contribution to sustainable development, democracy, and peace.

There are many different opinions on whether or not aid is a good solution for solving the poverty situation (Kwemo, 2017). Still, most agree that using development aid in an effective manner can contribute to solving problems in the developing world. According to Paul Collier, a well-recognized aid expert, shifting aid to support business is the right decision (Collier, 2016). However, in order to do business, knowledge is needed. There are two major sides of the equation for Africa to become sustainable; the people factor and the system factor. The people factor is about developing human capital and involvement. Handling something that is not anchored or originated from the beneficiary does not work.

So far, too much focus has been on the macro level interventions in Africa, and too little on micro interventions like human empowerment and educating people. The focus has to move from giving fish to teaching how to fish. Overall, collaboration with developed countries and aid has to be people centered rather than focused on exploiting natural resources. With this as a basis, the following are five key issues to take into account in the development of sustainable business in Africa.

1. Reduce export of non-manufactured natural resources
2. Involve stakeholders and collaborate throughout the supply chain
3. Manufacture products from local resources for own consumption and export
4. Make being a farmer more attractable
5. Reflect on the goal for the development

In a sustainability setting, these five issues are closely related to a change in mindset in addition to knowledge and education in the field of sustainability. The concepts of sustainability, environmental and social issues, have to be integrated into education, especially business education. A long-term focus is also crucial for projects and initiatives. In line with the Maslow's hierarchy, all people tend to be short sighted when their physiological needs are not met. This is more often the case in Africa. People who are hungry and struggling to satisfy basic human needs are less concerned about biological diversity than people with secure access to food, water, and shelter. In the following section, I will address the five issues introduced above and provide examples to illustrate their relevance and importance.

11.3 Reduce Export of Non-manufactured Natural Resources

The African continent is endowed with an abundance of natural resources from diamonds, platinum, and gold to bauxite, cobalt, and many other valuable minerals. The majority of foreign direct investment has been directed to the exploration and exploitation of these extractive resources. In 2020, almost 70 percent of what was imported to Africa from the EU were manufactured goods, whereas over 60 percent of export from Africa to EU were raw materials, commodities (Eurostat, 2021).

Many argue for instance that Africa's oil resources have been a curse, rather than a "blessing", because it spurred environmental degradation and lowered local living conditions. The revenues have mainly enriched a select cadre of corrupt politicians (BBC News, 2012).

Most of what is extracted is done under poor working conditions and exported to be processed outside the continent, particularly to developed countries. The case of cobalt illustrates the consequences of political instability, breaches of human rights principles, illegal processes, mismanagement, corruption, exploitation, lack of people focus and negative economic consequences. The case furthermore illustrates that the situation is gradually improving and moving toward more sustainable processes.

Case Cobalt

The use of electric cars (EV) has increased tremendously. Much of the green energy transition will hinge on the availability and affordability of the metals required to make the EV battery.[3] Cobalt is critical and comprises half the cost.[4] Making up 10–30 percent of the cathodes, it prevents corrosion that can lead to overheating and fires. Technically, it has been difficult to find super heat resistant substitutes without major trade-offs in battery life and performance.[5]

(continued)

[3] Ben Jones, Robert J. R. Elliott, Viet Nguyen-Tien, The EV revolution: The road ahead for critical raw materials demand, Applied Energy, Volume 280, 2020, 115072, ISSN 0306-2619,, https://doi.org/10.1016/j.apenergy.2020.115072.

[4] https://www.sciencedaily.com/releases/2020/07/200716101612.htm.

[5] https://pubs.usgs.gov/periodicals/mcs2020/mcs2020-cobalt.pdf.

(continued)

The issue is that global cobalt supply is constrained, and while demand is skyrocketing, it has become quite expensive.[6] Politically unstable,[7] Democratic Republic of the Congo (DRC) supplies 70 percent of the world's cobalt, a byproduct from copper and nickel mining. It is transported by trucks to South Africa, so vulnerable to disruptions and shipped out of Durban[8] for processing in China, which controls 80 percent of the commercial cobalt refining industry.[9] Demand is projected to surge by 400 percent in the next 10 years with rising demand for smartphones and electric cars.[10]

The reason it is problematic is that DRC sourced cobalt has been linked to severe human rights abuses. An estimated 10 to 30 percent of DRC production comes from 2 million Congolese, artisanal, small-scale miners, digging by hand.[11]. They frequently mine illegally, use child labor, and work in hazardous and sometime fatal working conditions. EV producers have a major dilemma with really few options. Future projects to expand supply are limited. Recycling rates can be economically improved, currently at 32 percent,[12] but additional cobalt supply will come from expanding existing mining operations in DRC. Mining companies in Norway, the UK, Belgium, and others are accessing deepsea mining projects, but Google, BMW, Volvo, and Samsung support a moratorium, vowing not to buy nor finance deepsea mined minerals.[13]

BMW, is the only car company in the industry that has signed agreements directly with mines in Australia and Morrocco to supply its cobalt to bypass the DRC and ensure its sourced responsibly.[14,15] Avoiding DRC cobalt is unrealistic and unsustainable for any company; even BMW in the future without major technological breakthroughs will have to source from the DRC. Other companies such as Tesla and CATL, China's largest EV battery maker, have made public statements that they plan to engineer cobalt out

(continued)

[6] https://tradingeconomics.com/commodity/cobalt.

[7] https://travel.state.gov/content/travel/en/traveladvisories/traveladvisories/democratic-republic-of-the-congo-travel-advisory.html#:~:text=Violent%20crime%2C%20such%20as%20murder,%2C%20Kasai%20Central%2C%20and%20Kasai

[8] https://www.wsj.com/articles/electric-vehicle-surge-sends-cobalt-prices-soaring-11611333538.

[9] https://www.bloomberg.com/graphics/2018-china-cobalt/.

[10] https://theconversation.com/as-cobalt-demand-booms-companies-must-do-more-to-protect-congolese-miners-149486.

[11] https://www.raconteur.net/corporate-social-responsibility/cobalt-mining-human-rights/.

[12] https://www.iisd.org/sites/default/files/publications/sustainability-second-life-cobalt-lithium-recycling.pdf.

[13] https://www.mining.com/bmw-volvo-google-and-samsung-call-for-ban-on-deep-sea-mining/.

[14] https://www.mining.com/cobalt-price-bmw-avoids-the-congo-conundrum-for-now/.

[15] https://www.ft.com/content/3ab6b934-202e-11ea-92da-f0c92e957a96.

(continued)

of the battery. Telsa has also partnered with Panasonic, dramatically lowering cobalt content in their next generation EV battery, down to 5 percent.[16] Further, they are striving to completely eliminate its use to dramatically lower the cost of the battery, which could make the EV affordable to the mass market.

In response, cobalt suppliers have launched a number of different initiatives. Chinese industry launched the Responsible Cobalt Initiative, partnering with companies such as Daimler, Volvo, and Apple to address child labor risks in the supply chain via due diligence. Mine owners such as Tesla's supplier, Glencore, have created the Fair Cobalt Alliance,[17] which will work directly with artisan miners to improve working conditions, eradicate child labor, and engage in community building to provide locals with other opportunities.[18]

Realizing the importance of moving away from the resource extraction approach, there has been a focus on supporting local entrepreneurs to develop new and more sustainable business. It is argued that the solution for Africa's greatest challenges needs to come from within, specifically using local expertise and resources (Gatesfoundation, n.d.).

Developing a country's own culture with pride needs focus. Omoyemi Akerele, a driving force behind Nigeria's fashion industry, works with local brands. She provides a good example of how local products and design can gain a national and international footing. African nationals and international celebrities have been seen wearing locally designed garments, bringing great pride to the local people.

There are many examples of promising businesses based on local knowledge and local people. Reviewing 650 nominations, *Forbes* magazine identified the 30 Most Promising Young Entrepreneurs in Africa. The list includes businesses ranging from affordable access to solar

[16] https://asia.nikkei.com/Business/Technology/Tesla-strikes-new-Panasonic-battery-deal-as-sales-and-shares-soar.

[17] https://www.ft.com/content/9194c7ee-9726-4462-ae04-e7c72c0818d4.

[18] https://www.theimpactfacility.com/commodities/cobalt/fair-cobalt-alliance/.

energy in areas where 87 percent of the population live without electricity, to a footwear brand becoming very popular within the urban populations, cashew processing companies, a mobile phone application to support rural crop farmers, and so on (Nsehe, 2018).

11.4 Involve Stakeholders and Collaborate Throughout the Supply Chain

Lack of infrastructure and the need for collaborative efforts have often been identified as other reasons for business project failures in Africa. In the agriculture business, post-harvest loss (PHL) is a significant problem among small hold farmers and the main cause is the lack of infrastructure to transport produce to market. This is the main reason why approximately 32 percent of crops and 24 percent of calories produced are not consumed. This waste amounts to the equivalent amount of food to feed 1.6 billion people (Deloitte, 2015).

Appropriate use of fertilizer is critical for ensuring good harvests. It is estimated that there is a need for eight times more fertilizer than what is currently used in Africa (Goedde et al., 2019). Yara, a Norwegian company and the world's leading fertilizer company, realized that the lack of infrastructure to take goods to market was a major challenge. They began collaborating in various initiatives across different sectors and institutions to make progress, based on Porter's Shared Value Concept (see Chap. 3). This collaboration across the supply chain led to the establishment of the Southern Agricultural Growth Corridor of Tanzania (SAGCOT).

SAGCOT is an international public-private partnership launched at the World Economic Forum on Africa in May 2010 in Dar es Salaam. Its founding objective was to foster inclusive, commercially successful agribusinesses that would benefit the region's small-scale farmers, and in so doing, improve food security, reduce rural poverty, and ensure environmental sustainability. Yara, Unilever, the Agriculture Council of Tanzania, the Tanzanian government, and USAID have all become key actors since its inception in 2009.

By 2014, SAGCOT had more than 60 partners, 38 from the private sector including a number of local companies and governments. The success of this initiative generated interest in investing in broader social and economic issues on a long-term horizon. Educating small-scale, Tanzanian farmers take time, but it later pays off with increased crop yields, incomes, and food security. These considerations were integral in Yara's approach to business development in Tanzania, despite the risks associated with upfront financing to realize future profits. The SAGCOT approach is a venue that illustrates the importance of, as well as how to address, stakeholder management in the supply chain. It is a good model for business development in rural Africa. Still, Tanzania imports fertilizer from abroad, rather than producing it domestically, forgoing local jobs and knowledge creation. Developing a self-managed circular bioeconomy has a great potential in Sub-Sahara Africa.[19] Respect, trust, transparency, listening to business partners, and learning about the local culture needs to be the foundation of any business collaboration and venture. Developed countries need to explicitly take the voice of local people into account when doing business in Africa.

11.5 Manufacture Products from Local Resources for Local Consumption and Export

Business development in Africa is centered on importing goods from abroad. Even products developed for use in development projects in Africa tend to be imported. Solar power is a great business opportunity in Africa. Still, the bulk of solar power equipment is imported (Cross & Murray, 2018).

When a country lacks a manufacturing base, it later lacks the in-country knowledge on how to make repairs and access to spare parts. This shortens the life span of the imported technology. Importing manufactured products and exporting raw materials is a trade dynamic that not only puts Africa in debt, but also creates opportunity costs in terms of employment and growth.

[19] Circular Bioeconomy Research for Development in Sub-Saharan Africa: Innovations, Gaps, and Actions.

To develop sustainable businesses in Africa, local resources need to be developed in a sustainable manner involving the local people. Coffee is a well-known, high value commodity from Africa. Ethiopia has managed to develop a brand as one of the five countries in the world with the highest quality coffee beans (May, 2018). There are many more business opportunities based on local and relatively unknown and unique resources. The prickly pear, sisal, and shea butter are three such examples.

The prickly pear, or *Opuntia*, is a cactus plant indigenous to Mexico, which found its way to Africa more than 100 years ago. Today, it is perceived as an invasive species and resources are spent on its eradication. Since the plant thrives in arid, drought prone areas and grows easily without the need for irrigation on marginal land, there are numerous business opportunities, which could be derived from its various applications. It can be eaten by people and animals, can be used as biofuel or to sequester carbon, and provides a promising alternative medicine for diabetes therapy.

Sisal is cultivated in Africa and Tanzania is the third largest producer in the world (Food and Agriculture Organization of the United Nations, 2019). Sisal, also a plant indigenous to Mexico, is a stiff natural fiber plant that has been commercially grown for decades. It is exported as a raw material for the production of ropes, twines, carpets, and other applications. Sisal production in Tanzania has never completely recovered from its peak production in the 1960s due to a number of factors: competing with synthetic substitutes, poor economic policies, technological innovations dampening demand, and trade barriers. However, sisal today warrants attention as we re-evaluate products and look for sustainable substitutes. Sisal is a very environmentally friendly product. There is great potential in Africa to begin processing sisal and creating value-added products. It can be used to make designer goods like bags and wallets for the tourism market. Today a large portion of goods available for tourists are manufactured in China.

Shea butter is extracted from the nuts of the shea tree growing on the Savannas South of the Sahara. These nuts have an edible pulp, rich in vitamins and minerals. The oil provides a high quality basis for skin repairing cream. Harvesting and processing the nuts are labor intensive and thus provide work. These nuts have "enormous opportunities" for local business (Okojie, 2015).

All three of these potential business opportunities are based on local, naturally occurring species which are abundant and hold great potential.

Countries outside Africa have less experience with these resources and they thus entail a great opportunity for African countries to harvest and develop by themselves.

There are advantages to doing business in emerging markets. Specifically, they can leapfrog directly to the latest technologies (Schroeder & Anantharaman, 2017). Whereas the analog telephone network in developed countries was constructed using insulated copper cables and wooden or concrete posts, this infrastructure is no longer necessary with digital solutions. Erecting a few cellphone towers provides the same utility as building thousands of kilometers of analog telephone lines. Through the MFarm mobile application, farmers can now check the market price of goods to ensure that when they travel, they secure a favorable price. Through the ICow app, cows can be registered individually, so small-scale dairy farmers can easily keep track of their cattle with regard to for example milking schedules, immunization, nutrition, breeding, and so on. This application, a sustainable business initiative, was developed by a Kenyan farmer, who was familiar with the local farmers' needs.

With the right strategy, countries in Sub-Sahara Africa may be able to leapfrog from charcoal to renewable energy such as wind and/or solar power—skipping the oil and gas industry. This will require major investments, but since it would result in reduced CO_2 emissions, it might actually be an efficient approach for developed countries to deal with the climate challenges.

Not only can African countries skip non-sustainable stages of development, some African states are far ahead of countries in Europe and the United States with regard to environmental laws and regulations. By 2020, 34 African states had passed laws banning the use of plastic bags. These initiatives are closely followed up (Center for Biological Diversity, n.d.).

11.6 Make Being a Farmer More Attractable

Agriculture in Africa has a massive social and economic footprint. More than 60 percent of the population of Sub-Saharan Africa is engaged in smallholder farming, and about 23 percent of Sub-Saharan Africa's GDP comes from agriculture (Goedde et al., 2019). Still, crop yields in Africa are far behind compared to other less developed countries like South America and Asia. Often the yield is less than half of that of these countries (Shah, 2021). Increasing the use of fertilizers, improved seed, irrigation, storage, infrastructure are all key to realizing the agricultural potential of Africa (Goedde et al., 2019).

Due to the hardships inherited by most smallholder farmers, it is generally not considered a very attractive future to young Africans, who often leave the villages for the big cities only to end up as unemployed and poor. This can lead to frustration, anger, and violence. There is a great potential for better farming and increased yield. According to the World Bank, "Africa can feed itself, earn billions and avoid food crises by unblocking regional food trade" (The World Bank, 2012). It is argued that Africa has the potential of more than doubling production through relatively simple improvements (Goedde et al., 2019).

Knowledge on how to run a small farm in a profitable manner can make being a farmer an attractive job, but this will require education. Access to basic primary school has increased farmers productivity by almost ten percent (United Nations Educational Scientific and Cultural Organization (UNESCO), n.d.). Imagine the effect of agricultural education. Such education needs to cover topics related to financing, efficient marketing, best practices, sales contracts, use of digital technology, and better collaboration throughout the supply chain. Integrating sustainability issues in this proposed farmer business education would have a long-term positive effect.

11.7 Reflect on What Is the Goal for Development

Last, but not least, it is necessary to reflect on what are the goals of development. It is assumed that most people want to live like people in the developed world. So far development aid has to a large extent been based on and fostered paternalism, as opposed to collaboration and partnership (Kwemo, 2017).

Living alone in an apartment and spending most of the day in an office, which is the case for a large portion of people in developed countries, might not necessarily be the goal for most people. There should be a larger interest in, and focus on, what local people actually prefer. European involvement in Africa began with Christian missionaries, who worked to convert the population with little respect for local religion. Now it is important to ensure that developed countries are not pushing developing countries into doing business in the same unsustainable way as they have.

What is the perfect life? Anecdote story

"One day a fisherman was lying on a beautiful beach, enjoying the warmth of the afternoon sun with his fishing pole propped up in the sand and his line cast out. Then a businessman came walking trying to relieve some of the stress of his workday. He noticed the fisherman and said "You aren't going to catch many fish that way. You should be working rather than lying on the beach!"

The fisherman smiled and replied, "And what will my reward be?"

The businessman replied, "You'll be able to buy a boat and catch more fish!"

"And then what will my reward be?" asked the fisherman again.

The businessman, getting a little irritated, said "You can buy a bigger boat, and hire some people to work for you!"

"And then what will my reward be?" repeated the fisherman.

The businessman, now angry shouted, "Don't you understand that you can become so rich that you will never have to work for your living again! You can spend all your days sitting on this beach, looking at the sunset."

The fisherman looked up, "And what do you think I'm doing right now?"

References

Acemoglu, D. (2014, January 25). Why foreign aid fails—and how to really help Africa. *The Spectator*. https://www.spectator.co.uk/article/why-foreign-aid-fails%2D%2D-and-how-to-really-help-africa

African Development Bank. (2021). *African Economic Outlook 2021*. https://www.afdb.org/en/knowledge/publications/african-economic-outlook

BBC News. (2012, October 25). Nigeria: 'Oil-gas sector mismanagement costs billions'. https://www.bbc.com/news/world-africa-20081268

Bjergaard, A. P. (2020, February 8). Nytt blodbad for «milliardeventyret» i Afrika. *Finansavisen*. https://finansavisen.no/nyheter/industri/2020/02/08/7496064/nytt-blodbad-for-green-resources

Boseley, S. (2017). How Bill and Melinda Gates helped save 122m lives—and what they want to solve next. *The Guardian*. https://www.theguardian.com/world/2017/feb/14/bill-gates-philanthropy-warren-buffett-vaccines-infant-mortality

Center for Biological Diversity. (n.d.). *10 Facts about single-use plastic bags: The problem with plastic bags*. https://www.biologicaldiversity.org/programs/population_and_sustainability/sustainability/plastic_bag_facts.html

Collier, P. (2007). *The bottom billion: Why the poorest countries are failing and what can be done about it*. Oxford University Press.

Collier, P. (2016, December 11). Shifting aid to support business is the right decision. *Financial Times*. https://www.ft.com/join/licence/31c81148-b0e9-4815-bcdd-74f2bbf99304/details?ft-content-uuid=63f8341a-be22-11e6-8b45-b8b81dd5d080

Cross, J., & Murray, D. (2018). The afterlives of solar power: Waste and repair off the grid in Kenya. *Energy Research & Social Science, 44*, 100–109.

Deloitte. (2015). Reducing food loss along African agricultural value chains. https://www2.deloitte.com/content/dam/Deloitte/za/Documents/consumer-business/ZA_FL1_ReducingFoodLossAlongAfricanAgriculturalValueChains.pdf

Eurostat. (2021, April). Africa-EU—international trade in goods statistics: Imports, exports and trade balance between the EU and African countries, 2010–2020. https://ec.europa.eu/eurostat/statistics-explained/index.php?title=Africa-EU_-_international_trade_in_goods_statistics

Food and Agriculture Organization of the United Nations. (2019). *Committee on commodity problems*. http://www.fao.org/fileadmin/templates/est/COMM_MARKETS_MONITORING/Jute_Hard_Fibres/Documents/IGG_40/19 CRS_1_Current_Situation_and_Outlook_01.pdf

Gatesfoundation. (n.d.). *Africa*. https://www.gatesfoundation.org/our-work/places/africa

Global Footprint Network. (n.d.-b). *Ecological footprint*. https://www.footprintnetwork.org/our-work/ecological-footprint/

Goedde, L., Ooko-Ombaka, A., & Pais, G. (2019, February 15). Winning in Africa's agricultural market. *McKinsey*. https://www.mckinsey.com/industries/agriculture/our-insights/winning-in-africas-agricultural-market

Goldin, I. (2019). Why do some countries develop and others not? In P. Dobrescu (Ed.), *Development in turbulent times* (p. 13). Springer. https://doi.org/10.1007/978-3-030-11361-2_2

Jolis, A. (2012, September 7). Mohammed Ibrahim: The philanthropist of honest government. *Wall Street Journal.* https://www.wsj.com/articles/SB10000872396390444318104577587641175010510

Kubania, J. (2015, July 6). How second-hand clothing donations are creating a dilemma for Kenya. *The Guardian.* https://www.theguardian.com/world/2015/jul/06/second-hand-clothing-donations-kenya

Kwemo, A. B. (2017, April 20). Making Africa great again: Reducing aid dependency. *Brookings.* https://www.brookings.edu/blog/africa-in-focus/2017/04/20/making-africa-great-again-reducing-aid-dependency/

Lyons, K., & Westoby, P. (2013, November). Carbon markets and the failed promise of new green gold: Plantation forestry in Uganda. *Friends of the Earth, Australia.* https://www.foe.org.au/carbon-markets-and-failed-promise-new-green-gold-plantation-forestry-uganda

May, O. (2018, March 4). 5 countries with the highest quality coffee beans. *Barefoot Coffee Roasters.* https://barefootcoffeeroasters.com/countries-with-the-best-coffee-beans/

Moyo, D. (2009, March 21). Why foreign aid is hurting Africa. *The Wall Street Journal.* https://www.wsj.com/articles/SB123758895999200083

NBC News. (2007, December 24). Examples of failed aid-funded projects in Africa. https://www.nbcnews.com/id/wbna22380448

Nsehe, M. (2018, April 18). 30 most promising young entrepreneurs In Africa 2018. *Forbes.* https://www.forbes.com/sites/mfonobongnsehe/2018/04/18/30-most-promising-young-entrepreneurs-in-africa-2018/?sh=ae35a477474e

Nsehe, M. (2019, January 9). The philanthropy of Africa's billionaires. *Forbes.* https://www.forbes.com/sites/mfonobongnsehe/2019/01/09/the-philanthropy-of-africas-billionaires/?sh=4caff8247fd9

OECD. (2020). *Aid by DAC members increases in 2019 with more aid to the poorest countries.* https://www.oecd.org/dac/financing-sustainable-development/development-finance-data/ODA-2019-detailed-summary.pdf

Okojie, J. (2015, November 25). Shea butter: Local business with enormous opportunities. *Business Day.* https://businessday.ng/agriculture/article/shea-butter-local-business-with-enormous-opportunities/

Okonjo-Iweala, N. (2007). Want to help Africa? Do business here. *TED Talk*. https://www.ted.com/talks/ngozi_okonjo_iweala_want_to_help_africa_do_business_here

Philanthropy News Digest. (2016, July 19). Gates foundation to invest $5 Billion in Africa over five years. https://philanthropynewsdigest.org/news/gates-foundation-to-invest-5-billion-in-africa-over-five-years

Reality Check Team. (2018, July 27). Reality check: Why some African countries don't want charity clothes. *BBC*. https://www.bbc.com/news/world-africa-44951670

Schroeder, P., & Anantharaman, M. (2017). "Lifestyle Leapfrogging" in emerging economies: Enabling systemic shifts to sustainable consumption. *Journal of Consumer Policy, 40*(1), 3–23. https://doi.org/10.1007/s10603-016-9339-3

Shah, S. (2021, March 29). It's time to expand fertilizer manufacturing across Africa. *The Breakthrough Institute*. https://thebreakthrough.org/issues/food/expand-fertilizer-manufacturing-across-africa

Short, J. L., Toffel, M. W., & Hugill, A. R. (2020). Improving working conditions in global supply chains: The role of institutional environments and monitoring program design. *ILR Review, 73*(4), 873–912.

The Economist. (2020, March 28). Africa's population will double by 2050. https://www.economist.com/special-report/2020/03/26/africas-population-will-double-by-2050

The World Bank. (2012, October 24). *Africa can feed itself, earn billions, and avoid food crises by unblocking regional food trade*. https://www.worldbank.org/en/news/press-release/2012/10/24/africa-can-feed-itself-earn-billions-avoid-food-crises-unblocking-regional-food-trade

United Nations Educational Scientific and Cultural Organization (UNESCO). (n.d.). *Linking education to food security*. http://www.fao.org/3/x0262e/x0262e20.htm

Wharton University of Pennsylvania. (2007). African aid projects that work: Partnerships on the ground, not donations from a distance. *Knowledge@Wharton*. https://knowledge.wharton.upenn.edu/article/african-aid-projects-that-work-partnerships-on-the-ground-not-donations-from-a-distance/

Wilson, H., & Hopewell, A. (2018, May 11). Buy one, give one: What TOMS shoes tells us about the west's urge to help Africa. *The Urge To Help*. https://theurgetohelp.com/articles/buy-one-give-one-what-toms-shoes-tells-us-about-the-wests-urge-to-help-africa/

12

The Way Forward: Is Sustainable Development Realistic?

Given that today's business and our way of consumption are not sustainable, this book looks into how we can change the direction of this destructive trajectory. Technically, it is feasible to develop a sustainable society, but we need new ways of doing business and changes in consumer behavior.

In Chap. 3 "Economic Theories and sustainable development", I presented and discussed some key economists' views on economic development, as well as society's development in lieu of sustainability from a business point of view. Different models for approaching sustainable development and corporate responsibility were presented. It becomes evident that the "warnings" from economists like Thomas Malthus, Stanley Jevons, Thorstein Veblen, and so on were "true" and that major changes have to occur in our society in order to get on a more sustainable track. New emerging economic models taking sustainability, including environmental and social issues, were also presented.

Global awareness and concern for environmental and social issues is not enough—neither are new economic theories that are not being implemented. The IPCC report launched in August 2021 (IPCC, 2021) documents that we are failing to act on the climate crisis and the climate gas emissions caused by human activities are irreversible. As of now, we

C. D. Ditlev-Simonsen, *A Guide to Sustainable Corporate Responsibility*,
https://doi.org/10.1007/978-3-030-88203-7_12

are not acting in line with the Paris agreement, and if we continue on the same track, global warming could reach over five degrees by the end of the century. The uncontrollable fires, rising water levels, extreme weather, and temperatures hitting new records in many countries are warnings of the negative effects of greenhouse gas (GHG) emissions. These climate challenges associated with fossil fuels have been announced repeatedly over the past two decades, with a stronger and stronger voice and warnings containing more devastating consequences. Still, during this time, we have witnessed continuous growth in GHG emissions. We are also witnessing biological degradation and loss of species across the world. Similar to global warming, we become increasingly aware of the challenges at the same time as the situation is getting worse.

So, we are aware of the challenges, we know how to attenuate the problems—by reducing consumption—but still, we are not acting enough on it. Very few people in the industrialized world are willing to make adjustments to their lifestyles that are necessary to achieve a sustainable ecological footprint, moving from five planets to one—which is what is sustainable for the current world population. Much of the individual GHG emissions can be reduced by simply increasing energy efficiency. However, for society as a whole to become sustainable will require major reductions in energy consumption. As 62 percent of greenhouse gas emissions today comes from fossil fuels, it will take time before we have replaced this with low or zero CO2 emission alternatives. Increases in energy efficiency has been impressive, illustrating the power of research and technology. From 2007 to 2017 the average emission per km from new cars in the EU went down from almost 160 g CO2 per km to 120 g CO3 per km. Today, zero emission electronic vehicles are available too and the price of producing solar based electricity is competitive with electricity produced from coal. Still, even though new technologies have increased energy efficiency tremendously, many sustainability challenges are escalating. Echoing Jevon Paradox, even though energy efficiency has increased and new energy technologies are emerging, the efficiency is being "eaten up" with greater volumes of consumption. Political parties suggesting significant increases in fossil fuel tax, integrating the environmental cost of using these resources, become less popular and are to a lesser degree elected. Economic growth *can* however also be associated with sustainable development, but we need to price products in such a way that includes the external costs of negative environmental impacts and the social costs. One high quality, sustainably produced handbag made by a well-known and expensive brand can provide much more satisfaction than the corresponding 25 cheap and unsustainable bags produced by a fast fashion company. With regards to climate challenges, we think too much about the cost of reducing emissions, and less about the costs associated with the negative effects of *not* reducing emissions. According to the IEA, even though the transition to clean energy will cost USD 4 trillion per year over the next decades, the negative effect of not acting is estimated to cost up to USD 10 trillion annually. The "social cost of carbon" includes issues like mass migration, armed conflicts, cost destruction, weather damage and air pollution. So it is actually "way cheaper to save the planet than to ruin it".

Collaboration between stakeholders such as business, government, NGOs, suppliers, media, customers, and so on is crucial to achieve a sustainable future. Still, the most important stakeholders in this process are people in general in developed countries. We need to change behavior and consumption patterns. Are we willing to do that? People in general claim that they actually are willing to change consumption—and even pay more for environmentally friendly products and steer away from consuming environmental damaging products and products which are not produced under acceptable social conditions. Many customers are becoming more sustainable, and new customer groups like LOHAS (Lifestyles of Health and Sustainability) are coming forward. Still, when we are in a store, the majority of us do not act in line with what we claim (Ditlev-Simonsen, 2015). There is a gap between attitude and behavior. The younger generation which often claims to be more sustainability concerned than the older generations, is actually often less environmentally responsible than today's seniors. People under 60 throw away more waste than old people (Faltin, 2016).

So, to make a sizable amount of people to change behavior, we need companies to provide products which are sustainable—and which customers will actually choose. In addition, it is necessary to reduce consumption. The fact that people in rich countries have an ecological footprint which goes way beyond our "allowance" for a sustainable future strongly implies a need for change. More knowledge and research across subject areas is crucial to understand human behavior relative to social and environmental impact. The often unpredictable and irrational human behavior and marked imperfection need more attention. Integrating sustainability throughout education and ensuring dialogue and communication between fields is crucial.

Governments are probably the stakeholders with the largest opportunity to redirect society to a more sustainable future. Only regulations can ensure that the prices of the products reflect the environmental impact (full cost pricing of resources which will increase the price of products), and even rule out products that are not sustainable. We need to discuss alternative ideas of measuring growth and human progress with less focus on consumption and material dimension.

But what about us, the population, will we be content with increased prices? Based on major market opposition on simple initiatives such as toll roads and CO_2 taxes on fossil fuels, it does not seem as though we are that willing to shift behavior to become more sustainable when it requires a lower material standard of living.

On the other hand, we have seen that people actually do accept situations and changes we thought we would never accept. During the oil crisis in 1973, we had to accept and survive with limited access to travelling and driving cars. During the COVID-19 pandemic, people across the world experienced and survived the closure of stores, restaurants, schools, curfew, and so on.

The commonality between these two events, the oil crisis, COVID-19 pandemic, and also other incidents which have led to situations that could be perceived as unacceptable, was that they were imposed on us from nature, not drafted by politicians and governments. In the future, will our society act as the frog in the slowly heating water? The frog jumps right out if it was put into boiling water, but if the frog is gradually being heated in a saucepan it would not jump out but die as the water starts boiling. I hope I am wrong with this extreme and pessimistic hypothesis on what is happening as we adapt to global warming.

12.1 What Do We Really Want?

Peoples have survived in a sustainable manner for thousands of years prior to the industrial revolution and the shift to an unsustainable society. The level of need is well described in Maslow's Hierarchy of Needs (Maslow, 1943), see Fig. 12.1. In this model, it is only the first level, the physiological needs which actually require direct consumption of natural resources: food, water, shelter, air, and so on. The following needs: security, social needs, esteem needs, and self-actualization are psychological and not based on material and resource consumption. So, human needs can actually be covered at the same time as we are living sustainably. But does this make us happy?

The purpose and goal of society has been to make people happy. This was claimed already by Aristotle before 350 years B.C. At the same time, the concept of happiness and what happiness includes has been discussed ever since. Still, the ultimate goal for most of us is to be happy. From a

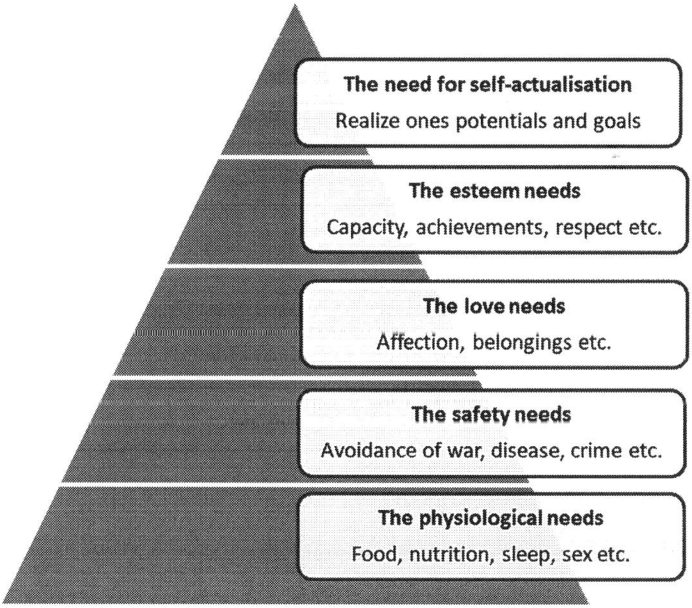

Fig. 12.1 Maslow's hierarchy of needs

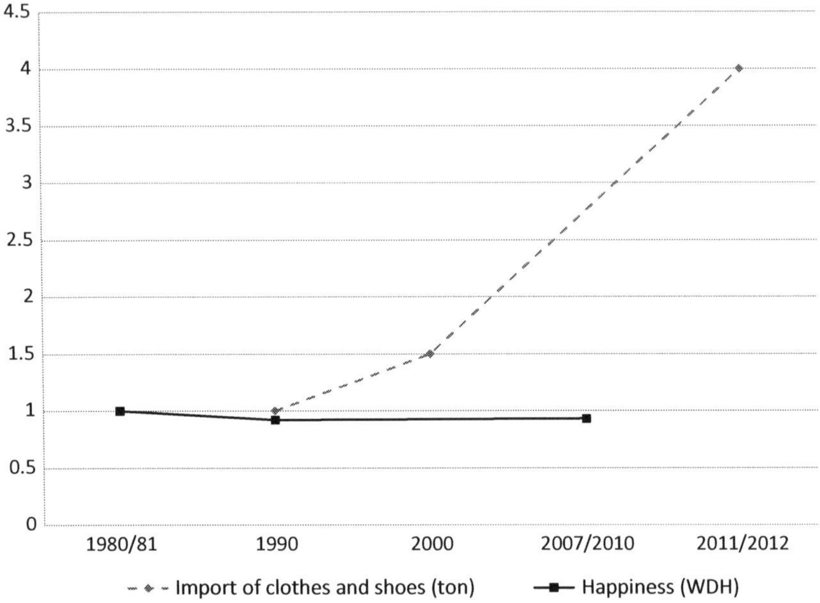

Fig. 12.2 Happiness versus consumption among Norwegians

sustainability perspective, happiness is especially relevant: Is it possible to have a sustainable living style and consumption and still be happy? More knowledge and research across subject areas are crucial.

So far, we know that consumption and happiness are not necessarily correlated. Figure 12.2 shows that in Norway, one of the richest countries in the world and with a very unsustainable per capita consumption, levels of happiness have stayed rather constant at the same time as consumption has quadrupled. The fact that increased consumption is not directly correlated with happiness is positive news for realizing a sustainable future—with a happy population.

12.2 Happiness

Government and politicians work for a happy population, but what is measured is the country's development in GDP. GDP is used to measure a country's "success", while such growth does not necessarily make people happier. As addressed in Chap. 3, using the GDP as a goal is contrary to sustainable development. A big oil spill actually contributes to GDP as the cleanup requires production and work. This does not mean that we do not want growth; it just means that growth must be measured in another way and toward another goal(s).

In light of the fact that society's ultimate goal is happy people, not increased consumption, several countries and organizations have begun to measure a population's well-being, life satisfaction and happiness with regards to its development. The OECD measures well-being through the Better Life Index (BLI). Key variables or topics in the country score include: housing, income, jobs, community, education, environment, civic engagement, health, life satisfaction, safety and work-life balance. Bhutan measures Gross National Happiness (GNH). GNH is based on the following four pillars: sustainable and equitable socio-economic development, environmental conservation, preservation and promotion of culture, and good governance. The Happy Planet Index (HPI) is another approach to assess happiness and rank countries. It measures "what matters: sustainability for all". This tells us how well nations are doing at achieving long, happy and sustainable lives. HPI was developed by the New Economics Foundation and its key purpose is to contribute an alternative measure to GDP. A country's HPI is measured by multiplying the level of well-being, life expectancy and inequality of outcome, and then divide the result by the ecological footprint. The countries that rank the highest are the ones with the least relative amount of consumption. In 2016, Costa Rica was at the top of the list, followed by Mexico, Columbia, Vanuatu and Vietnam. Common to these measurements are that they define what happiness is from the outside (predefined variables), and measure happiness through indicators such as income, work, life expectancy, culture, government, external environment, and security. The UN's World Happiness Report is also published annually, but in this report the degree of "best possible life" is measured, and not "happiness". "Happiness", "best possible life", and "well-being" are three different things.

According to the World Happiness Report, Norway is number eight on the list. Keeping in mind that happiness in Norway has not been correlated with growth in consumption. This can be argued as supporting Jevons argument for marginal utility. I conducted a study to identify what Norwegians claim to make them happy. Social issues (family, friends, love, relationships, etc.) turned out to be on the top of the list. In second place were health issues and, far down the list, came financial issues like income, salary, money, and so on (Ditlev-Simonsen, 2020). Asking Norwegians how happy they were, 79 percent answered Very happy or Rather Happy. The response to the same question in Tanzania showed that 85 percent were Very Happy and Rather Happy. Having sustainable consumption indicates that one can be equally or even more Happy than people with very unsustainable consumption.

What can we learn from this? This indicates that we can be both happy and live sustainably. More focus must be on how we can achieve this. So, even though we today might think that a sustainable future is unrealistic, it might still be possible. It will, however, require major changes, and hopefully this book has contributed a nanometer in the right direction.

The world will not evolve past its current state of crisis by using the same thinking that created the situation.—Albert Einstein

References

Ditlev-Simonsen, C. D. (2015). The gap between attitude and behavior in environmental protection—the case of Norway. In P. E. Stoknes & K. A. Eliassen (Eds.), *Science based activism*. Fagbokforlaget.

Ditlev-Simonsen, C. D. (2020). *What is happiness to Norwegians—And how happy are they*? Working Paper—BI Forum for Stiftelser (Forum for Foundations)(1/2020). https://papers.ssrn.com/sol3/papers.cfm?abstract_id=3721884

Faltin, T. (2016, September 7). Matsvinn: Tre grupper nordmenn kaster mest mat. *Dagbladet*. https://www.dagbladet.no/mat/tre-grupper-nordmenn-kaster-mest-mat/62315143

IPCC. (2021). *AR6 climate change 2021: The physical science basis*.

Maslow, A. H. (1943). A theory of human motivation. *Psychological Review, 50*(4), 370–396.

References

Acemoglu, D. (2014, January 25). Why foreign aid fails—and how to really help Africa. *The Spectator*. https://www.spectator.co.uk/article/why-foreign-aid-fails%2D%2D-and-how-to-really-help-africa

Achor, S., Reece, A., Kellerman, G. R., & Robichaux, A. (2018). 9 out of 10 people are willing to earn less money to do more-meaningful work. *Harvard Business Review Digital Articles,* 1–7. https://hbr.org/2018/11/9-out-of-10-people-are-willing-to-earn-less-money-to-do-more-meaningful-work

African Development Bank. (2021). *African Economic Outlook 2021*. https://www.afdb.org/en/knowledge/publications/african-economic-outlook

Ambrose, J. (2021, June 23). Most new wind and solar projects will be cheaper than, coal reports finds. *The Guardian*.

Apple. (2021). *Environment: We're carbon neutral. And by 2030, every product you love will be too. How it's designed*. https://www.apple.com/environment/

Ariely, D. (2012). *The honest truth about dishonesty: How we lie to everyone*. HarperCollins Publishers.

Atasu, A., Agrawal, V., Rinaldi, M., Herb, R., & Ülkü, S. (2018, July 3). Rethinking sustainability in light of the EU's new circular economy policy. *Harvard Business Review*. https://hbr.org/2018/07/rethinking-sustainability-in-light-of-the-eus-new-circular-economy-policy

C. D. Ditlev-Simonsen, *A Guide to Sustainable Corporate Responsibility*,
https://doi.org/10.1007/978-3-030-88203-7

Baral, N., & Pokharel, M. P. (2017). How sustainability is reflected in the S&P 500 companies' strategic documents. *Organization & Environment, 30*(2), 122–141. https://doi.org/10.1177/1086026616645381. https://login.ezproxy.library.bi.no/login?qurl=https://search.ebscohost.com/login.aspx?direct=true&db=bth&AN=123161373&site=ehost-live&scope=site

BBC News. (2012, October 25). Nigeria: 'Oil-gas sector mismanagement costs billions'. https://www.bbc.com/news/world-africa-20081268

Bergin, T. (2012, October 15). Special Report: How Starbucks avoids UK taxes. *Reuters.* https://www.reuters.com/article/us-britain-starbucks-tax-idUKBRE89E0EX20121015

Bhattacharya, C. B., Sen, S., & Korschun, D. (2008). Using corporate social responsibility to win the war for talent. *MIT Sloan Management Review, 49*(2), 37.

Bjergaard, A. P. (2020, February 8). Nytt blodbad for «milliardeventyret» i Afrika. *Finansavisen.* https://finansavisen.no/nyheter/industri/2020/02/08/7496064/nytt-blodbad-for-green-resources

Bloomberg Professional Services. (n.d.). Sustainable finance. *Bloomberg Professional Services.* https://www.bloomberg.com/professional/solution/sustainable-finance/?gclid=Cj0KCQjwhr2FBhDbARIsACjwLo2mRzuHPuTxpfY9WBNFF9YL6_p7G-qDvwAUNCipzqv8Hb-HtTiBKWwaAriZEALw_wcB#scores/?utm_medium=Adwords&utm_campaign=ESG&utm_source=pdsrch&utm_content=esgscores&tactic=342352

Blyth, N. (2020). Sustainable development goals and the business community. *DailyFT.* http://www.ft.lk/opinion/Sustainable-development-goals-and-the-business-community/14-695549

Boseley, S. (2017). How Bill and Melinda Gates helped save 122m lives—and what they want to solve next. *The Guardian.* https://www.theguardian.com/world/2017/feb/14/bill-gates-philanthropy-warren-buffett-vaccines-infant-mortality

Bowen, H. R. (1953). *Social responsibilities of the businessman.* Harper.

Boztas, S. (2016). Phone companies release too many new models, say consumers. *The Guardian.* https://www.theguardian.com/sustainable-business/2016/aug/15/phone-companies-release-too-many-new-models-consumer-survey-greenpeace

BP. (2020). *Statistical review of world energy 2020* (69th edition). https://www.bp.com/content/dam/bp/business-sites/en/global/corporate/pdfs/energy-economics/statistical-review/bp-stats-review-2020-full-report.pdf

Brand Finance. (2015, September 25). VW risks its $31 billion brand and Germany's national reputation. https://brandfinance.com/press-releases/vw-risks-its-31-billion-brand-and-germanys-national-reputation

Broom, D. (2019). Millennials are transforming African farming. https://www.weforum.org/agenda/2019/06/the-millennials-giving-african-farming-an-image-boost/

Business Call to Action. (n.d.). *More than philanthropy: SDGs present an estimated US$12 trillion in market opportunities for private sector through inclusive business.* https://www.businesscalltoaction.org/resources/more-philanthropy-sdgs-present-estimated-us12-trillion-market-opportunities-private-sector

Business Roundtable. (n.d.). *One year later: Purpose of a corporation.* https://purpose.businessroundtable.org/

Canon Global. (2021). *CSR activities: Materiality and SDGs.* https://global.canon/en/csr/sdgs/index.html

Carroll, A. B. (1991). The Pyramid of corporate social responsibility: Toward the moral management of organizational stakeholders. *Business Horizons, 34*(4), 39–48. http://search.ebscohost.com/login.aspx?direct=true&db=bth&AN=9707074820&site=ehost-live

Carson, R. (1962/2012). *Silent spring* (50th anniversary ed.). Penguin Classics.

Center for Biological Diversity. (n.d.). *10 Facts about single-use plastic bags: The problem with plastic bags.* https://www.biologicaldiversity.org/programs/population_and_sustainability/sustainability/plastic_bag_facts.html

Charbatke-Church, C. S., & Chigas, D. (2019). *Understanding social norms: A reference guide for policy and practice.* https://sites.tufts.edu/ihs/social-norms-reference-guide/

Chrisafis, A. (2016). French law forbids food waste by supermarkets. *The Guardian.* https://www.theguardian.com/world/2016/feb/04/french-law-forbids-food-waste-by-supermarkets

Civita. (2013). Korrupsjon og norsk næringsliv. *Civita-notat* (4). https://www.civita.no/assets/2013/03/Civita-notat_4_2013.pdf

Clark, J. M. (1916). The changing basis of economic responsibility. *The Journal of Political Economy, 24*(3), 209–229. https://doi.org/10.1086/252799

Coady, D., Parry, I. W. H., Sears, L., & Shang, B. (2015). *How large are global energy subsidies?* IMF Working Paper, 15 (105). https://www.imf.org/external/pubs/ft/wp/2015/wp15105.pdf

Collier, P. (2007). *The bottom billion: Why the poorest countries are failing and what can be done about it.* Oxford University Press.

Collier, P. (2016, December 11). Shifting aid to support business is the right decision. *Financial Times*. https://www.ft.com/join/licence/31c81148-b0e9-4815-bcdd-74f2bbf99304/details?ft-content-uuid=63f8341a-be22-11e6-8b45-b8b81dd5d080

Cross, J., & Murray, D. (2018). The afterlives of solar power: Waste and repair off the grid in Kenya. *Energy Research & Social Science, 44*, 100–109.

Dæhlen, M. (2016). Vet du hvor mange klesplagg du har? *forskning.no*. https://forskning.no/miljo-historie-naeringsliv/vet-du-hvor-mange-klesplagg-du-har/406500

Deloitte. (2015). Reducing food loss along African agricultural value chains. https://www2.deloitte.com/content/dam/Deloitte/za/Documents/consumer-business/ZA_FL1_ReducingFoodLossAlongAfricanAgriculturalValueChains.pdf

Deloitte. (2019). The Deloitte global millennial survey 2019. https://www2.deloitte.com/content/dam/Deloitte/global/Documents/About-Deloitte/deloitte-2019-millennial-survey.pdf

Devinney, T. M., Auger, P., Eckhardt, G., & Birtchnell, T. (2006, Fall). The other CSR: Consumer social responsibility. *Stanford Social Innovation Review*. https://doi.org/10.2139/ssrn.901863

Dieschbourg, M. T., & Nussbaum, A. P. (2017). No places to hide thanks to Morningstar, Bloomberg, MSCI and Multiple global data providers. *Investments & Wealth Monitor*. https://investmentsandwealth.org/getattachment/fdf4d0e3-adc0-487a-bbe0-624cdefb3b2f/IWM17NovDec-

DiMaggio, P. J., & Powell, W. W. (1983). The iron cage revisited: Institutional isomorphism and collective rationality in organizational fields. *American Sociological Review, 48*, 147–160.

Ditlev-Simonsen, C. D. (2009). Fordrer det noe spesielt å lede en samfunnsansvarlig bedrift. *Magma, 2*, 22–33.

Ditlev-Simonsen, C. D. (2010). From corporate social responsibility awareness to action? *Social Responsibility Journal, 6*(3), 452–468. https://doi.org/10.1108/17471111011064807

Ditlev-Simonsen, C. D. (2012). The relationship between Norwegian and Swedish employees' perception of corporate social responsibility and affective commitment. *Business & Society, 54*(2), 229–253. https://doi.org/10.1177/0007650312439534

Ditlev-Simonsen, C. D. (2013). Ny proposisjon om samfunnsansvarsrapportering. *Magma, 2*, 12–14. https://www.magma.no/ny-proposisjon-om-samfunnsansvarsrapportering

Ditlev-Simonsen, C. D. (2014). Are non-financial (CSR) reports trustworthy? A study of the extent to which non-financial reports reflect the media' perception of the company's behaviour. *Issues in Social and Environmental Accounting, 8*(2), 116–133. https://doi.org/10.22164/isea.v8i2.85

Ditlev-Simonsen, C. D. (2015). The gap between attitude and behavior in environmental protection—the case of Norway. In P. E. Stoknes & K. A. Eliassen (Eds.), *Science based activism*. Fagbokforlaget.

Ditlev-Simonsen, C. D. (2017). Beyond sponsorship—exploring the impact of cooperation between corporations and NGOs. *International Journal of Corporate Social Responsibility, 2*(6). https://doi.org/10.1186/s40991-017-0017-9

Ditlev-Simonsen, C. D. (2020). *What is happiness to Norwegians—And how happy are they*? Working Paper—BI Forum for Stiftelser (Forum for Foundations) (1/2020). https://papers.ssrn.com/sol3/papers.cfm?abstract_id=3721884

Ditlev-Simonsen, C. D., & Midttun, A. (2011). What motivates managers to pursue corporate responsibility? A survey among key stakeholders. *Corporate Social Responsibility and Environmental Management, 18*(1), 25–38.

Ditlev-Simonsen, C. D., & Wenstøp, F. (2016). Attitudes towards ethical pension management among Norwegians. *Beta (Oslo, Norway), 30*(2), 100–118. https://doi.org/10.18261/issn.1504-3134-2016-02-01

Doboczky, S. (2019). Ending the era of dirty textiles. *World Economic Forum*. https://www.weforum.org/agenda/2019/09/ending-the-era-of-dirty-textiles/

Edseth, R. F. (2009). *En kritisk vurdering av tobakksavgiften* [University of Oslo]. https://www.duo.uio.no/bitstream/handle/10852/17570/RemyxEdsethxtobakksavgift.pdf?sequence=1&isAllowed=y

Elkington, J. (1998). *Cannibals with Forks: The triple bottom line of 21st century business*. John Wiley & Sons, Ltd.

Elkington, J. (2018). 25 years ago i coined the phrase "Triple Bottom Line." Here's why it's time to rethink it. *Harvard Business Review Digital Articles*, 2–5.

Ellen MacArthur Foundation. (n.d.). *Infographic: Circular economy system diagram*. https://www.ellenmacarthurfoundation.org/circular-economy/concept/infographic

Ellen MacArthur Foundation, SUN, & McKinsey Center for Business and Environment. (2015). *Growth within: A circular economy vision for a competitive Europe*. https://www.ellenmacarthurfoundation.org/assets/downloads/publications/EllenMacArthurFoundation_Growth-Within_July15.pdf

Environmental Protection Agency. (2020). *Guide to greenhouse gas management for small business & low emitters* (August). https://www.epa.gov/sites/production/files/2017-01/documents/guide_to_greenhouse_gas_management_for_small_business_low_emitters.pdf

Epstein, P. R., Buonocore, J. J., Eckerle, K., Hendryx, M., Stout Iii, B. M., Heinberg, R., Clapp, R. W., May, B., Reinhart, N. L., & Ahern, M. M. (2011). Full cost accounting for the life cycle of coal. *Annals of the New York Academy of Sciences, 1219*(1), 73. https://doi.org/10.1111/j.1749-6632.2010.05890.x

EREK. (n.d.). Leasing extends end-of-life product cycles at Xerox. https://www.resourceefficient.eu/es/node/142

EU Technical Expert Group on Sustainable Finance. (2019). *Taxonomy technical report.* https://ec.europa.eu/info/sites/default/files/business_economy_euro/banking_and_finance/documents/190618-sustainable-finance-teg-report-taxonomy_en.pdf

Euronews. (2021, March 1). EU law requires companies to fix electronic goods for up to 10 years. https://www.euronews.com/2021/03/01/eu-law-requires-companies-to-fix-electronic-goods-for-up-to-10-years

European Coalition for Corporate Justice. (2017, February 23). *French corporate duty of vigilance law: FAQs.* https://corporatejustice.org/publications/faqs-french-duty-of-vigilance-law/

European Commission. (2020). *First circular economy action plan* https://ec.europa.eu/environment/topics/circular-economy/first-circular-economy-action-plan_en

European Commission. (n.d.-a). *Corporate sustainability reporting.* https://ec.europa.eu/info/business-economy-euro/company-reporting-and-auditing/company-reporting/corporate-sustainability-reporting_en

European Commission. (n.d.-b). *EU taxonomy for sustainable activities.* https://ec.europa.eu/info/business-economy-euro/banking-and-finance/sustainable-finance/eu-taxonomy-sustainable-activities_en

European Commission. (n.d.-c). *FAQ: What is the EU taxonomy and how will it work in practice?* https://ec.europa.eu/info/sites/default/files/business_economy_euro/banking_and_finance/documents/sustainable-finance-taxonomy-faq_en.pdf

European Commission. (n.d.-d). *Financing sustainable growth—factsheet.* https://ec.europa.eu/info/sites/default/files/business_economy_euro/banking_and_finance/documents/200108-financing-sustainable-growth-factsheet_en.pdf

European Commission. (n.d.-e). *Proposal for a Corporate Sustainability Reporting Directive (CSRD).* https://ec.europa.eu/info/business-economy-euro/company-reporting-and-auditing/company-reporting/corporate-sustainability-reporting_en#review

European Commission the European Economic and Social Committee. (n.d.). *European circular economy stakeholder platform: Good practices*. https://circulareconomy.europa.eu/platform/good-practices

Eurosif. (2018). *European SRI study 2018*.

Eurostat. (2021, April). Africa-EU—international trade in goods statistics: Imports, exports and trade balance between the EU and African countries, 2010–2020. https://ec.europa.eu/eurostat/statistics-explained/index.php?title=Africa-EU_-_international_trade_in_goods_statistics

Fairphone. (2016, July). Fairphone fact sheet. https://www.fairphone.com/wp-content/uploads/2016/08/Fairphone-factsheet_EN.pdf

Faltin, T. (2016, September 7). Matsvinn: Tre grupper nordmenn kaster mest mat. *Dagbladet*. https://www.dagbladet.no/mat/tre-grupper-nordmenn-kaster-mest-mat/62315143

Financial Accountability Transparency & Integrity. (2021, February 25). *UN Panel: End financial abuses to save people and planet* https://www.factipanel.org/press-release/un-panel-end-financial-abuses-to-save-people-and-planet

Fombrun, C. J. (2005). Building corporate reputation through CSR initiatives: Evolving standards. *Corporate Reputation Review, 8*(1), 7.

Food and Agriculture Organization of the United Nations. (2016, December 16). *Women hold the key to building a world free from hunger and poverty*. http://www.fao.org/news/story/en/item/460267/icode/

Food and Agriculture Organization of the United Nations. (2019). *Committee on commodity problems*. http://www.fao.org/fileadmin/templates/est/COMM_MARKETS_MONITORING/Jute_Hard_Fibres/Documents/IGG_40/19-CRS_1_Current_Situation_and_Outlook_01.pdf

Food and Agriculture Organization of the United States. (2020). *The state of world fisheries and aquaculture 2020*. http://www.fao.org/state-of-fisheries-aquaculture/en/

Freeman, R. E. (1984). *Strategic management: A stakeholder approach*. Pitman.

Friede, G., Busch, T., & Bassen, A. (2015). ESG and financial performance: Aggregated evidence from more than 2000 empirical studies. *Journal of Sustainable Finance & Investment, 5*(4), 210–233. https://doi.org/10.1080/20430795.2015.1118917

Friedman, M. (1970). A Friedman doctrine—The social responsibility of business is to increase its profits. *The New York Times*. https://www.nytimes.com/1970/09/13/archives/a-friedman-doctrine-the-social-responsibility-of-business-is-to.html

Gadgets Now. (2020, November 20). 10 highest-selling smartphones in the world. https://www.gadgetsnow.com/slideshows/10-highest-selling-smartphones-in-the-world/apple-iphone-11/photolist/77882296.cms

Gardner, T. (2020). Bill Gates' nuclear venture plans reactor to complement solar, wind power boom. *Reuters*. https://www.reuters.com/article/us-usa-nuclearpower-terrapower/bill-gates-nuclear-venture-plans-reactor-to-complement-solar-wind-power-boom-idINKBN25N2U8?edition-redirect=in

Gatesfoundation. (n.d.). *Africa*. https://www.gatesfoundation.org/our-work/places/africa

Gibbs, S. (2020). Fairphone 3+ review: Ethical smartphone gets camera upgrades. *The Guardian*. https://www.theguardian.com/technology/2020/aug/31/fairphone-3-review-ethical-smartphone-gets-camera-upgrades

Gillian, T. (2019). Governments won't fund sustainable development. Will private finance step in? *Financial Times*. https://www.ft.com/content/82ef5e8e-1ea1-11e9-b126-46fc3ad87c65

Gleckman, H. (1995). Transnational corporations' strategic responses to "sustainable development". In H. O. A. Bergesen (Ed.), *Green Global yearbook of international co-operation on environment and development 1995* (pp. 93–106). Oxford University Press.

Glick, D. (n.d.). The big thaw. *National Geographic,*. https://www.nationalgeographic.com/environment/article/big-thaw

Global Footprint Network. (n.d.-b). *Ecological footprint*. https://www.footprintnetwork.org/our-work/ecological-footprint/

Global Justice Now. (2018, October 17). 69 of the richest 100 entities on the planet are corporations, not governments, figures show. https://www.globaljustice.org.uk/news/69-richest-100-entities-planet-are-corporations-not-governments-figures-show/

Global Reporting Initiative. (2020, December 1). Sustainability reporting is growing, with GRI the global common language. https://www.globalreporting.org/about-gri/news-center/2020-12-01-sustainability-reporting-is-growing-with-gri-the-global-common-language

Goedde, L., Ooko-Ombaka, A., & Pais, G. (2019, February 15). Winning in Africa's agricultural market. *McKinsey*. https://www.mckinsey.com/industries/agriculture/our-insights/winning-in-africas-agricultural-market

Goldin, I. (2019). Why do some countries develop and others not? In P. Dobrescu (Ed.), *Development in turbulent times* (p. 13). Springer. https://doi.org/10.1007/978-3-030-11361-2_2

Gonçalves, A. (2018, October 26). Are ISO 14001 certified companies more competitive, efficient & sustainable? *Youmatter*. https://youmatter.world/en/are-iso-14001-certified-companies-are-more-competitive-and-efficient/

Grimstad, M. E., Jacobsen, G. E., & Bastiansen, J. E. (2019). Heller ut 25.000 liter drikke—hver dag. *NRK*. https://www.nrk.no/dokumentar/heller-ut-25.000-liter-drikke-_-hver-dag-1.14789395

Guinness World Records. (2016). *Smallest ecological footprint (per capita, country)*. https://www.guinnessworldrecords.com/world-records/637715-smallest-ecological-footprint-per-capita-country

Hankammer, S., Kleer, R., Mühl, L., & Euler, J. (2021). Principles for organizations striving for sustainable degrowth: Framework development and application to four B Corps. *Journal of Cleaner Production, 300*, N.PAG-N.PAG. https://doi.org/10.1016/j.jclepro.2021.126818. https://login.ezproxy.library.bi.no/login?qurl=https://search.ebscohost.com/login.aspx?direct=true&db=bth&AN=150008795&site=ehost-live&scope=site

Hannon, E. e. a. (2016). *The circular economy: Moving from theory to practice*. McKinsey Center for Business and Environment Special edition, Issue.

Hodak, M. (2007). Adam Smith's Folly. *Forbes*. https://www.forbes.com/2007/10/24/adam-smith-corporations-markets-marketsp07-cx_mh_1025hodak.html?sh=10d5a65e3c1b

Hodal, K. (2019, February 25). One in 200 people is a slave. Why? *The Guardian*. https://www.theguardian.com/news/2019/feb/25/modern-slavery-trafficking-persons-one-in-200

Hoffmann, A. J. (2018). The next phase of business sustainability. *Stanford Social Innovation Review, 16*(2), 34–39. https://ssir.org/articles/entry/the_next_phase_of_business_sustainability

Horton, R. (2014). Offline: Why the sustainable development goals will fail. *The Lancet, 383*(9936). https://www.thelancet.com/journals/lancet/article/PIIS0140-6736(14)61046-1/fulltext

Hursthouse, R. (1999). *On virtue ethics*. Oxford University Press.

IKEA. (2021). *IKEA culture and values*. https://about.ikea.com/en/about-us/ikea-culture-and-values

Ingraham, C. (2017, December 6). The richest 1 percent now owns more of the country's wealth than at any time in the past 50 years. *The Washington Post*. https://www.washingtonpost.com/news/wonk/wp/2017/12/06/the-richest-1-percent-now-owns-more-of-the-countrys-wealth-than-at-any-time-in-the-past-50-years/

Integrated Reporting. (n.d.). Frequently asked questions. https://integratedreporting.org/FAQS/#what-is-the-international-integrated-reporting-council-iirc

Investor Alliance for Human Rights. (n.d.). *About the investor alliance for human rights*. https://investorsforhumanrights.org/about

IPCC. (2021). *AR6 climate change 2021: The physical science basis*.

Jensen, M. (2001). Value maximisation, stakeholder theory, and the corporate objective function. *European Financial Management: The Journal of the European Financial Management Association, 7*(3), 297–317. https://doi.org/10.1111/1468-036x.00158

Jolis, A. (2012, September 7). Mohammed Ibrahim: The philanthropist of honest government. *Wall Street Journal*. https://www.wsj.com/articles/SB10000872396390444318104577587641175010510

Juetten, M. (2014). Pay attention to innovation and intangibles—They're more than 80% Of your business' value. *Forbes*. https://www.forbes.com/sites/maryjuetten/2014/10/02/pay-attention-to-innovation-and-intangibles-more-than-80-of-your-business-value/?sh=12c143b11a67

Kanter, R. M. (1999). From spare change to real change. The social sector as beta site for business innovation. *Harvard Business Review, 77*(3), 122–210.

Kapland, S. (2012). The business model innovation factory: How to stay relevant when the world is changing. In *Business models 101: Creating delivering, and capturing value*. Wiley. https://doi.org/10.1002/9781119205234

Karns, M. P. (n.d.). Nongovernmental organization. *Encyclopædia Britannica*. https://www.britannica.com/topic/nongovernmental-organization

Kershaw, S. (2005). Microsoft comes under fire for reversal on gay rights bill. *The New York Times*. https://www.nytimes.com/2005/04/22/us/microsoft-comes-under-fire-for-reversal-on-gay-rights-bill.html

Keynes, J. M. (1930/2010). Economic possibilities for our grandchildren. In *Essays in Persuasion* (pp. 321–332). Palgrave Macmillan. https://doi.org/10.1007/978-1-349-59072-8_25

Keynes, J. M. (1936/2018). *The general theory of employment, interest, and money*. Springer International Publishing AG. https://doi.org/10.1007/978-3-319-70344-2

Khan, M., Serafeim, G., & Yoon, A. (2016). Corporate sustainability: First evidence on materiality. *The Accounting Review, 91*(6), 1697–1724. https://doi.org/10.2308/accr-51383

Kolbert, E. (2014). No time: How did we get so busy? *New Yorker*. https://www.newyorker.com/magazine/2014/05/26/no-time

Kotter, J. P. (2012). *Leading change*. Harvard Business School Press.

KPMG. (2018). *How to report on the SDGs: What good looks like and why it matters.* https://home.kpmg/xx/en/home/insights/2018/02/how-to-report-on-the-sdgs.html

Kraft, A. G., Vashishtha, R., & Venkatachalam, M. (2018). Frequent financial reporting and managerial Myopia. *The Accounting Review, 93*(2), 249–275. https://doi.org/10.2308/accr-51838

Kubania, J. (2015, July 6). How second-hand clothing donations are creating a dilemma for Kenya. *The Guardian.* https://www.theguardian.com/world/2015/jul/06/second-hand-clothing-donations-kenya

Kwemo, A. B. (2017, April 20). Making Africa great again: Reducing aid dependency. *Brookings.* https://www.brookings.edu/blog/africa-in-focus/2017/04/20/making-africa-great-again-reducing-aid-dependency/

Laramée de Tannenberg, V. (2019). Wealthy countries still failing on $100 billion climate finance pledge. *Le Journal de l'environnement.* https://www.euractiv.com/section/climate-environment/news/wealthy-countries-still-failing-on-100-billion-climate-finance-pledge/

Lemus, E. (2014). The financial collapse of the Enron Corporation and its impact in the United States capital market. *Global Journal of Management and Business Research: Accounting and Auditing, 14*(4) https://globaljournals.org/GJMBR_Volume14/3-The-Financial-Collapse-of-the-Enron.pdf

Lindsey, R. (2021). Climate change: Global sea level. *Climate.gov.* https://www.climate.gov/news-features/understanding-climate/climate-change-global-sea-level

Lyons, K., & Westoby, P. (2013, November). Carbon markets and the failed promise of new green gold: Plantation forestry in Uganda. *Friends of the Earth, Australia.* https://www.foe.org.au/carbon-markets-and-failed-promise-new-green-gold-plantation-forestry-uganda

Martin, J., & Sherr, I. (2019). How Apple's Daisy iPhone recycling robot works. *CNET.* https://www.cnet.com/news/how-apples-daisy-phone-recycling-robot-works/

Maslow, A. H. (1943). A theory of human motivation. *Psychological Review, 50*(4), 370–396.

Mattilsynet. (2019, November 7). Slik tar du vare på maten: Matsvinn. *Matportalen.* https://www.matportalen.no/matsmitte_og_hygiene/matsvinn-1

May, O. (2018, March 4). 5 countries with the highest quality coffee beans. *Barefoot Coffee Roasters.* https://barefootcoffeeroasters.com/countries-with-the-best-coffee-beans/

Mayer, M. L. (2017). Slik blir garderoben din mer miljøvennlig. *Putsj*. https://putsj.no/artikkel/slik-blir-garderoben-mer-miljovennlig

Mayor, T. (2019). Why ESG ratings vary so widely (and what you can do about it). *MIT Thinking Forward Newsletter*. https://mitsloan.mit.edu/ideas-made-to-matter/why-esg-ratings-vary-so-widely-and-what-you-can-do-about-it

McCartney, P. (2009, December 8). Meat free Monday—the facts. https://www.paulmccartney.com/news-blogs/news/meat-free-monday-the-facts

McClimon, T. J. (2020). Corporate giving by the numbers. *Forbes*. https://www.forbes.com/sites/timothyjmcclimon/2020/01/16/corporate-giving-by-the-numbers/?sh=18375d1a6c51

McGoey, S. (2021). Panama papers revenue recovery reaches $1.36 billion as investigations continue. *ICIJ International Consortium of Investigative Journalists*. https://www.icij.org/investigations/panama-papers/panama-papers-revenue-recovery-reaches-1-36-billion-as-investigations-continue/

McMaster, A. (2017). 3 ways your iPhone could be bad for the environment & workers. *Global Citizen*. https://www.globalcitizen.org/fr/content/iphone-x-apple-environment-pollution-smartphones-k/

Menke, A. (2017, October 19). Working conditions in the textile industry. *globalEDGE*. https://globaledge.msu.edu/blog/post/54484/working-conditions-in-the-textile-indust

Meyersohn, N. (2019). Walmart settles with US government over international bribery. *CNN*. https://edition.cnn.com/2019/06/20/business/walmart-bribery-mexico-brazil-fcpa-sec

Morris, D. Z. (2016, October 15). Mercedes-Benz's self-driving cars would choose passenger lives over bystanders. *Fortune*. https://fortune.com/2016/10/15/mercedes-self-driving-car-ethics/

Moyo, D. (2009, March 21). Why foreign aid is hurting Africa. *The Wall Street Journal*. https://www.wsj.com/articles/SB123758895999200083

National Centers for Environmental Information. (n.d.). Billion-Dollar weather and climate disasters: Overview. *National Centers for Environmental Information*. https://www.ncdc.noaa.gov/billions/

NBC News. (2007, December 24). Examples of failed aid-funded projects in Africa. https://www.nbcnews.com/id/wbna22380448

Neate, R. (2017, November 14). Richest 1% own half the world's wealth, study finds. *The Guardian*. https://www.theguardian.com/inequality/2017/nov/14/worlds-richest-wealth-credit-suisse

Nijland, H., & van Meerkerk, J. (2017). Mobility and environmental impacts of car sharing in the Netherlands. *Environmental Innovation and Societal Transitions, 23*, 84–91. https://doi.org/10.1016/j.eist.2017.02.001

Nike News. (2018, May 15). Nike's latest sustainable innovations and environmental impact. https://news.nike.com/news/sustainable-innovation-air-bag-manufacture

Njarga, B. B. (2016). Derfor bør ikke vrakpanten økes. *Dagbladet*. https://www.dagbladet.no/tema/derfor-bor-ikke-vrakpanten-okes/61663256

Nogrady, B. (2016). Your old phone is full of untapped precious metals. *BBC*. https://www.bbc.com/future/article/20161017-your-old-phone-is-full-of-precious-metals

Norges Bank Investment Management. (2016). *Guidelines for observation and exclusion from the fund*. https://www.nbim.no/en/organisation/governance-model/guidelines-for-observation-and-exclusion-from-the-fund/

Norges Bank Investment Management. (2019, February 27). *About the fund*. https://www.nbim.no/en/the-fund/about-the-fund/

Nsehe, M. (2018, April 18). 30 most promising young entrepreneurs In Africa 2018. *Forbes*. https://www.forbes.com/sites/mfonobongnsehe/2018/04/18/30-most-promising-young-entrepreneurs-in-africa-2018/?sh=ae35a477474e

Nsehe, M. (2019, January 9). The philanthropy of Africa's billionaires. *Forbes*. https://www.forbes.com/sites/mfonobongnsehe/2019/01/09/the-philanthropy-of-africas-billionaires/?sh=4caff8247fd9

OECD. (2011). *OECD guidelines for multinational enterprises*. https://www.oecd.org/daf/inv/mne/48004323.pdf

OECD. (2020a). *Aid by DAC members increases in 2019 with more aid to the poorest countries*. https://www.oecd.org/dac/financing-sustainable-development/development-finance-data/ODA-2019-detailed-summary.pdf

OECD. (2020b). *Corporate anti-corruption compliance drivers, mechanisms, and ideas for change*. https://www.oecd.org/corruption/anti-bribery/corporate-anti-corruption-compliance.htm

Okojie, J. (2015, November 25). Shea butter: Local business with enormous opportunities. *Business Day*. https://businessday.ng/agriculture/article/shea-butter-local-business-with-enormous-opportunities/

Okonjo-Iweala, N. (2007). Want to help Africa? Do business here. *TED Talk*. https://www.ted.com/talks/ngozi_okonjo_iweala_want_to_help_africa_do_business_here

Pandey, K. (2020). Sustainable development goals: 36 changes in global indicator framework. *Down to Earth*. https://www.downtoearth.org.in/news/climate-change/sustainable-development-goals-36-changes-in-global-indicator-framework-69716

Philanthropy News Digest. (2016, July 19). Gates foundation to invest $5 Billion in Africa over five years. https://philanthropynewsdigest.org/news/gates-foundation-to-invest-5-billion-in-africa-over-five-years

Philips. (n.d.). *Lighting services has moved to signify*. https://www.lighting.philips.com/main/services

Pistilli, M. (2021, January 13). What was the BP stock price before the deepwater Horizon spill? *Investing News*. https://investingnews.com/daily/resource-investing/energy-investing/oil-and-gas-investing/bp-oil-stock-price-before-spill/

Porter, M. E. (1998). Clusters and the new economics of competition. *Harvard Business Review, 76*(6), 77–90.

Porter, M. E., & Kramer, M. R. (2011). Creating shared value: How to reinvent capitalism—and unleash a wave of innovation and growth. *Harvard Business Review, 89*(1–2), 62.

Prather, C. W., & Turrell, M. C. (2002). Managers at work: Involve everyone in the innovation process. *Research-Technology Management, 45*(5), 13–16.

PwC. (2020). *PwC's global economic crime and fraud survey 2020*. https://www.pwc.com/fraudsurvey

Reality Check Team. (2018, July 27). Reality check: Why some African countries don't want charity clothes. *BBC*. https://www.bbc.com/news/world-africa-44951670

Reike, D., Vermeulen, W. J. V., & Witjes, S. (2018). The circular economy: New or Refurbished as CE 3.0?—Exploring Controversies in the Conceptualization of the Circular Economy through a Focus on History and Resource Value Retention Options. *Resources. Conservation and Recycling, 135*, 246–264. https://doi.org/10.1016/j.resconrec.2017.08.027

Rhenman, E. (1968). *Industrial democracy and industrial management*. Tavistock.

Ritchie, H., Hasell, J., Appel, C., & Roser, M. (2019, November). Terrorism. *Our World in Data*. https://ourworldindata.org/terrorism

Ritchie, H., & Roser, M. (n.d.). CO2 emissions. *Our World in Data*. https://ourworldindata.org/co2-emissions

Roser, M. (2013). Employment in agriculture. *Our World in Data*. https://ourworldindata.org/employment-in-agriculture

Sandin, G., Roos, S. R., Spak, B., Zamani, B., & Peters, G. (2019). Environmental assessment of Swedish clothing consumption. *Mistra Future Fashion Report* (2019:05). http://mistrafuturefashion.com/wp-content/uploads/2019/08/G.Sandin-Environmental-assessment-of-Swedish-clothing-consumption.MistraFutureFashionReport-2019.05.pdf

Schmelzer, R. (2020, October 1). Automating data collection for AI at Morningstar. *Forbes*.

Schokkaert, E. (2019, Spring). Review of Kate Raworth's Doughnut economics. *Erasmus Journal for Philosophy & Economics, 12*(1), 125–132. https://doi.org/10.23941/ejpe.v12i1.412. https://search.ebscohost.com/login.aspx?direct=true&db=bth&AN=137859877&site=ehost-live&scope=site

Schroeder, P., & Anantharaman, M. (2017). "Lifestyle Leapfrogging" in emerging economies: Enabling systemic shifts to sustainable consumption. *Journal of Consumer Policy, 40*(1), 3–23. https://doi.org/10.1007/s10603-016-9339-3

Shah, S. (2021, March 29). It's time to expand fertilizer manufacturing across Africa. *The Breakthrough Institute*. https://thebreakthrough.org/issues/food/expand-fertilizer-manufacturing-across-africa

Shindell, D. T. (2015). The social cost of atmospheric release. *Climatic Change, 130*(2), 313–326.

Short, J. L., Toffel, M. W., & Hugill, A. R. (2020). Improving working conditions in global supply chains: The role of institutional environments and monitoring program design. *ILR Review, 73*(4), 873–912.

Si, S., Ahlstrom, D., Wei, J., & Cullen, J. (2020). Business, entrepreneurship and innovation toward poverty reduction. *Entrepreneurship & Regional Development, 32*(1/2), 1–20. https://doi.org/10.1080/08985626.2019.1640485. https://search.ebscohost.com/login.aspx?direct=true&db=bth&AN=140851015&site=ehost-live&scope=site

Sivertsen, E. V., & Zakariassen, G. (2016). Svensk kleskjede lar deg lease garderoben. *NRK*. https://www.nrk.no/kultur/filippa-k-lar-deg-lease-klaer-1.12835784

Smith, A. (1776/2008). *An inquiry into the nature and causes of the wealth of nations*. Oxford University Press.

Smithers, R. (2016). England's plastic bag usage drops 85% since 5p charge introduced. *The Guardian*. https://www.theguardian.com/environment/2016/jul/30/england-plastic-bag-usage-drops-85-per-cent-since-5p-charged-introduced

Spash, C. L. (2013). The shallow or the deep ecological economics movement? *Ecological Economics, 93*, 351–362. https://doi.org/10.1016/j.ecolecon.2013.05.016. https://login.ezproxy.library.bi.no/login?qurl=https://search.ebscohost.com/login.aspx?direct=true&db=bth&AN=89436681&site=ehost-live&scope=site

Spraul, K., & Thaler, J. (2019). Partnering for good? An analysis of how to achieve sustainability-related outcomes in public–private partnerships. *Business Research, 13*, 1–27.

Spurlock, M. (2004). *Super Size Me* [Film]. https://www.imdb.com/title/tt0390521/

Straffeloven [The Penal Code]. (2005). *Lov om straff* (LOV-2005-05-20-28). Lovdata. https://lovdata.no/dokument/NL/lov/2005-05-20-28/KAPITTEL_2-15#%C2%A7387

Sustainable Brands. (2019, July 3). Measuring and managing brand reputation: How CSR and other factors influence reputational value [Video]. *YouTube*. https://www.youtube.com/watch?v=JKzZlyJD1Z0

Sustainable Development Report. (2020). *Country profiles*. https://dashboards.sdgindex.org/profiles

Sweet, P. (2019, September 23). Listed companies increase use of integrated reporting, says IIRC. *Accountancy Daily*. https://www.accountancydaily.co/listed-companies-increase-use-integrated-reporting-says-iirc

Sykes, G., & Matza, D. (1957). Techniques of neutralization: A theory of delinquency. *American Sociological Review, 22*(6), 664–670. https://doi.org/10.2307/2089195

Taraldsen, L. E., Poulsson, L., & Starn, J. (2020). Wind farm backlash grows in oil-rich Norway ahead of election. *Bloomberg*. https://www.bloomberg.com/news/articles/2020-12-09/wind-farm-backlash-grows-in-oil-rich-norway-ahead-of-election

The Economist. (2020, March 28). Africa's population will double by 2050. https://www.economist.com/special-report/2020/03/26/africas-population-will-double-by-2050

The Irish News. (2018, March 02). How our smartphones are hurting the environment. https://www.irishnews.com/magazine/science/2018/03/02/news/how-our-smartphones-are-hurting-the-environment-1268849/

The Nano Membrane Toilet Project. (n.d.). The nano membrane toilet. http://www.nanomembranetoilet.org/

The Pulitzer Prizes. (2013). The 2013 Pulitzer prize winner in investigative reporting: David Barstow and Alejandra Xanic von Bertrab of The New York Times. https://www.pulitzer.org/winners/david-barstow-and-alejandra-xanic-von-bertrab

The World Bank. (2012, October 24). *Africa can feed itself, earn billions, and avoid food crises by unblocking regional food trade*. https://www.worldbank.org/en/news/press-release/2012/10/24/africa-can-feed-itself-earn-billions-avoid-food-crises-unblocking-regional-food-trade

The World Bank. (n.d.-a). Imports of goods and services (% of GDP): 1960–2019. https://data.worldbank.org/indicator/NE.IMP.GNFS.ZS

The World Bank. (n.d.-b). Metadata glossary. *Databank*. https://databank.worldbank.org/metadataglossary/gender-statistics/series/SI.POV.GINI

The World Bank. (n.d.-c). Trends in solid waste management. *WHAT A WASTE 2.0: A Global Snapshot of Solid Waste Management to 2050*. https://datatopics.worldbank.org/what-a-waste/trends_in_solid_waste_management.html

Transparency International. (2019, July 5). *Siemens: Corruption made in Germany*. https://www.transparency.org/en/news/25-corruption-scandals#Siemens

Transparency International. (2020). *Corruption perceptions index*. https://www.transparency.org/en/cpi/2020/index/nzl#

Transparency International. (n.d.). *What is corruption?* https://www.transparency.org/en/what-is-corruption

Tyson, J. (2020). Cooking up a solution to Uganda's deforestation crisis with mud stoves. *The Guardian*. https://www.theguardian.com/global-development/2020/jun/29/cooking-up-a-solution-to-ugandas-deforestation-crisis-with-mud-stoves

UN Sustainable Development Goals. (2016). The sustainable development agenda. https://www.un.org/sustainabledevelopment/development-agenda-retired/

UNDP Seoul Policy Centre for Knowledge Exchange through SDG Partnerships. (n.d.). *Goal 15: Life on land*. https://www1.undp.org/content/seoul_policy_center/en/home/sustainable-development-goals/goal-15-life-on-land.html

UNECE Sustainable Development Goals. (n.d.). Methane management: The challenge. https://unece.org/challenge

Unilever. (2020, December 14). *Unilever to seek shareholder approval for climate transition action plan*. https://www.unilever.com/news/press-releases/2020/unilever-to-seek-shareholder-approval-for-transition-action-plan.html

United Nations. (1945). Chapter I: Purposes and principles. *United Nations Charter*. https://www.un.org/en/about-us/un-charter/chapter-1

United Nations. (1948). *Universal declaration of human rights*. https://www.un.org/en/about-us/universal-declaration-of-human-rights

United Nations. (2015). *The millennium development goals report 2015*. https://www.un.org/millenniumgoals/2015_MDG_Report/pdf/MDG%202015%20rev%20(July%201).pdf

United Nations Educational Scientific and Cultural Organization (UNESCO). (n.d.). *Linking education to food security*. http://www.fao.org/3/x0262e/x0262e20.htm

United Nations Global Compact. (2017, December 5). *Enact: What, how and why?* https://www.sa.is/media/2864/erika.pdf

United Nations Global Compact. (2021). *Our finances*. https://www.unglobalcompact.org/about/finances

United Nations Human Rights. (2011). *Guiding principles on business and human rights*. https://www.ohchr.org/documents/publications/guidingprinciplesbusinesshr_en.pdf

United Nations News. (2019, March 25). UN launches drive to highlight environmental cost of staying fashionable. https://news.un.org/en/story/2019/03/1035161

United Nations Office on Drugs and Crime. (2003). *United Nations convention against corruption*. https://www.unodc.org/unodc/en/corruption/uncac.html

United Nations Office on Drugs and Crime. (2013). *An anti-corruption ethics and compliance programme for business: A practical guide*. https://www.unodc.org/documents/corruption/Publications/2013/13-84498_Ebook.pdf

United Nations Secretary-General. (2018, December 5). *Cost of corruption at least 5 per cent of global gross domestic product, secretary-general says in International Day message* [Press Release]. https://www.un.org/press/en/2018/sgsm19392.doc.htm

United Nations Sustainable Development. (2020). *About major groups and other stakeholders*. Division for Sustainable Development Goals. https://sustainabledevelopment.un.org/mgos

United Nations Sustainable Development. (n.d.). *Goals.13: Take urgent action to combat climate change and its impacts*. https://sdgs.un.org/goals/goal13

US SIF: The Forum for Sustainable and Responsible Investment. (2020, November 16). The US SIF foundation's biennial "trends report" finds that sustainable investing assets reach $17.1 trillion. https://www.ussif.org/blog_home.asp?Display=155

Visser, W. (2005). Revisiting Carroll's CSR pyramid: An African perspective. In E. R. Pedersen & M. Huniche (Eds.), *Corporate citizenship in developing countries: New partnership perspectives* (pp. 29–56). Samfundslitteratur.

Wass, S. (2019). Paperless port system prompts import revenue growth in Ghana. *Global Trade Review*. https://www.gtreview.com/news/africa/paperless-port-system-prompts-import-revenue-growth-in-ghana/

Wenden, A. (2008). Discourses on poverty: Emerging perspectives on a caring economy. *Third World Quarterly, 29*(6), 1051–1067. https://doi.org/10.1080/01436590802201030. https://search.ebscohost.com/login.aspx?direct=true&db=bth&AN=33158069&site=ehost-live&scope=site

Wharton Magazine. (2007, July 1). Inventor of GNP Measure: Simon Kuznets Hon56 Hon76. https://magazine.wharton.upenn.edu/issues/anniversary-issue/inventor-of-gross-national-product-measure-simon-kuznets-hon-56-hon-76-professor/

Wharton University of Pennsylvania. (2007). African aid projects that work: Partnerships on the ground, not donations from a distance. *Knowledge@Wharton*. https://knowledge.wharton.upenn.edu/article/african-aid-projects-that-work-partnerships-on-the-ground-not-donations-from-a-distance/

Whelan, T., & Douglas, E. (2021). How to talk to your CFO about sustainability. *Harvard Business Review, 99*(1), 86–93.

Williamson, O. E. (1964). *The economics of discretionary behavior: Managerial objectives in a theory of the firm*. Prentice Hall.

Willige, A. (2020). 4 challenges we need to solve to protect our ocean. *World Economic Forum*. https://www.weforum.org/agenda/2020/09/oceans-coral-reefs-climate-change-pollution-overfishing/

Willums, J.-O. a. (1992). *From ideas to action—Business and sustainable development*. adNotam Gyldendal.

Wilson, H., & Hopewell, A. (2018, May 11). Buy one, give one: What TOMS shoes tells us about the west's urge to help Africa. *The Urge To Help*. https://theurgetohelp.com/articles/buy-one-give-one-what-toms-shoes-tells-us-about-the-wests-urge-to-help-africa/

Wilson, I. H. (1975). What one company is doing about today's demands on business. In G. A. Steiner (Ed.), *Changing business society interrelationship*. Graduate School of Management, UCLA.

World Bank Group. (2020, March 19). *Wastewater a resource that can pay dividends for people, the environment, and economies, says World Bank* [Press release]. https://www.worldbank.org/en/news/press-release/2020/03/19/wastewater-a-resource-that-can-pay-dividends-for-people-the-environment-and-economies-says-world-bank

World Commission on Environment and Development. (1987). *Our common future*. https://sustainabledevelopment.un.org/content/documents/5987our-common-future.pdf

World Health Organization. (2019, June 18). 1 in 3 people globally do not have access to safe drinking water—UNICEF, WHO. https://www.who.int/news/item/18-06-2019-1-in-3-people-globally-do-not-have-access-to-safe-drinking-water-unicef-who

Zadek, S. (2004, December). The path to corporate responsibility. *Harvard Business Review*. https://hbr.org/2004/12/the-path-to-corporate-responsibility

Index

C. D. Ditlev-Simonsen, *A Guide to Sustainable Corporate Responsibility*,
https://doi.org/10.1007/978-3-030-88203-7